Accounting

for Cambridge International AS & A Level

WORKBOOK

Sharon Elan-Puttick

CAMBRIDGE
UNIVERSITY PRESS

Shaftesbury Road, Cambridge CB2 8EA, United Kingdom

One Liberty Plaza, 20th Floor, New York, NY 10006, USA

477 Williamstown Road, Port Melbourne, VIC 3207, Australia

314–321, 3rd Floor, Plot 3, Splendor Forum, Jasola District Centre, New Delhi – 110025, India

103 Penang Road, #05–06/07, Visioncrest Commercial, Singapore 238467

Cambridge University Press is part of the University of Cambridge.

It furthers the University's mission by disseminating knowledge in the pursuit of education, learning and research at the highest international levels of excellence.

www.cambridge.org
Information on this title: www.cambridge.org/9781108828710

© Cambridge University Press & Assessment 2022

This publication is in copyright. Subject to statutory exception and to the provisions of relevant collective licensing agreements, no reproduction of any part may take place without the written permission of Cambridge University Press.

First published
Second edition 2016
Third edition 2022

20 19 18 17 16 15 14 13 12 11 10 9 8 7 6 5 4

Printed in Poland by Opolgraf

A catalogue record for this publication is available from the British Library

ISBN 978-110-882871-0 Paperback with Digital Access (2 Years)

Additional resources for this publication at www.cambridge.org/9781108828710

Cambridge University Press has no responsibility for the persistence or accuracy of URLs for external or third-party internet websites referred to in this publication, and does not guarantee that any content on such websites is, or will remain, accurate or appropriate. Information regarding prices, travel timetables, and other factual information given in this work is correct at the time of first printing but Cambridge University Press does not guarantee the accuracy of such information thereafter.

....

NOTICE TO TEACHERS IN THE UK

It is illegal to reproduce any part of this work in material form (including photocopying and electronic storage) except under the following circumstances:
(i) where you are abiding by a licence granted to your school or institution by the Copyright Licensing Agency;
(ii) where no such licence exists, or where you wish to exceed the terms of a licence, and you have gained the written permission of Cambridge University Press;
(iii) where you are allowed to reproduce without permission under the provisions of Chapter 3 of the Copyright, Designs and Patents Act 1988, which covers, for example, the reproduction of short passages within certain types of educational anthology and reproduction for the purposes of setting examination questions.

....

Cambridge International copyright material in this publication is reproduced under licence and remains the intellectual property of Cambridge Assessment International Education.

Cambridge Assessment International Education bears no responsibility for the example answers to questions taken from its past question papers which are contained in this publication.

Exam-style questions and sample answers have been written by the authors. In examinations, the way marks are awarded may be different. References to assessment and/or assessment preparation are the publisher's interpretation of the syllabus requirements and may not fully reflect the approach of Cambridge Assessment International Education.

Cambridge International recommends that teachers consider using a range of teaching and learning resources in preparing learners for assessment, based on their own professional judgement of their students' needs.

Past examination paper questions throughout are reproduced by permission of Cambridge Assessment International Education.

Cover image: MirageC/Getty Images

DEDICATED TEACHER AWARDS

Teachers play an important part in shaping futures. Our Dedicated Teacher Awards recognise the hard work that teachers put in every day.

Thank you to everyone who nominated this year; we have been inspired and moved by all of your stories. Well done to all of our nominees for your dedication to learning and for inspiring the next generation of thinkers, leaders and innovators.

Congratulations to our incredible winner and finalists!

WINNER
Patricia Abril
New Cambridge School, Colombia

Stanley Manaay
Salvacion National High School, Philippines

Tiffany Cavanagh
Trident College Solwezi, Zambia

Helen Comerford
Lumen Christi Catholic College, Australia

John Nicko Coyoca
University of San Jose-Recoletos, Philippines

Meera Rangarajan
RBK International Academy, India

For more information about our dedicated teachers and their stories, go to
dedicatedteacher.cambridge.org

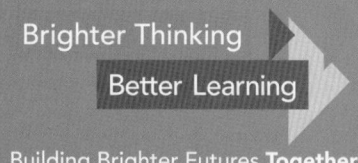

Contents

How to use this book — vii

Introduction — viii

Introducing command words — x

Part 1 The accounting system

1. Double-entry bookkeeping: Cash transactions — 2
2. Double-entry bookkeeping: Credit transactions — 7
3. Books of prime entry — 13
4. Balancing accounts — 19
5. The classification of accounts and division of the ledger — 25
6. The trial balance — 29

Part 2 Financial accounting

7. The statement of profit or loss for sole traders — 36
8. Statements of financial position for sole traders — 44
9. Accounting concepts — 49
10. Accruals and prepayments (the matching concept) — 52
11. Accounting for the depreciation of non-current assets — 59
12. Irrecoverable and doubtful debts — 67
13. Bank reconciliation statements — 73
14. Control accounts — 80
15. The correction of errors — 86
16. Incomplete records — 93
17. Incomplete records: Further considerations — 100

18 Partnership accounts	108
19 Partnership changes	117
20 Manufacturing accounts	127
21 An introduction to limited company accounts	136
22 Limited companies: Further considerations	144
23 Clubs and societies	151
24 Statements of cash flows	160
25 Auditing and stewardship	170
26 International Accounting Standards	176
27 Computerised accounting systems	185
28 Business acquisition and merger	187
29 Ethics and the accountant	201
30 Accounting information for stakeholders	204
31 Analysis and communication of accounting information	215

Part 3 Cost and management accounting

32 Costing of materials and labour	225
33 Absorption costing	230
34 Unit, job and batch costing	238
35 Marginal costing	245
36 Activity based costing	254
37 Budgeting and budgetary control	262
38 Standard costing	270
39 Investment appraisal	279

> How to use this book

Throughout this workbook, you will notice recurring features that are designed to help your learning. Here is a brief overview of what you will find.

LEARNING INTENTIONS

Learning intentions open each chapter. These help you with navigation through the workbook and indicate the important concepts in each topic. The learning intentions also map to the content in our *Cambridge International AS & A Level Accounting coursebook*.

KEY TERMS

These provide a reminder of the key definitions that you need to recall for each chapter topic.

Key skills exercises

These are scaffolded exercises that support your progression through the course and enable you to put into practice what you have learnt so far. The exercises have been linked to the key skills that you need for accounting.

- For knowledge and understanding exercises, there will be key content that you need to know and understand.

- For application exercises, you should use the context provided either by the question or the data response material in your answer.

- For analysis exercises, you need to explain why or how something is important, or why or how it is an advantage or disadvantage.

- For evaluation exercises, you are required to make supported decisions, draw conclusions and give recommendations.

TIPS

Tips are provided throughout this workbook to help with your learning. The tips provide you with additional practical guidance and advice in preparing the answers to exercises and exam-style questions.

WORKED EXAMPLES

Worked examples provide you with sample answers in order to help you understand how to respond to questions using key skills. In Accounting, the Worked examples offer a clear step-by-step breakdown of complex accounting processes to show learners how an outcome is achieved.

EXAM-STYLE QUESTIONS

More demanding exam-style questions provide you with an opportunity to further practise what you have learnt in each topic. Some of the questions in these sections are past paper questions. These include a reference to the past paper they are taken from. Some past paper questions are also included in the activities found in this resource.

Improve this answer

This offers you an opportunity to evaluate a sample answer to a question. Advice and guidance are provided in order to help you assess the answer. All sample answers have been written by the authors.

Your challenge

After completing 'Improve this answer', you are then asked to apply the advice to your own answer.

> Introduction

This Workbook is designed to help you develop your knowledge as you study for your Cambridge International AS & A Level Accounting qualifications. Each Workbook chapter gives you support as you put into practice knowledge and skills learnt in the corresponding Coursebook chapter. Working through the many exercises in this book will help you to feel more confident about what you need to be a successful Accounting student.

The Workbook covers a range of exercises in every chapter to help you build up your core skills. It is important that you gain as much practice as possible in developing the following skills:

- Knowledge and understanding
- Application of knowledge and understanding
- Analysis
- Evaluation

You will benefit mostly from the Workbook by using it together with the following Coursebook:

Endorsed Coursebook: *Cambridge International AS & A Level Accounting Coursebook*, published by Cambridge University Press.

Answers to all of the exercises and exam-style questions are provided online. These allow you to access a response for each question. The accounting statements are presented fully using standard layouts, and international accounting terms and formats are used where appropriate.

Complete your own answers before referring to the online answers. The more you practise exam-style questions, the better your answers will become.

Enjoy your Accounting course and use this book as an invaluable resource, guide and support towards achieving success in your studies.

Introducing command words

The command words and definitions in this section are taken from the Cambridge International syllabus (9706) for examination from 2023. You should always refer to the appropriate syllabus document for the year of your examination to confirm the details and for more information. The syllabus document is available on the Cambridge International website at www.cambridgeinternational.org. The guidance that appears in the tables has been written by the authors.

Questions in exam papers typically start with a command word. For Cambridge International AS & A Level Accounting, the command words are shown in the table. In time, and with experience, it will become easy to understand which skills need to be demonstrated in response to different types of question.

Command word	Definition
Advise	write down a suggested course of action in a given situation
Analyse	examine in detail to show meaning, identify elements and the relationship between them
Assess	make an informed judgement using evidence
Comment	give an informed opinion
Compare	identify/comment on similarities and/or differences
Define	give precise meaning
Describe	state the points of a topic/give characteristics and main features
Discuss	write about issue(s) or topic(s) in depth in a structured way that develops each point
Evaluate	judge or calculate the quality, importance, amount or value of something
Explain	set out purposes or reasons/make the relationships between things evident/provide why or how and support with evidence
Identify	name/select/recognise
Justify	support a case with evidence/argument
State	express in clear terms
Suggest	apply knowledge and understanding to situations where there are a range of valid responses in order to make proposals/put forward considerations

There are a number of command words that relate more to the numerical elements of examinations – and in some cases, to particular topics. These are provided in the table next:

Command word	Definition
Allocate	charge overheads that can be directly attributed to a specific cost centre to that centre
Apportion	charge overheads that cannot be directly attributable to a cost centre, to other centres using that overhead, on an appropriate basis
Re-apportion	recharge overheads from non-production cost centres on an appropriate basis
Calculate	work out from given facts, figures or information
Prepare	present information in a suitable format
Reconcile	process two sets of figures to confirm their agreement

> Part 1

The accounting system

Chapter 1
Double-entry bookkeeping: Cash transactions

LEARNING INTENTIONS

In this chapter you will:

- understand that double-entry bookkeeping is used to record the two sides of a transaction
- know what ledgers and ledger accounts are
- understand cash transactions
- use the double-entry system to record cash transactions.

KEY TERMS

Accounting system   Capital   Capital account   Credit side   Debit side   Double-entry bookkeeping   Drawings
Ledger   Ledger account   Purchases   Purchases returns   Sales returns

Key skills exercises

Knowledge and understanding

To answer the questions in this chapter, you need to know and understand:

- each financial transaction has two entries (giving and receiving) into the ledger system, hence the name double-entry system
- a ledger system records each financial transaction that takes place in a business
- one entry is on the debit side of an account and the second entry is on the credit side of an account for each transaction
- cash transactions involve money being paid or received straightaway.

You also need to be able to apply your knowledge and understanding of the double-entry system to the ledger accounts.

ARHAM'S CELL PHONE REPAIRS

Arham has decided to open his own cell phone repair shop.

He finds a shop location in Lahore, Pakistan, which is central and easy access for people. He rents the shop to get the business started and, if the business becomes successful, he will consider buying the premises.

To start the business, he needs shop fittings and equipment. In order to pay for these items, he needs some capital, which he deposits into the business bank account. Arham realises that his capital contribution will not cover all of his initial costs and so applies for a bank loan.

1 Double-entry bookkeeping: Cash transactions AS Level

> **WORKED EXAMPLE 1**
>
> Before Arham opens his shop to the public the following financial transactions take place.
>
> State the accounts that will be debited and credited for each transaction (double-entry system).

Transaction	Account to debit (received into the account)	Account to credit (what is given)
Arham deposits his capital contribution into the business bank account	Bank	Capital
Paid rent by debit card	Rent expense	Bank
Purchased cell phones, chargers, cell phone covers for resale purposes	Purchases	Bank
Receives the bank loan via a bank transfer	Bank	Bank loan
Purchased equipment (tools etc.) and paid by cheque	Equipment	Bank
Returned some damaged phone covers he had bought for resale purposes	Bank	Purchases returns
Bought furniture for the shop by debit card	Furniture	Bank
Carriage inwards paid by debit card	Carriage inwards	Bank

TIP

We are dealing with cash transactions, which means money is either being spent or received by the business. The bank account will always be affected by these transactions.

1 Arham has now set up his shop and is ready to open his business to the public. In his first two weeks of business, the following financial transactions took place.

State the account to debit and credit for each transaction.

Transaction	Account to debit (received into the account)	Account to credit (what is given)
Sold a cell phone and cover to a customer who paid by cheque		
Carriage outwards paid by cheque		
Banked the takings from selling goods		
Repaired a customer's cell phone and received the payment by a debit card payment		
A customer returned goods and was refunded from the bank account		
Paid light and heating by debit card		
Purchased new office equipment and paid by cheque		
Withdrew money from bank account for personal use		
Paid general expenses by cheque		
Returned unwanted goods to supplier and received refund by bank transfer		

3

WORKED EXAMPLE 2

These are the financial transactions that took place in the first week of August 2019, the second month of Arham's business venture.

Prepare the ledger accounts for these transactions.

Aug 1 Arham paid rent by bank transfer, $2 500
2 Cash purchases of more stock for his shop to the value of $3 000 for resale
3 Cash purchases of shop fittings for $1 000
4 Received $400 by debit card from selling cell phones
5 Arham returned some damaged goods to the value of $60
6 Arham withdrew $200 from the business bank account for private use

Answer

Bank account

Debit			Credit		
		$			$
Aug 4	Sales	400	Aug 1	Rent expense	2 500
5	Purchases returns	60	2	Purchases	3 000
			3	Shop fittings	1 000
			6	Drawings	200

Rent expense

Debit			Credit	
		$		$
Aug 1	Bank	2 500		

Purchases account

Debit			Credit	
		$		$
Aug 2	Bank	300		

Sales account

Debit		Credit		
	$			$
		Aug 4	Bank	400

Purchases returns account

Debit		Credit		
	$			$
		Aug 5	Bank	60

Drawings account

Debit			Credit	
		$		$
Aug 6	Bank	200		

1 Double-entry bookkeeping: Cash transactions AS Level

> **CONTINUED**
> - Each transaction is entered into the bank account as these are cash transactions.
> - The debit side is for cash received whereas the credit side is for cash paid.
> - The double-entry from the bank account is to the account for which the cash was either received or spent.

2 Arham has now been in business for six months. He is so busy he can't run the shop on his own. He decides to employ an assistant. The following financial transactions took place in January 2020.

Prepare the ledger accounts for the following financial transactions.

Jan 1   Arham deposited $5 000 into the business bank account as additional capital
    2   Purchased equipment for business use to the value of $6 700, paid by cheque
    3   Purchased $4 800 worth of stock for resale, paid by debit card
    4   Received $360 by bank transfer for goods sold
    5   Returned $230 worth of damaged goods
    6   Paid light and heat account $790 by cheque
    7   Paid carriage outwards $450 by bank transfer

3 Arham has owned his own business for a year now and it is very successful. He has decided not to buy his business premises yet but has bought another premises elsewhere, which he is renting out. The following financial transactions took place in July 2020.

Complete the table by stating which account to debit and which account to credit for each transaction, *then* prepare the ledger accounts by recording the transactions in the necessary ledger accounts.

	Transaction	Account to debit (received into the account)	Account to credit (what is given)
1	Purchased for cash a motor vehicle for $3 600		
2	Received $280 cash for sales		
3	Paid wages in cash $1 200 for the shop assistant		
4	Returned damaged goods to a supplier, received a refund of $270		
5	Carriage inwards paid in cash, $180		
6	Received $2 500 cash from Hazeem for rent		
7	Cash purchases of shop fittings, $690		
8	Withdrew $560 cash for personal use		
9	Paid $38 cash for stationery		
10	A dissatisfied customer returned goods worth $470		

EXAM-STYLE MULTIPLE CHOICE QUESTIONS

1   Liyana owns a bakery. She recently bought an oven for business use and paid by cheque. Which entries in Liyana's books record this transaction?

	Debit account	Credit account
A	Bank	Purchases
B	Equipment	Bank
C	Purchases	Bank
D	Bank	Equipment

[1]

2   Souma is a plumber. He ordered some plumbing materials from Plumbing Requirements and discovered some were damaged when they were delivered. He returned the damaged materials and received a refund. How would this transaction be recorded in Souma's books of account?

	Debit account	Credit account
A	Purchases returns	Bank
B	Bank	Sales returns
C	Sales returns	Bank
D	Bank	Purchases returns

[1]

> Chapter 2

Double-entry bookkeeping: Credit transactions

LEARNING INTENTIONS

In this chapter you will:

- understand credit transactions
- use the double-entry system to record credit transactions
- know the difference between trade and cash discounts and how to treat them in the ledger accounts
- use the double-entry system to record payments to trade payables and receipts from trade receivables

KEY TERMS

Cash discount   Credit transaction   Discount allowed   Discount received   Trade discount   Trade payable   Trade receivable

Key skills exercises

Knowledge and understanding

To answer the questions in this chapter, you need to know and understand:

- credit transactions are when a purchase or sale occurs but the payment or receipt of money happens later
- what a trade payable and trade receivable are
- a trade discount is a reduction in the selling price made by one trader to another
- a cash discount is an allowance given to encourage a customer to pay quickly.

You also need to be able to apply your knowledge and understanding of trade payables, trade receivables, trade discount and cash discount to the ledger accounts.

> **OMAR'S GROCERY STORE**
>
> Chocoholics Malaysia is one of the leading companies in Kuala Lumpur. They manufacture products and sell them to many shops throughout Malaysia for resale purposes. Due to the large quantities of inventory being bought by businesses throughout Malaysia, Chocoholics offers its customers credit transactions.
>
> Omar owns a grocery store in Mont Kiara and buys goods from Chocoholics Malaysia to be resold in his store. Omar has a deal with Chocoholics to make all his purchases on credit (trade payables), with the agreement that he will pay for the goods within 30 days of purchase.
>
> Omar also allows his customers to buy on credit from his store (trade receivables); he allows a 30-day period in which payments need to be made for goods purchased on credit.

CAMBRIDGE INTERNATIONAL AS & A LEVEL ACCOUNTING: WORKBOOK

WORKED EXAMPLE 1

The following financial transactions took place in Omar's grocery store books of account in the month of May 2020.

State the accounts that will be debited and credited for each transaction (using the double-entry system) and then prepare the ledger accounts by recording the transactions in their ledger accounts.

Transaction		Account to debit (received into the account)	Account to credit (what is given)
May 3	Omar purchased goods on credit from Chocoholics to the value of $1 800	Purchases	Chocoholics
8	Omar sold on credit to a customer, Sari, for $460	Sari	Sales
13	Omar sold goods on credit valued at $890 to Raj	Raj	Sales
20	Omar returned damaged goods to Chocoholics, $230	Chocoholics	Purchases returns
26	Sari returned some unwanted goods that she bought on 8 May, $56	Sales returns	Sari

Purchases

Debit			Credit		
		$			$
May 3	Chocoholics	1800			

Chocoholics

Debit			Credit		
		$			$
May 20	Purchases returns	230	May 3	Purchases	1 800

Sari

Debit			Credit		
		$			$
May 8	Sales	460	May 26	Sales returns	56

Sales

Debit			Credit		
		$			$
			May 8	Sari	460

Purchases returns

Debit			Credit		
		$			$
			May 20	Chocoholics	230

Sales returns

Debit			Credit		
		$			$
May 26	Sari	56			

2 Double-entry bookkeeping: Credit transactions AS Level

1 Omar's grocery store had the following financial transactions in June 2020.

State which two accounts are affected by each transaction and then prepare the ledger accounts by recording the transactions in their ledger accounts.

Jun 2   Omar sold goods on credit to Zamrud for $3 400

      6   Omar bought goods on credit from Chocoholics for $5 890

     10   Omar sold goods to Nawar on credit for $2 370

     16   Omar returned some unwanted goods to Chocoholics for $270

     21   Omar sold goods to Demak on credit for $4 680

     29   Nawar returned $360 worth of goods that she purchased on 10 June as they were damaged

WORKED EXAMPLE 2

Omar's grocery store is struggling to get some trade receivables to pay their accounts on time. He decides to offer cash discounts to some of his credit customers to encourage them to pay their debts early.

Chocoholics also offers Omar trade discount on his large orders and also offers a cash discount to Omar to pay his account early.

State which two accounts are affected by each financial transaction and then prepare the ledger accounts by recording the transactions in their ledger accounts.

Date	Transaction	Account to debit	Account to credit
Jul 3	Omar bought equipment from We Equip You for business use on credit for $1 300	Equipment	We Equip You
9	Hitam bought goods on credit from Omar's grocery store for $3 400; Omar offered Hitam a 5% cash discount if he paid his account by 31 July	Hitam	Sales
12	Omar returned some goods to Chocoholics worth $450	Chocoholics	Purchases returns
15	Omar bought goods on credit to the value of $6 500 from Chocoholics; they offered him a 4% trade discount as well as a 5% cash discount if he pays his account by 31 July	Purchases	Chocoholics
21	Azura bought goods from Omar's grocery store worth $3 650; Omar agreed to a 6% cash discount if Azura can pay her account by 31 July	Azura	Sales
23	Hitam returned damaged goods to Omar's grocery store worth $320; he originally purchased these goods on 9 July	Sales returns	Hitam
25	Omar paid Chocoholics for the goods purchased on 15 July	Chocoholics	Bank Discount received
28	Azura paid her account for the goods purchased on 21 July	Bank Discount allowed	Azura
29	Omar withdrew money for his own personal use, $1 240	Drawings	Bank
30	Hitam paid his account for the goods purchased on 9 July	Bank Discount allowed	Hitam

CONTINUED

Equipment

Debit			Credit		
		$			$
Jul 3	We Equip You	1 300			

We EquipYou

Debit			Credit		
		$			$
			Jul 3	Equipment	1 300

Hitam

Debit			Credit		
		$			$
Jul 9	Sales	3 400	Jul 23	Returns	320
			30	Bank	2 926
			30	Discount allowed	154

Sales

Debit			Credit		
		$			$
			Jul 9	Hitam	3 400
			21	Azura	3 650

Chocoholics

Debit			Credit		
		$			$
Jul 12	Returns	450	Jul 15	Purchases	624
25	Bank	5 928			
25	Discount received	312			

Purchases returns

Debit			Credit		
		$			$
			Jul 12	Chocoholics	450

Purchases

Debit			Credit		
		$			$
Jul 15	Chocoholics	6 240			

> **TIP**
> For example, Omar purchased equipment on credit for resale purposes: the purchases account will be debited however; Omar purchased equipment on credit for office use: the equipment will be debited.

CONTINUED

Azura

Debit		$	Credit		$
Jul 21	Sales	3650	Jul 28	Bank	3431
			28	Discount allowed	219

Sales returns

Debit		$	Credit		$
Jul 23	Hitam	320			

Bank

Debit		$	Credit		$
Jul 28	Azura	3431	Jul 25	Chocoholics	6432
30	Hitam	2926	29	Drawings	1240

Discount allowed

Debit		$	Credit		$
Jul 28	Azura	219			
30	Haziq	154			

Drawings

Debit		$	Credit		$
Jul 29	Bank	1240			

Omar has found that offering cash discounts is helping his business receive money owed faster. He decides to offer trade discount to some of his customers as well, like he has been receiving from Chocoholics.

2   The following financial transactions took place at Omar's grocery store in August 2020.

State which account to debit and which account to credit for each transaction to complete the table. Prepare the ledger accounts by recording the transactions in the necessary ledger accounts.

Date	Transaction	Account to debit	Account to credit
Aug 1	Omar deposited an additional capital contribution of $15 000		
4	Sold goods on credit to Fajar for $2 300, offered her a 3% trade discount		
9	Bought furniture on credit from Furniture World for $6 950		

CAMBRIDGE INTERNATIONAL AS & A LEVEL ACCOUNTING: WORKBOOK

Date	Transaction	Account to debit	Account to credit
13	Bought goods on credit from Chocoholics for $4 360, they offered a cash discount of 5% if the amount is paid by 31 August		
18	Fajar returned $400 worth of goods purchased 4 August		
22	Sold goods to Maya for $6 500, offered her a 2% cash discount if her account was settled by 31 August		
24	Refunded money to Maya for damaged goods purchased on 22 August to the value of $250		
27	Paid the amount owed to Chocoholics on 13 August by cheque		
31	Received a cheque from Maya for the goods purchased on 22 August		

3   Shown are the financial transactions for Omar's grocery store for September 2020.

Prepare the ledger accounts for the transactions. All goods are bought and sold on credit.

Sep 2	Bought goods from Chocoholics for $3 000 less trade discount of $33\frac{1}{3}$%
6	Sold goods to Bayu for $5 600
11	Returned goods costing $240 to Chocoholics; originally bought on 2 September
18	Purchased goods from Chocoholics that cost $7 500 before trade discount of 6%
23	Paid Chocoholics all the money owed for this month.
29	Received full payment from Bayu

TIP

For the transactions where Fajar returns goods on 18 August, which she originally purchased on 4 August, the discount offered on 4 August must be deducted.

EXAM-STYLE MULTIPLE CHOICE QUESTIONS

1   Muda bought goods on credit to the value of $2 340 and received a trade discount of 5%. Which double-entry in Muda's business books is correct?

	Account to debit	**Account to credit**
A	Sales $2 340	Bank $2 340
B	Bank $2 223	Muda $2 223
C	Purchases $2 223	Trade payables $2 223
D	Trade receivables $2 340	Sales $2 340

[1]

2   Zakaria sold goods on credit to Zamrud to the value of $9 600. Zakaria offered Zamrud a 5% trade discount as well as another 5% cash discount if Zamrud paid his account within 10 days. Zamrud paid his account within the time to receive the cash discount. Which entries record the payment in Zakaria's books?

	Account(s) to debit	**Account(s) to credit**
A	Purchases $9 600	Zamrud $9 600
B	Bank $8 664 Discount allowed $456	Zamrud $9 120
C	Zakaria $9 120	Bank $8 664 Discount received $456
D	Zamrud $9 600	Sales $9 600

[1]

12

Chapter 3
Books of prime entry

LEARNING INTENTIONS

In this chapter you will:
- understand the purpose of books of prime entry
- know when to use each book of prime entry
- use books of prime entry to record transactions
- use the double-entry system to post transactions from the books of prime entry to ledger accounts

KEY TERMS

Books of prime entry   Cash book   Contra entry   Credit note   General journal   Invoice   Narrative
Purchases journal   Purchases returns journal   Sales journal   Sales returns journal

Key skills exercises

Knowledge and understanding

To answer the questions in this chapter, you need to know and understand:
- the different books of prime entry and when to use each one
- which transactions go into which book of prime entry.

You should also be able to apply your knowledge and understanding of books of prime entry and post the records to the ledger accounts.

> **Zimbo Beverages**
> Zimbo Beverages is a company in Harare, Zimbabwe, that sells beverages. They buy beverages from the manufacturer and sell them to customers for resale. Their accounting system includes all the books of prime entry.

WORKED EXAMPLE 1

The following transactions took place at Zimbo Beverages during the first week of October 2019.

Oct 1   Received an invoice from Soda-pop for beverages purchased, $5 600
     3   Purchased equipment on credit for $3 780 from We Equip You, invoice no. 124
     6   Cheque stub showed the payment of goods purchased on 1 October

a   State which book of prime entry should be used for each transaction and enter all the transactions for the week into their relevant book of prime entry.

Answer

Date	Transaction	Book of prime entry
1	Received an invoice from Soda-pop for beverages purchased, $5 600	Purchases journal
3	Purchased equipment on credit for $3 780 from We Equip You, invoice no. 124	General journal
6	Cheque stub showed the payment of goods purchased on 1 October	Cash book

Transaction 1 October is entered in the purchases journal as an invoice was received, which means it was purchased on credit. It is entered as follows:

Purchases journal

Date	Supplier	$
Oct 1	Soda-pop	5 600
	Total purchases	5 600

Transaction 3 October is entered in the general journal as a non-current asset and was purchased on credit. It is entered as follows:

General journal

Date	Details	Dr $	Cr $
Oct 3	Equipment	3 780	
	We Equip You		3 780
	Purchase of new equipment on credit, invoice no.124		

Transaction 6 October is entered in the cash book as the beverages purchased on 1 October are now being paid for. It is entered as follows:

Cash book

	Debit				Credit		
	Discounts allowed $	Cash $	Bank $		Discounts received $	Cash $	Bank $
				Oct 6 Soda-pop			5 600

b Prepare the ledger accounts for these transactions.

Answer

Transaction 1 October: Double-entry accounts are Debit Purchases (what is received) and Credit Soda-pop (what is given).

Transaction 3 October: Double-entry accounts are Debit Equipment (what is received) and Credit We Equip You (what is given).

Transaction 6 October: Double-entry accounts are Debit Soda-pop (what is received) and Credit Bank (what is given).

CONTINUED

Soda-pop

Debit			Credit		
		$			$
Oct 6	Bank	5 600	Oct 1	Purchases	5 600

Purchases

Debit			Credit		
		$			$
Oct 1	Soda-pop	5 600			

Equipment

Debit			Credit		
		$			$
Oct 3	We Equip You	3 780			

We Equip You

Debit			Credit		
		$			$
			Oct 3	Equipment	3 780

Bank

Debit			Credit		
		$			$
			Oct 6	Soda-pop	5 600

---

1 The following transactions took place in the rest of October 2019 at Zimbo Beverages.

Oct 10	Bought beverages from Soda-pop for $9 500 less 10% trade discount; Soda-pop allowed 2% cash discount
12	Zimbo Beverages returned damaged goods to Soda-pop, which had cost $640
15	Sold beverages to Vimbai for $3 400, invoice sent to her
19	Sold goods for cash to Garai, $2 300, less 20% trade discount and 5% cash discount
23	Vimbai returned some unwanted goods, $260
26	Purchased beverages from Soda-pop, $7 800 less 20% trade discount; Soda-pop allowed another 5% cash discount
31	Beverages sold on credit to Masimba for $890 were incorrectly posted to Simba's account

a State which book of prime entry should be used for each transaction and enter all the transactions for the week into their relevant book of prime entry.

Date	Transaction	Book of prime entry
Oct 10	Bought beverages from Soda-pop for $9 500 less 10% trade discount; Soda-pop allowed 2% cash discount	
12	Zimbo Beverages returned damaged goods to Soda-pop, which had cost $640	
15	Sold beverages to Vimbai for $3 400, invoice sent to her	
19	Sold goods for cash to Garai, $2 300, less 20% trade discount and 5% cash discount	
23	Vimbai returned some unwanted goods, $260	
26	Purchased beverages from Soda-pop, $7 800 less 20% trade discount; Soda-pop allowed another 5% cash discount	
31	Beverages sold on credit to Masimba for $890 were incorrectly posted to Simba's account	

b Prepare the ledger accounts for these transactions.

2 During November 2019 the following transactions took place at Zimbo Beverages. Prepare the books of prime entry and post the journals to the ledger.

Nov 2   Sold beverages to Tinashe for $6 800, invoice sent to her

4   Paid Soda-pop an amount of $2 350

8   Purchased beverages from Soda-pop, $6 290, received invoice

11   Tinashe paid her account less 6% cash discount

15   Purchased beverages for cash from Soda-pop; received a 10% trade discount and further 5% cash discount, $2 600

16   Zimbo Beverages returned damaged goods to Soda-pop, which had cost $760

19   Sold goods for cash to Runako, $6 000, less 5% trade discount and 2% cash discount

22   Runako returned some unwanted goods, $600, refund given to him

27   Purchased a motor vehicle on credit, $12 000, received invoice no. 421

30   Purchased goods on credit from Soda-pop, $3 200; it was incorrectly posted to Pop-Soda's account

WORKED EXAMPLE 2

The following transactions took place in the month of December 2019:

a Zimbo Beverages discovered that they had credited $100, which they had received from N. Dube on 1 December to an account for M. Dube in error.

b On 8 December Zimbo Beverages bought office furniture from We Got Furniture on credit for $400, invoice no. 654.

c On 19 December Zimbo Beverages bought a delivery van from Vans 4 U. An amount of $2 300 has been debited to the purchases account in error.

Prepare general journal entries with suitable narratives.

3 Books of prime entry AS Level

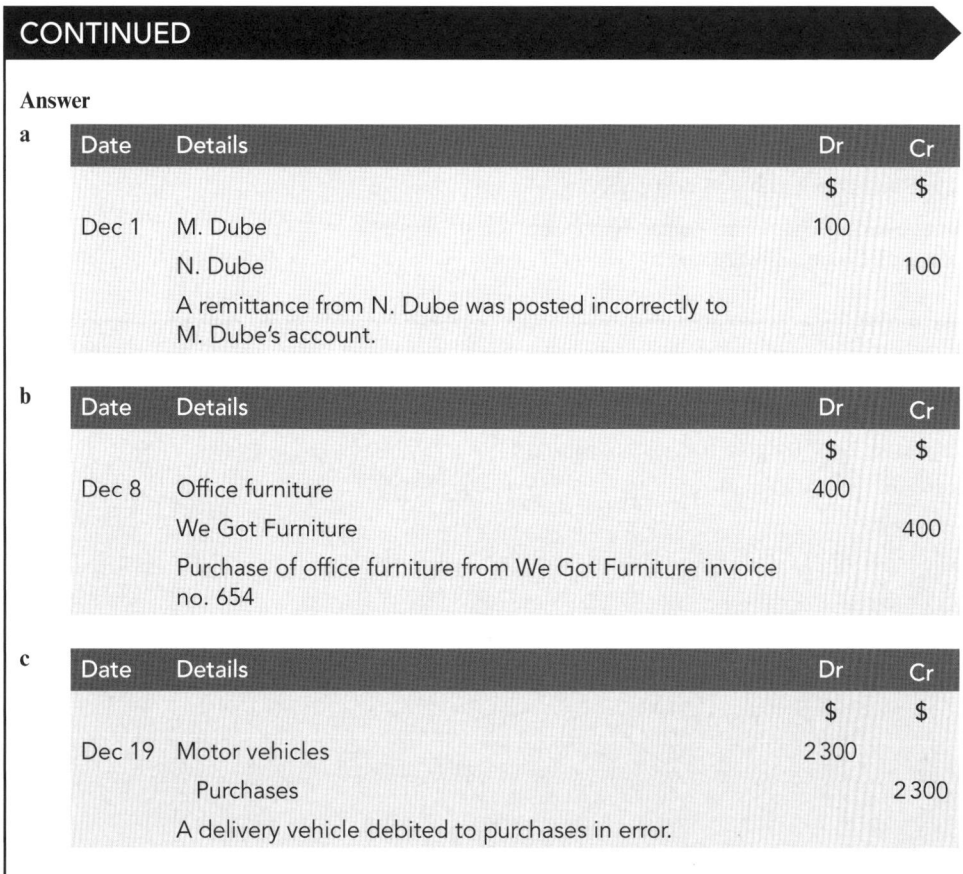

3   Prepare general journal entries with suitable narratives.

   a   Received invoice no. 52 from Machines Galore, dated 15 December for $10 000. This was in respect of the purchase of a machine on credit.

   b   Credit note no. 203, dated 18 December for $190, sent to Tinashe but omitted from the sales returns journal.

   c   Invoice no. 753, dated 21 December for $675, for goods sold to Runako. The invoice has been entered twice in the sales journal.

   d   Invoice no. 649, dated 27 December for $1 300, for goods purchased from Soda-pop. The invoice has been posted to Popsicles account in error.

4   During January 2020 the following transactions took place at Zimbo Beverages. Prepare the books of prime entry and post the journals to the ledger.

   Jan 1   Bought goods from Soda-pop for $3 000 less 20% trade discount; Soda-pop allowed Zimbo Beverages 5% cash discount

   5   Sold goods to Tinashe for $800 less 10% trade discount; allowed Tinashe 5% cash discount

   8   Bought goods from Soda-pop for $1 300 less 20% trade discount; Soda-pop allowed 5% cash discount

   12   Purchased a delivery van on credit from We Got Motors for $6 000; The invoice for the van was no. 489

   16   Returned goods that had cost $100 to Soda-pop

20 Sold goods to Runako for $1 100 less 20% trade discount; allowed Runako 5% cash discount

23 Tinashe returned goods which that cost $60

25 Purchased goods from Soda-pop, for $4 000 less 25% trade discount; Soda-pop allowed 5% cash discount

28 Returned goods to Soda-pop which had cost $300

30 Settled all accounts owed by cheque and received cheques for all amounts owing by customers; all discounts were taken

EXAM-STYLE MULTIPLE CHOICE QUESTIONS

1   Which of these transactions should be entered in the general journal?
    A   Purchase of new motor vehicle by bank transfer
    B   Return of goods by a customer
    C   Cash drawings by owner
    D   Purchase of equipment on credit [1]

2   Tendai purchased goods from Zimbo Beverages for $9 000. She received 25% trade discount and 10% cash discount. How much should she pay?
    A $6 750
    B $8 100
    C $6 075
    D $5 850 [1]

3   Chiedza purchased goods from Zimbo Beverages on credit. A few days later, she returned a few items to Zimbo Beverages. At the end of the month, she paid her outstanding balance. Which is the correct order of documents issued to Chiedza?
    A   Receipt, invoice, credit note
    B   Credit note, receipt, invoice
    C   Invoice, credit note, receipt
    D   Invoice, receipt, credit note [1]

> Chapter 4
Balancing accounts

LEARNING INTENTIONS

In this chapter you will:
- understand debit and credit balances
- know that accounts are balanced regularly
- calculate and record ledger accounts balances
- calculate and record cash and bank balances using a cash book

KEY TERMS

Balancing an account   Credit balance   Debit balance   Overdraft

Key skills exercises

Knowledge and understanding

To answer the questions in this chapter, you need to know and understand:
- the difference between the debit and credit side of a ledger account
- the different methods of balancing accounts and which one is used for which situation.

You should also be able to apply your knowledge of the different methods of balancing accounts to the ledger accounts.

> **Zimbo Beverages**
>
> Zimbo Beverages in Harare, Zimbabwe (continued from Chapter 3), sells local and international brands in beverages. Zimbo Beverages buy in products from other companies and then distribute these products. Therefore, Zimbo Beverages has many trade receivables and trade payables accounts as well as expense and income accounts. It is important for them to know on a regular basis what money is owed to them, what money is owed by them, and what their expenses and income totals are. Some of the supermarkets they distribute to are Food Market, Stop & Shop and Hungry Harvest.

WORKED EXAMPLE 1

Calculate and balance each of the following accounts.

Answers

Account 1

	Debit		Machinery	Credit	
		$			$
Aug 15	Bank	15 000	Aug 31	Balance c/d	15 000
		15 000			15 000
Sep 1	Balance b/d	15 000			

CONTINUED

Account 2

Soda-pop

Debit			Credit		
		$			$
Aug 8	Purchases returns	520	Aug 3	Purchases	2 300
15	Purchases returns	630	11	Purchases	1 400
31	Bank	4 200	20	Purchases	1 070
31	Discount received	380	28	Purchases	2 100
31	Balance c/d	1 140			
		6 870			6 870
			Sep 1	Balance b/d	1 140

Account 3

Tinashe

Debit			Credit		
		$			$
Aug 12	Sales	1 400	Aug 21	Sales returns	200
			31	Balance c/d	1 200
		1 400			1 400
Aug 31	Balance b/d	1 200			

Account 4

Discounts allowed

Debit			Credit		
		$			$
Aug 1	Balance b/d	310	Aug 31	Balance c/d	580
13	Cash book	270			
		580			580
Sep 1	Balance c/d	580			

1 Calculate and balance each account using the correct method.

Account 1

Purchases

Debit			Credit		
		$			$
Oct 1	Soda-pop	5 600			
10	Bank	8 379			
26	Bank	5 928			

Account 2

Best Buys				
Debit		Credit		
	$			$
Oct 14 Bank	1 250	Oct 14	Purchases	1 250

2 Calculate and balance the following accounts.

Motor vehicles			
Debit		Credit	
	$		$
Apr 1 Balance	12 540		
22 Bank	5 410		

Sales			
Debit		Credit	
	$		$
		Apr 1 Balance	14 786
		10 Bank	5 170
		17 Stop & Shop	4 230
		23 Hungry Harvest	2 740

Wages			
Debit		Credit	
	$		$
Apr 25 Bank	9 530		

Soda-pop			
Debit		Credit	
	$		$
Apr 20 Bank	4 320	Apr 4 Purchases	4 320

WORKED EXAMPLE 2

Zimbo Beverages makes use of a cash book for all their cash and bank transactions. The opening balances for 1 June 2020 are bank $25 460 and cash $7 530. The following transactions took place in the first week of June and have been recorded in the cash book.

Calculate and balance the cash book shown here and total the discount columns.

Cash book

		Debit					Credit		
		Discount allowed $	Cash $	Bank $			Discount received $	Cash $	Bank $
Jun 1	Balances		7 530	25 460	Jun 2	Stationery		456	
3	Sales		2 360		3	Soda-pop	763		5 621
4	Food Market	260		5 340	5	Bank		1 000	
5	Cash			1 000	6	Maizy drink	423		4 890
6	Stop & Shop	730		12 350	6	Snappysip	347		3 752
7	Hungry Harvest	140		3 580	7	Wages		3 450	
7	Sales		7 320						

Answer

Cash book

		Debit					Credit		
		Discount allowed $	Cash $	Bank $			Discount received $	Cash $	Bank $
Jun 1	Balances		7 530	25 460	Jun 2	Stationery		456	
3	Sales		2 360		3	Soda-pop	763		5 621
4	Food Market	260		5 340	5	Bank C		1 000	
5	Cash C			1 000	6	Maizy drink	423		4 890
6	Stop & Shop	730		12 350	6	Snappysip	347		3 752
7	Hungry Harvest	140		3 580	7	Wages		3 450	
7	Sales		7 320		8	Balances c/d		12 304	33 467
		1 130	17 210	47 730			1 533	17 210	47 730
8	Balances b/d		12 304	33 467					

Method 1 is applied to balance the cash book. The cash column will always have the debit side as the side with the higher amount as cash can never have a negative amount of cash. However, the bank balance can be on the credit side as the bank offers an overdraft. In this example, both the cash and bank accounts have debit (positive) balances.

4 Balancing accounts AS Level

3 Calculate and balance the cash book shown here from the second week of June 2020 for Zimbo Beverages.

Cash book

		Debit					Credit		
		Discount allowed $	Cash $	Bank $			Discount received $	Cash $	Bank $
Jun 8	Balances		12 304	33 467	Jun 8	Equipment			2 300
9	Hungry Harvest	450		3 789	9	Electricity		360	
10	Sales		2 800		10	Snappysip	85		3 512
11	Cash			2 500	11	Bank expenses		2 500	
12	Food Market	590		4 780	12	Maizy drink	97		2 874
13	Sales		4 650		14	Wages		4 890	
14	Hungry Harvest	780		10 260					

4 The following transactions took place in the first two weeks of November 2020 at Zimbo Beverages. The opening balances for 1 November are cash $13 458 and bank $20 680.

Prepare the cash book and nominal ledger accounts and balance both the cash book and nominal ledger accounts.

Opening balances for trade receivables and trade payables:

Soda-pop	$10 740
Hungry Harvest	$6 987
Snappysip	$9 830
Stop & Shop	$4 217
Maizy drink	$3 692

Nov 1	Zimbo Beverages paid Soda-pop $4 350 by debit card and received a 2% cash discount
2	Cash sales of $2 890
3	Bought a new motor vehicle for distribution purposes, $12 780, paid by bank transfer
3	Received payment from Hungry Harvest for $1 260 via bank transfer and gave them a 5% cash discount
4	Paid for postage $45 by cash
5	Cash sales of $1 567
6	Paid cash into the bank account $1 200
6	Paid Snappysip $6 280 by debit card and received 5% trade discount
7	Received payment from Stop & Shop $1 300 by bank transfer and gave them a 3% cash discount
7	Paid Maizy drink by cheque $2 400 less 4% cash discount
7	Paid wages $2 650 by cash
8	Hungry Harvest bought goods on credit to the value of $3 590
9	Returned goods to Soda-pop, $460
10	Bought goods on credit from Maizy drink, $6 530
11	Paid stationery $230 by cash
12	Paid Soda-pop $580 by cheque, less 5% cash discount
13	Returned damaged goods to Snappysip worth $470
14	Stop & Shop returned goods to Zimbo Beverages to the value of $150

CAMBRIDGE INTERNATIONAL AS & A LEVEL ACCOUNTING: WORKBOOK

EXAM-STYLE STRUCTURED QUESTION

1. Zira owns a toy shop and needs to complete her accounting records at the end of the year in order to complete her statements of financial position. She has prepared the nominal ledger.

    Calculate and balance the accounts at the end of the month.

Sales

Debit			Credit	
	$			$
		Dec 1 Balance		3 678
		7 The Play Castle		1 780
		18 Bank		3 472
		27 The Play Castle		3 654

Stationery

Debit			Credit	
	$			$
Dec 12 Bank	2 540			

Tawana

Debit			Credit	
	$			$
Dec 1 Balance b/d	4 650	Dec 17 Bank		5 210
5 Sales	3 780	17 Discount allowed		360
23 Sales	2 760	22 Sales returns		840
28 Sales	1 730			

Kids Toys

Debit			Credit	
	$			$
Dec 16 Bank	1 650	Dec 4 Purchases		1 780
16 Discount received	130			

[4]

Chapter 5
The classification of accounts and division of the ledger

LEARNING INTENTIONS

In this chapter you will:

- know that ledger accounts can be classified into assets, liabilities, income, expenses, capital and drawings
- understand that debit balances are common to asset, expense and drawings accounts while credit balances are common to liability, income and capital accounts
- understand how a single ledger can be divided into several ledgers, each containing transactions of a similar nature

KEY TERMS

Asset   Creditor   Current assets   Current liability   Expenses   Impersonal account   Nominal account
Non-current assets   Non-current liability   Personal account   Purchases ledger   Sales ledger

Key skills exercises
Knowledge and understanding

To answer the questions in this chapter, you need to know and understand:
- the different classifications of ledger accounts and what accounts fall under each classification (e.g. motor vehicle is an asset)
- which side of the account the balances go for each of the classifications
- ledgers are separated into more individualised accounts, understanding which accounts go into which ledgers.

You should also be able to apply your knowledge and understanding of ledgers and their classification to prepare sales and purchases ledger accounts.

> **THANDEKA'S HAIR PRODUCTS**
>
> Thandeka has recently completed a hairdressing course at a Hairdressing Salon and Training Centre in Manzini, Swaziland. She would like to open her own hair product shop and needs to calculate what it will cost her. Thandeka decides to write a business plan where she needs to state the assets, liabilities, income, expenses and capital for her business.
>
> Thandeka identifies the following assets for her shop: desk for the reception area, display shelves for sale of retail products, cash register and phone.
>
> She identifies the following expenses: electricity, products, rent, telephone bill and cleaning materials. The income would be from the sale of retail products.
>
> The capital she is able to put together is not sufficient for her to start the business so she will need to take a loan from the bank, which will be a liability.

Once Thandeka has all this information, she decides to open her shop. Sfiso, the accountant, advises Thandeka to keep a record of all her money spent (expenses), received (income), withdrawn for herself (drawings), money owed (trade payables) and money owed to her (trade receivables) through ledger accounts.

Sfiso also advised Thandeka to divide her ledger accounts into the three types of ledger: *nominal ledger* for assets, liabilities, income and expenses; *sales ledger* for individual trade receivable accounts and *purchases ledger* for individual trade payable accounts.

1 Identify whether the following accounts are assets, liabilities, revenue (income) or expenses. Tick the correct column in the table. The first one has been completed as an example.

Account	Asset	Liability	Revenue (Income)	Expense
Stationery				✓
Bank overdraft				
Equipment				
Discount received				
Trade receivables				
Bank loan				
Furniture and fittings				
Heat and light				
Rent receivable				
Salaries				
Trade payables				
Interest received				
Discount allowed				
Insurance				
Inventory				
Water charges				

2 Identify whether the following assets and liabilities are non-current or current.

Account	Non-current asset	Current asset	Non-current liability	Current liability
Premises				
Long-term bank loan				
Trade payable				
Bank				
Machinery				
Short-term bank loan				
Inventory				
Trade receivables				
Bank overdraft				
Cash in hand				

5 The classification of accounts and division of the ledger AS Level

WORKED EXAMPLE 1

Thandeka buys products from Hairlicious on a monthly basis. On 1 June 2020, she owed Hairlicious $1 480. During June, the following transactions took place.

Jun 2   Bought goods on credit $3 270, less 20% trade discount

     7   Made a bank transfer to Hairlicious in full settlement of amount owed on 1 June, less 5% cash discount

    16   Returned goods $450 bought on credit on 2 May

    26   Bought goods on credit $690, less $33\frac{1}{3}\%$ trade discount

Prepare Hairlicious' account in the purchases ledger. Balance the account at the end of the month and bring the new balance down for the start of July.

Answer

Purchases ledger — Hairlicious

Debit		$				$
Jun 7	Bank	1 406	Jun 1	Balance		1 480
7	Discount received	74	2	Purchases		2 616
16	Purchases returns	360	26	Purchases		460
30	Balance c/d	2 716				
		4 556				4 556
			Jul 1	Balance b/d		2 716

TIP

Trade payables are a liability as it is money the business owes. Therefore, the opening balance and purchases are on the credit side. Any money paid, returns or cash discounts received are on the debit side.

TIP

The purchases returns made on 16 June must still take the trade discount received on the purchase of the goods on 2 June into account.

---

3   Thandeka buys products from Hairlicious on a monthly basis. On 1 September 2020, she owed Hairlicious $2 220. During September, the following transactions took place.

     Sep 1   Bought goods on credit $2 560, less 20% trade discount

         12   Returned goods $520 bought on credit on 1 September

         21   Made a bank transfer to Hairlicious in full settlement of the amount owed on 1 September, less 5% cash discount

         27   Bought goods on credit $960, less $33\frac{1}{3}\%$ trade discount

Prepare Hairlicious' account in the purchases ledger. Balance the account at the end of the month and bring the new balance down for the start of July.

WORKED EXAMPLE 2

Appliances Galore, sells appliances on credit. One of Appliances Galore's customers, Maita, owes Appliances Galore $2 800 on 1 November 2019. During November, the following transactions took place.

Nov 2   Maita purchased appliances $1 700, less 15% trade discount

     8   Maita purchased appliances $2 300, less 10% trade discount

    16   Maita returned some damaged appliances bought on 2 November, $500

    25   Paid a cheque to Appliances Galore in settlement of the amount owed on 20 November, less 4% cash discount.

CONTINUED

Prepare Maita's account in the sales ledger for Appliances Galore. Balance the account at the end of the month and bring the new balance down for the start of September.

Answer

Sales ledger Maita					
Debit			**Credit**		
		$			$
Nov 1	Balance	2 800	Nov 16	Sales returns	440
2	Sales	1 445	25	Bank	5 640
16	Sales	2 070	28	Discount allowed	235
		6 315			6 315

TIP

Trade receivables are an asset as it is money owed to the business. The opening balance and sales will be on the debit side. Any payment, returns or discount allowed will be on the credit side. It works the opposite way to the purchases ledger shown in Worked example 2.

4 First in Furniture sells furniture on credit. One of First in Furniture's customers, Sambulo, owes First in Furniture $3200 on 1 August 2020. During August, the following transactions took place.

Aug 3   Sambulo purchased furniture $2900, less 16% trade discount
9   Sambulo returned some damaged furniture bought on 3 August, $700
17   Sambulo purchased furniture $1430, less 10% trade discount
28   Paid a cheque to First in Furniture in settlement of the amount owed 1 August, less 3.5% cash discount

Prepare Sambulo's account in the sales ledger for First in Furniture. Balance the account at the end of the month and bring the new balance down for the start of September.

TIP

The nominal ledger is used to record assets, liabilities, income, expenses and drawings. The sales ledger is used for individual trade receivable accounts and the purchases ledger for individual trade payable accounts.

EXAM-STYLE MULTIPLE CHOICE QUESTIONS

1   Which type of account will have a debit balance?
  A   Sales
  B   Discount received
  C   Purchases
  D   Income [1]

2   Which ledger will store the discount allowed account?
  A   Nominal
  B   Purchases
  C   Sales
  D   Cash book [1]

⟩ Chapter 6
The trial balance

LEARNING INTENTIONS

In this chapter you will:
- know what a trial balance is
- understand the purpose of a trial balance
- prepare a trial balance
- analyse the benefits and limitations of a trial balance
- explain the types of error that do or do not affect the agreement of the debit and credit totals on a trial balance

KEY TERMS

Overadded   Sole trader   Trial balance   Underadded

Key skills exercises

Knowledge and understanding

To answer the questions in this chapter. you need to know and understand:
- a trial balance is a list of the balances on each account at a particular date
- the purpose of a trial balance is to check that the debit and credit totals balance.

You should also be able to apply your knowledge and understanding of what a trial balance is and its purpose in order to prepare a trial balance.

> **CUSTOM FURNITURE**
>
> Siyabonga is a sole trader who owns a custom furniture business in Cape Town, South Africa. His business name is Crafted with Care. Siyabonga supplies the tourism industry (hotels, guest houses etc.) with custom made furniture for their establishments.
>
> Siyabonga's clients are able to specify what furniture they need and what it should look like. Siyabonga is then able to make as many of the custom made furniture pieces required by each establishment for the number of rooms they have.
>
> Siyabonga bought his equipment by taking out a bank loan. His wife, Karabo, keeps track of his expenses, income, assets, liabilities, capital and drawings using books of prime entry. She posts the information to the nominal, sales and purchases ledger every month. She also draws up a trial balance every six months. If she has made errors, this will become evident in the trial balance and she can go back to rectify the errors.

1   Siyabonga has the following balances on 30 June 2020.

    Prepare his trial balance.

Account	$
Electricity	694
Drawings	1 750
Sales	11 842
Motor vehicle	23 780
Advertising	238
Equipment	8 350
Bank loan	20 000
Cash	840
Sales returns	547
General expenses	1 306
Capital	25 000
Tools	11 470
Fuel	451
Bank (Dr)	7 416

WORKED EXAMPLE 1

Siyabonga's wife, Karabo, has prepared the following trial balance at 31 December 2020, but it does not balance.

Prepare the trial balance and correct the errors.

Crafted with Care
Trial balance at 31 December 2020

	$	$
Capital		27 000
Drawings		3 482
Trade payables	1 796	
Sales	13 691	
Equipment	8 620	
Advertising	537	
Discount allowed		287
Motor vehicle	23 523	
Bank (debit)	7 572	
Electricity	963	
Sales returns		368
Discount received	249	
General expenses	1 982	
Cash		1 340
Tools		11 486
Fuel	576	
Bank loan	18 000	
	77 509	43 963

CONTINUED

Answer

Drawings should be in the debit column as it is money leaving the business.

Trade payables are a liability and therefore should be in the credit column.

Sales is an income and so should be entered in the credit column.

Discount allowed is considered an expense and so should be in the debit column.

Sales returns is money the business is no longer going to receive and goes in the debit column.

Discount received is considered an income and therefore should go in the credit column.

Cash can never be negative and therefore should always be in the debit column.

Tools are an asset to Siyabonga and so should be in the debit column.

Bank loan is a liability and so should be in the credit column.

Crafted with Care Trial balance at 31 December 2020		
	$	$
Capital		27 000
Drawings	3 482	
Trade payables		1 796
Sales		13 691
Equipment	8 620	
Advertising	537	
Discount allowed	287	
Motor vehicle	23 523	
Bank (debit)	7 572	
Electricity	963	
Sales returns	368	
Discount received		249
General expenses	1 982	
Cash	1 340	
Tools	11 486	
Fuel	576	
Bank loan		18 000
	60 736	60 736

2 Correct Siyabonga's trial balance at 30 June 2021 and correct the errors.

Crafted with Care
Trial balance at 30 June 2021

	$	$
Discount allowed		351
Sales returns	140	
Drawings	5 100	
Fuel		870
Equipment	8 910	
Cash	3 454	
Electricity		1 063
Trade payables		2 670
Tools	14 780	
Advertising	749	
Capital	31 300	
Discount received	467	
General expenses	1 200	
Sales	14 800	
Bank (debit)	5 620	
Bank loan	16 000	
Motor vehicle		23 000
	102 520	27 954

3 Identify the type of error in each of these situations:

	Error	Type of error
a	Karabo entered the payment, $580, for motor vehicle repairs into the motor vehicle account	
b	A stationery payment by cheque of $89 was entered as $98	
c	A payment of $749 made by J. Dlamini was credited to A. Dlamini's account	
d	Siyabonga made cash drawings of $400, which was omitted from the records	
e	Payment of $280 for wages should have been $300 and a receipt for sales was $20 underadded	
f	A payment made for general expenses, $267, was debited to the bank account and credited to general expenses	

WORKED EXAMPLE 2

Prepare the general journal and correct the errors from Question 3.

Answer

	General journal	$	$
a	Motor vehicle repairs	580	
	Motor vehicle		580
	Correction of entry of motor vehicle repairs into motor vehicles account		
b	Bank	9	
	Stationery		9
	Correction of error of stationery of $89 posted as $98		
c	A. Dlamini	749	
	J. Dlamini		749
	Correction of amount credited to A. Dlamini instead of J. Dlamini		
d	Drawings	400	
	Cash		400
	Correction of error of omission of cash drawings		
e	Wages	20	
	Sales		20
	Correction of the error made recording wages of $300 as $280 and the incorrect under casting of sales by $20		
f	General expenses	534	
	Bank		534
	Correction of General expenses credited and bank debited instead of general expenses debited and bank credited.		

> **TIP**
>
> In error f, which is the error of complete reversal, the amount is doubled as the one amount cancels the original error and the second amount puts the amount in the correct place.

4 Prepare the general journal and correct the following errors:

    a   Advertising expenses of $670 was debited to administrative expenses.

    b   A petty cash voucher for postage $27 was mislaid.

    c   Rent receivable was entered as $650 instead of $660. Heat and light was entered as $340 instead of $350.

    d   The receipt from paying a trade payable was entered as debit bank $1 034, credit trade payables $1 034.

    e   The purchase of office equipment was debited to the purchases account, $2 780.

    f   A credit note received from A. Dlamini for $290 was entered in the purchases returns journal as $390.

EXAM-STYLE MULTIPLE CHOICE AND STRUCTURED QUESTIONS

1 A cheque received from H. Nkosi was posted to D. Nkosi's account. What type of error is this?

   A   Error of principle   C   Error of commission
   B   Compensating error   D   Error of complete reversal   [1]

2 A cheque received from a trade receivable for $450 was entered in the cash book as $540. What type of error is this?

   A   Error of omission   C   Error of commission
   B   Compensating error   D   Error of original entry   [1]

3 Jabulani runs a shoe shop and has provided the following information at the end of the financial year 31 December 2021.

Account	$
Electricity	632
Drawings	2 478
Purchases	3 489
Sales	15 923
Motor vehicle	19 560
Discount received	340
Advertising	461
Equipment	8 420
Purchases returns	179
Bank loan	14 000
Cash	1 698
Discount allowed	256
Sales returns	248
General expenses	2 630
Capital	32 000
Rent expense	2 893
Tools	10 463
Fuel	852
Commission receivable	783
Bank (Dr)	9 145

REQUIRED

a   Prepare the trial balance of Jabulani's shoe shop at 31 December 2021.   [5]
b   State two reasons why a trial balance is prepared.   [2]
c   Identify four types of error that are not revealed by a trial balance. Prepare an example of each.   [8]

[Total: 15]

Part 2
Financial accounting

> Chapter 7

The statement of profit or loss for sole traders

LEARNING INTENTIONS

In this chapter you will:

- know what a statement of profit or loss is and what it shows
- understand what is meant by the term sole trader
- know why a statement of profit or loss is important for a sole trader
- prepare a basic statement of profit or loss from a trial balance
- account for returns, discounts and other income
- know how to treat goods taken by a business owner for their own use

KEY TERMS

Carriage inwards   Carriage outwards   Cost of sales   Discounts   Drawings   Expenses   Gross profit   Inventory
Loss for the year   Other income   Profit   Profit for the year   Revenue   Sole trader   Statement of profit or loss
Unlimited liability   Identify the discounts

Key skills exercises

Knowledge and understanding

To answer the questions in this chapter, you need to know and understand:

- the statement of profit or loss is an account prepared periodically, for one year
- a statement of profit or loss shows gross profit and the profit or loss for the year
- statements of profit or loss account for a variety of day-to-day issues including changing inventory levels, returns, carriage costs and discounts
- statements of profit or loss account for a variety of less common issues including alternative incomes, drawings involving inventory and costs incurred in making sure that goods are in a condition where they can be sold.

You should also be able to apply your knowledge and understanding of what a statement of profit or loss is and what its purpose is when preparing a statement of financial position.

7 The statement of profit or loss for sole traders AS Level

VIV'S PHARMACY

Vivaan owns a pharmacy, Viv's Pharmacy, in Kolkata, West Bengal. His pharmacy is a leading specialist in health and well-being, healthy food and beauty products. He purchases his products from a leading pharmaceutical company, whose head office is based in Mumbai, Maharashtra.

Vivaan has to pay the delivery costs (carriage inwards) for the products he purchases from the pharmaceutical company but has decided he will not charge his customers for the delivery of products (carriage outwards); his pharmacy will cover those costs.

Running a pharmacy has many day-to-day expenses and it is important for Vivaan to know whether his business is making a profit or loss.

WORKED EXAMPLE 1

Vivaan has a trial balance at 30 April 2019.

Viv's Pharmacy Trial balance at 30 April 2019		
	$	$
Carriage inwards	612	
Carriage outwards	876	
Discount allowed	1 416	
Discount received		2 827
Heat and light	2 734	
Insurance	1 557	
Inventory 1 May 2018	34 500	
Motor expenses	5 350	
Purchases	74 454	
Purchases returns		1 593
Rent and rates	12 850	
Revenue		273 582
Sales returns	2 060	
Wages and salaries	24 117	

TIP

The first two columns of the statement of profit or loss are used for calculations and the final column is used for the totals.

Note: The inventory was valued at $26 700 at 30 April 2019.

a Prepare the trading section of the statement of profit or loss, calculate the gross profit for the company.

Answer

Viv's Pharmacy Statement of profit or loss for the year ended 30 April 2019			
	$	$	$
Revenue		273 582	
Less sales returns		(2 060)	
			271 522

37

CONTINUED

Cost of sales			
Opening inventory		34 500	
Purchases	74 454		
Carriage inwards	612		
	75 066		
Less purchases returns	(1 593)		
		73 473	
		107 973	
Less closing inventory		(26 700)	
Cost of sales			(81 273)
Gross profit			190 249

b Prepare the statement of profit or loss for Viv's Pharmacy, adding any extra income and subtracting his expenses from the gross profit to see whether he has made a profit or loss for the year.

Answer

Gross profit (as above)		190 249
Add discount received		2 827
		193 076
Less expenses		
Carriage outwards	876	
Discount allowed	1 416	
Heat and light	2 734	
Insurance	1 557	
Motor expenses	5 350	
Rent and rates	12 850	
Wages and salaries	24 117	
		(48 900)
Profit for the year		144 176

1 Vivaan has a trial balance at 30 April 2020.

Viv's Pharmacy Trial balance at 30 April 2020		
	$	$
Carriage inwards	827	
Carriage outwards	742	
Discount allowed	1 278	
Discount received		1 956
Heat and light	2 147	

	$	$
Insurance	1 368	
Inventory 1 May 2019	31 078	
Motor expenses	4 612	
Purchases	68 453	
Purchases returns		1 752
Rent and rates	13 470	
Revenue		125 186
Sales returns	2 136	
Wages and salaries	2 783	

Note: The inventory was valued at $22 750 at 30 April 2020.

a Prepare the trading section of the statement of profit or loss, calculate the gross profit for the company.

b Prepare the statement of profit or loss for Viv's Pharmacy, adding any extra income and subtracting his expenses from the gross profit to see whether he has made a profit or loss for the year.

WORKED EXAMPLE 2

Vivaan wants to know halfway through the year whether his business is making a profit or loss.

Viv's Pharmacy
Trial balance at 31 October 2020

	$	$
Administrative expenses	1 070	
Carriage inwards	5 000	
Carriage outwards	3 724	
Discount allowed	5 020	
Discount received		3 160
Drawings	20 527	
Heat and light	6 450	
Insurance	1 143	
Inventory 1 May 2020	17 770	
Motor expenses	2 496	
Purchases	120 000	
Purchases returns		4 440
Rent and rates	8 000	
Revenue		224 000
Sales returns	3 600	
Wages and salaries	36 800	

CONTINUED

Notes:
a   Inventory on 31 October 2020 was valued at $25 380
b   Vivaan took goods valued at $1 750 for his own use
c   10% of the wages and salaries had been paid to staff for working to get the goods into a saleable condition

Prepare the statement of profit or loss for the half-year ended 31 October 2020.

Answer

Viv's Pharmacy
Statement of profit or loss for the six months ending 31 October 2020

	$	$	$
Revenue		224 000	
Less sales returns		(3 600)	
			220 400
Cost of sales			
Opening inventory		17 770	
Purchases	120 000		
Carriage inwards	5 000		
	125 000		
Less purchases returns	(4 440)		
Less drawings	(1 750)		
Add wages paid to prepare goods (10% × $36 800)	3 680		
		122 490	
Less closing inventory		(25 380)	
Cost of sales			(114 880)
Gross profit			105 520
Add income			
Discount received			3 160
			108 680
Less expenses			
Administrative expenses		1 070	
Carriage outwards		3 724	
Discount allowed		5 020	
Heat and light		6 450	
Insurance		1 143	
Motor expenses		2 496	
Rent and rates		8 000	
Wages and salaries (90% × $36 800)		33 120	
			(61 023)
Profit for the half-year			47 657

2 Vivaan is happy with the work you did for him in 2020 and would like you to complete his statement of profit or loss for 30 April 2021. He has supplied you with a trial balance to complete this work.

Viv's Pharmacy Trial balance at 30 April 2021		
	$	$
Administrative expenses	2 449	
Carriage inwards	815	
Carriage outwards	914	
Discount allowed	1 410	
Discount received		1 902
Drawings	18 432	
Heat and light	1 008	
Insurance	1 240	
Inventory 1 May 2020	26 700	
Motor expenses	2 753	
Purchases	92 743	
Purchases returns		1 559
Rent and rates	8 763	
Revenue		108 647
Sales returns	3 489	
Wages and salaries	65 400	

Notes:

a   Inventory on 30 April 2021 was valued at $45 870

b   Vivaan took goods valued at $2 900 for his own use

c   15% of the wages and salaries had been paid to staff for working to get the goods into a saleable condition.

TIP

Subtract the goods Vivaan took for his personal use and add the 15% of wages and salaries in the trading section of the statement of profit or loss when calculating the cost of sales.

3 Vivaan was very pleased with your work from the past two years. He couldn't believe the company made a loss in the previous year and was determined to improve that to a profit this year. In order to help his business make a profit this year, he ran an advertising campaign. The campaign did cost him money, but he is hoping the benefits of the campaign will outweigh the costs. He would like you to complete his statement of profit or loss for 30 April 2022. He has supplied you with a trial balance with profit or loss for the year ended.

Viv's Pharmacy Trial balance at 30 April 2022		
	$	$
Administrative expenses	5 964	
Advertising	26 740	
Bank	54 798	
Carriage inwards	567	
Carriage outwards	843	
Discount allowed	1 654	

	$	$
Discount received		1 082
Drawings	12 568	
Equipment	32 852	
Heat and light	5 236	
Insurance	3 512	
Inventory 1 May 2021	45 870	
Motor expenses	2 589	
Purchases	98 752	
Purchases returns		3 564
Rent and rates	9 635	
Revenue		453 698
Sales returns	2 540	
Wages and salaries	56 230	

Notes:

a Inventory on 30 April 2022 was valued at $26 430

b Vivaan took goods valued at $1 700 for his own use

Prepare the statement of profit or loss for the year ended 30 April 2022.

EXAM-STYLE MULTIPLE CHOICE AND STRUCTURED QUESTIONS

1 The following information has also been extracted from Vivaan's books for 2021.

	$
Carriage inwards	3 651
Inventory 1 May 2020	25 716
Inventory 30 April 2021	32 450
Purchases	23 984
Purchases returns	3 570
Revenue	89 560

What was Vivaan's cost of sales for 30 April 2021?

A $ 72 229   C $ 27 148
B $ 17 331   D $ 13 680   [1]

2 At 30 April 2022, Viv's Pharmacy showed a gross profit of $167 350. It was later discovered that the opening inventory had been underadded by $5 700 and the closing inventory had been underadded by $4 800.

What is the correct gross profit for the year?

A $ 177 850   C $ 166 450
B $ 156 850   D $ 168 250   [1]

CONTINUED

3 The following trial balance has been extracted from the books of Grayson, a sole trader, at 30 April 2022.

	$	$
Premises	60 000	
Office equipment	12 000	
Revenue		104 000
Sales returns	3 700	
Purchases	59 000	
Purchases returns		2 550
Inventory at 1 May 2021	6 000	
Heating and lighting	2 700	
Interest on loan	750	
Rent expense	2 000	
Rent income		1 800
Discount received		770
Discount allowed	1 030	
Wages	13 000	
Stationery	4 100	
Trade receivables	1 624	
Trade payables		1 880
Bank	5 000	
Drawings	10 096	
Bank loan		15 000
Capital		55 000
	181 000	181 000

Inventory at 30 April 2022 was $10 000.

REQUIRED

Prepare Grayson's statement of profit or loss for the year ended 30 April 2022. [15]

> Chapter 8
Statements of financial position for sole traders

> **LEARNING INTENTIONS**
>
> In this chapter you will:
>
> - know what a statement of financial position is and what it shows
> - explain why a business will produce a statement of financial position
> - know how the statement of financial position and the statement of profit or loss are linked
> - prepare a statement of financial position for a sole trader

> **KEY TERMS**
>
> Accounting equation   Capital   Current asset   Current liability   Drawings   Non-current asset
> Non-current liability   Statement of financial position

Key skills exercises

Knowledge and understanding

To answer the questions in this chapter, you need to know and understand:

- what a statement of financial position is and what it shows
- why a business will produce a statement of financial position
- how the statement of financial position and the statement of profit or loss are linked.

You should also be able to use your knowledge and understanding of a statement of financial position to prepare one for a sole trader.

> **VIV'S PHARMACY**
>
> Vivaan from Viv's Pharmacy believes you did a great job of calculating his pharmacy's statements of profit or loss and would like you to complete his statements of financial position, as well. During the financial year 2021–2022 Vivaan used an advertising campaign to help his company improve from a loss to a profit. At the end of April 2022 he asked you to calculate whether it was worth the money he spent on the advertising campaign, and the statement of profit or loss showed a big improvement as the company made a healthy profit.

1 Shown next is a table with a list of assets, liabilities, capital, income and expenses at 31 July 2019. Identify whether each item belongs in the statement of profit or loss or statement of financial position. The first one has been completed as an example.

	Statement of profit or loss	Statement of financial position
Advertising	✓	
Bank account		
Bank loan		
Capital account		
Carriage inwards		
Carriage outwards		
Discount received		
Discount allowed		
Drawings		
Equipment		
Inventory at 1 August 2018		
Light and heat		
Motor expenses		
Motor vehicles		
Office expenses		
Purchases		
Purchases returns		
Rent and rates		
Sales		
Sales returns		
Stationery		
Trade payables		
Trade receivables		
Wages and salaries		

2 Viv's Pharmacy's statement of profit or loss for 30 April 2019 had a profit for the year of $144 176 and closing inventory of $ 26 700. Using the information shown, prepare the statement of financial position for Viv's Pharmacy at 30 April 2019.

TIP

First, classify each item as to whether it is an asset or liability and whether it is non-current or current.

	$	$
Bank	55 120	
Bank loan (repayable 2024)		22 000
Capital at 1 May 2018		156 120
Drawings	21 690	
Equipment	58 790	
Furniture and fittings	26 146	
Trade receivables	11 430	
Trade payables		7 980
Motor vehicle	130 400	

WORKED EXAMPLE

Prepare Vivaan's statement of financial position at 30 April 2021. This was the year his company made a loss of $46 806. The closing inventory at 30 April 2021 was $45 870.

	$	$
Bank overdraft		3 654
Bank loan (repayable 2024)		20 500
Capital at 1 May 2019		196 000
Drawings	18 432	
Equipment	36 540	
Furniture and fittings	14 415	
Trade receivables	9 870	
Trade payables		15 329
Motor vehicle	90 250	

Answer

Viv's Pharmacy
Statement of financial position at 30 April 2021

	$	$
Non-current assets		
Motor vehicle	90 250	
Equipment	36 540	
Furniture and fittings	14 415	
		141 205
Current assets		
Inventory	45 870	
Trade receivables	9 870	
		55 740
Total assets		196 945
Capital at 1 May 2020	222 700	
Less loss for the year	(46 806)	
	175 894	
Less drawings	(18 432)	
		157 462
Non-current liabilities		
Bank loan (repayable 2024)		20 500
Current liabilities		
Bank overdraft	3 654	
Trade payables	15 329	
		18 983
Total capital and liabilities		196 945

TIP

Subtract the loss from the opening capital and bank overdraft is a current liability.

3 Prepare the statement of financial position for Viv's Pharmacy at 30 April 2022. The company made a profit of $226 342 and the closing inventory was $26 430.

Viv's Pharmacy
Trial balance at 30 April 2022

	$	$
Administrative expenses	4 264	
Advertising	26 740	
Bank	54 798	
Bank loan (repayable August 2024)		11 000
Capital at 1 May 2021		255 870
Carriage inwards	567	
Carriage outwards	843	
Discount allowed	1 654	
Discount received		1 082
Drawings	12 568	
Equipment	32 852	
Furniture and fittings	18 279	
Heat and light	5 236	
Insurance	3 512	
Inventory 1 May 2021	45 870	
Motor expenses	2 589	
Motor vehicles	32 560	
Premises	310 435	
Purchases	98 752	
Purchases returns		3 564
Rent and rates	9 635	
Sales		453 698
Sales returns	2 540	
Trade receivables	8 490	
Trade payables		3 200
Wages and salaries	56 230	
	728 414	728 414

> **TIP**
>
> Decide which items from the trial balance belong in the statement of financial position and then classify which category they belong to.

EXAM-STYLE MULTIPLE CHOICE AND STRUCTURED QUESTIONS

1 Aditi bought a motor vehicle for $5 600. The transaction was debited to the motor vehicle repairs account in error. What effect does this error have on the following items?

	Non-current assets	Profit for the year	Capital
A	Underadded	Overadded	No effect
B	No effect	Underadded	No effect
C	Overadded	No effect	Underadded
D	Underadded	Underadded	Underadded

[1]

CONTINUED

2   Muhammad has the following information available as he does not keep complete accounting records.

	$
Capital introduced during the year	12 000
Drawings	21 000
Capital at the start of the year	48 000
Capital at the end of the year	32 000

What is the profit or loss for the year?

A   profit $7 000
B   loss $25 000
C   loss $7 000
D   profit $25 000 [1]

3   The following trial balance has been extracted from Alisha's books at 30 November 2022.

	$	$
Advertising	4 023	
Bank	12 369	
Capital		95 070
Discounts received		1 450
Drawings	34 800	
Equipment	65 790	
Fixtures and fittings	24 753	
Heat and light	6 420	
Inventory at 1 December 2021	37 610	
Loan from bank (repayable 2024)		39 400
Motor vehicles	21 780	
Office expenses	37 050	
Trade payables		20 740
Trade receivables	21 790	
Purchases	145 655	
Purchases returns		2 400
Revenue		286 300
Sales returns	1 760	
Wages and salaries	31 560	
	445 360	445 360

Inventory at 30 November 2022 was $32 480. Profit for the year was $58 552.

REQUIRED

Prepare Alisha's statement of financial position for the year ended 30 November 2022. [7]

> Chapter 9
Accounting concepts

> **LEARNING INTENTIONS**
>
> In this chapter you will:
> - learn why it is necessary to have generally accepted rules for accounting
> - understand the most important rules and what they aim to achieve

> **KEY TERMS**
>
> Accounting concepts   Consistency   Depreciation   Duality   Going concern   Goods on sale or return
> Historic cost   Inflation   Prudence   Realisation   Substance over form   True and fair view

Key skills exercises

Knowledge and understanding

To answer the questions in this chapter, you need to know and understand:

- the importance of having generally accepted rules for accounting that accountants worldwide are expected to follow
- the 11 most important accounting principles and concepts and what they aim to achieve.

You should also be able to use your knowledge and understanding of the accounting principles and what each one stands for, and apply this knowledge to each situation.

> **A NEW GYM**
>
> Olivia and Thomas are a married couple in Ontario, Canada. They both have a passion for health and fitness and have recently completed a level 1 fitness certificate. They have decided to open their own gym and turn their passion into their business.
>
> Before opening their gym, they consult with an accountant as their accounting knowledge is very limited, but they understand the importance of it and want to have a better understanding and grasp of things before they open their business.
>
> Felix, the accountant, explains the importance of accounting rules and the most important accounting concepts, being: duality, business entity, money measurement, historic cost, realisation, consistency, materiality, matching, prudence, going concern and substance over form.
>
> Felix has set up a few questionnaires for Olivia and Thomas to complete to test their knowledge of the accounting concepts. They would like your help in completing these questionnaires.

WORKED EXAMPLE 1

Olivia and Thomas have owned their gym for a year. In celebration of their one-year anniversary, they decide to go on a much needed holiday. They pay for the trip using business money but aren't sure which account to record it in and so decide to record it in the general expenses account.

State the accounting concept that applies to the situation and explain how it should have been dealt with.

Answer

The concept that should be applied is business entity. Business entity states that every business is regarded as having an existence separate from that of its owner(s).

Olivia and Thomas are entitled to their holiday and may make use of business money if they choose to do so. Their mistake is recording it as a general expense instead of recording it as drawings. This error will affect the profit of the business as well as the capital contribution as profit will be underadded (due to expenses being too high) and capital will be overadded (due to drawings being too low).

1 State which accounting concept is being applied in each of these situations.

   a   If the owner takes goods for their own use and it is treated as drawings.

   b   An adjustment is made to an account to record a prepayment for the statement of profit or loss.

   c   The business is successful but no record has been made of their reputation and workers' skill levels.

   d   When a business owner purchases equipment and pays by cheque, two accounts are affected: equipment is debited and bank is credited.

   e   A business owner always uses a specific method of depreciating their non-current assets.

2 Identify and match the name of the concept that is being applied in each case. The first one has been done as an example.

	Transaction		Concept
a	Businesses should value their inventory at the net realisable value or lower of cost value.		duality
b	The owner of a business paid her private telephone account from the business bank account. The amount was debited to her drawings account.		business entity
c	A trader has included rent that was due but not paid in their statement of profit or loss.		money measurement
d	The payment of stationery has resulted in two entries being made in the accounting system.		historic cost
e	A trader purchases a new machine on hire purchase and this machine appears as a non-current asset in the statement of financial position.		realisation
f	A stapler is purchased by a business. The decision is made to write the cost off as an expense in the statement of profit or loss rather than showing it as a depreciating non-current asset.		consistency
g	Machinery bought a few years ago cost $3 700. To replace that machinery today would cost $5 200. The machinery is valued at a cost of $3 700 in the statement of financial position.		materiality
h	A trader has a prime location for their business and highly skilled staff. These are both assets to the business; however, they do not appear in the statement of financial position.		matching (accruals)
i	A customer orders goods to be delivered in a week's time. The goods are not processed as sold until they have been paid for.		prudence
j	A trader uses the same method of deprecation each year.		going concern
k	Accounting records are prepared with the assumption that the business will continue to operate in the foreseeable future.		substance over form

WORKED EXAMPLE 2

Thomas orders protein shakes to sell to the gym's clients. He mentions this to the clients and a few clients place orders with him. He records these orders as sales in the accounting records even though the products haven't arrived yet and the clients haven't paid for them as yet.

State the accounting concept being applied and how it should be dealt with.

Answer

The accounting concept is realisation. This concept states that revenue should only be recorded once an invoice has been issued or cash has been received.

Thomas should not be recording these as sales yet as he has not received payment for them. Only once he has received payment should he then record the transaction in the accounting records.

3   State, in each situation, which accounting concept applies and explain how it should have been dealt with.

   a   Olivia bought stationery for the front desk of the gym. She recorded this transaction by only debiting the stationery account.

   b   When Olivia and Thomas opened the gym, they agreed on using the straight-line method of depreciation. At the end of the second year, Thomas worked out that they could increase their profit if they made use of the reducing balance method of depreciation.

   c   Thomas and Olivia receive great reviews about their gym from their customers. The customers are enjoying the positive attitude of their trainers and are impressed by their customer service. Olivia and Thomas view this as an asset and would like to include it in their statement of financial position.

EXAM-STYLE MULTIPLE CHOICE AND STRUCTURED QUESTIONS

1   Isabella adjusts her statements of financial position for an accrual expense of $2 500 for insurance. Which accounting concept has she applied?

   A   Materiality   C   Matching
   B   Prudence   D   Historical cost   [1]

2   Explain, briefly, the prudence concept.   [2]

   Improve this answer

   This is a sample answer to **Q2**.

   > The prudence concept states that profits and assets should be underadded rather than overadded. Rather have an underadded profit and get a surprise when you have more than you expected than have an overadded profit and have less than what you expected.

   Your challenge

   See whether you can improve this answer. It seems that this explanation of the prudence concept with regards to profit and assets is not entirely correct. A better answer is available online – but write yours out first!

> Chapter 10
Accruals and prepayments (the matching concept)

LEARNING INTENTIONS

In this chapter you will:
- understand the practical application of the matching concept
- record accruals and prepayments in ledger accounts
- account for inventories of consumables in both the ledger and statement of financial position
- adjust for accruals and prepayments when preparing a trial balance
- know the effect of accruals and prepayments on the expenses and income recorded in the statement of profit or loss
- show accruals and prepayments in the statement of financial position

KEY TERMS

Accrual   Commission earned   Interest earned   Prepayment   Rental income   Other payables   Other receivables

Key skills exercises

Knowledge and understanding

To answer the questions in this chapter, you need to know and understand:
- how to record accruals and prepayments in ledger accounts
- how to account for inventories of consumables in both the ledger and statement of financial position
- how to adjust for accruals and prepayments when dealing with a trial balance
- the effect of accruals and prepayments on the expenses and income recorded in the statement of profit or loss
- how to show accruals and prepayments in the statement of financial position.

You should also be able to use your knowledge and understanding of accruals and prepayments and apply it to ledger accounts, statements of profit or loss and statements of financial position.

JACK'S BUILDING COMPANY

Building supplies is a construction materials and equipment supplier in Dublin, Ireland. They supply products to builders, trades people, self-builders, DIY and householders. Builders who buy large quantities of materials and equipment will buy on credit and pay at a later stage. The builders will open accounts with the company and receive a statement of account at the end of every month stating what they owe.

Jack Byrne is a builder and a loyal customer of Building supplies. Jack hires certain equipment from Building Supplies as it doesn't warrant him buying every piece of equipment that is only used on specialised projects.

10 Accruals and prepayments (the matching concept) AS Level

WORKED EXAMPLE 1

Jack received a statement of account from Building supplies on 31 March 2019 (which is his business year end), stating that he owed $685 for equipment hire. At the start of the year (1 April 2020) Jack had a balance of $230 and made payments of $16 700 during the year.

Prepare the account for Jack to show what will appear in the statement of profit or loss.

Answer

Equipment hire

Debit			Credit		
		$			$
			2018		
Apr–Mar	Bank	16 700	Apr 1	Balance b/d	230
2019			2019		
Mar 31	Balance c/d	685	Mar 31	Statement of profit or loss	17 155
		17 385			17 385
			2019		
			Apr 1	Balance b/d	685

The balance at the start of the year appears on the credit side as it is an accrual balance. The opening balance at the start of the next year also appears on the credit side as it is also an accrual balance.

The statement of profit or loss total is calculated by taking the amount owed at the start of the year ($230) subtracting it from what was paid during the year ($16 700 − $230 = $16 470) and then adding what is still owed for this financial year ($16 470 + $685 = $17 155).

1. At the end of the following year (31 March 2020) Jack owed Building supplies $830 and had made payments of $22 360 during the year.

    Prepare the account for Jack to show what will appear in the statement of profit or loss.

WORKED EXAMPLE 2

During March 2021 Jack received early payment from his client who he was building for and decided to make an early payment on his equipment hire account with Building supplies. He hadn't received a statement of account from them yet for this month and therefore made a payment of $1 200, hoping it would cover his cost. At the end of the month, he received a statement of account and it stated that he had made an overpayment of $258, and therefore had made a prepayment for the next month. Jack had made payments of $23 490 during the year. Prepare the account for Jack to show what will appear in the statement of profit or loss.

CONTINUED

Answer

	Debit		Equipment hire	Credit	
		$			$
			2020		
Apr–Mar	Bank	23 490	Apr 1	Balance b/d	830
			2021		
			Mar 31	Statement of profit or loss	22 402
				Balance c/d	258
		23 490			23 490
2021					
Apr 1	Balance b/d	258			

At the start of the year Jack owed $830, which is why his balance is on the credit side. During the year he made payments of $23 490 and a prepayment of $258 at the end of the year, which is a debit balance.

To calculate the statement of profit or loss amount you take the payments during the year, subtract the $830 due from the previous year and subtract the prepayment for the next year of $258 ($23 490 − $830 − $258 = $22 402).

2   During the following year Jack made payments of $25 690. He had a prepayment of $587 at 31 March 2022.

Prepare the account for Jack to show what will appear in the statement of profit or loss.

WORKED EXAMPLE 3

Jack has an office building and land that he has to pay rates and insurance on each month. He stores all his machinery and equipment and excess construction materials at the office.

Jack groups these two accounts together in his nominal ledger to lessen the number of accounts in his ledger.

During the year ended 31 March 2021 Jack made payments for rates and insurance to the value of $21 560. The amount of accrued and prepaid expenses at 1 April 2020 and 31 March 2021 were as follows:

	1 April 2020	31 March 2021
Rates	$590 prepaid	$350 prepaid
Insurance	$780 accrued	$960 accrued

Prepare the rates and insurance account to show what would appear in the statement of profit or loss.

CONTINUED

Answer

Rates and insurance

Debit			Credit		
		$			$
2020			2020		
Apr 1	Balance b/d – rates	590	Apr 1	Balance b/d – ins	780
Apr – Mar	Bank	21 560			
2021			2021		
Mar 31	Balance c/d – ins	960	Mar 31	Statement of profit or loss	21 980
			31	Balance c/d – rates	350
		23 110			23 110
2021			2021		
Apr 1	Balance b/d – rates	350	Apr 1	Balance b/d – ins	960

Accrued balances are on the credit side and prepaid balances are on the debit side. To calculate the statement of profit or loss amount in this example, you start with the payment made during the year, $21 560, add the prepaid rates ($590) at the start of the year and subtract the accrued insurance expense ($780) from the start of the year ($21 560 + $590 − $780 = $21 370). At the end of the year, you add the accrued insurance of $960 and subtract the prepaid rates of $350 to get the final total for the statement of profit or loss ($21 370 + $960 − $350 = $21 980).

3   During the year ended 31 March 2022 Jack had made payments for rates and insurance to the value of $24 830. The amount of accrued and prepaid expenses at 1 April 2021 and 31 March 2022 were as follows:

	1 April 2021	31 March 2022
Rates	$350 prepaid	$340 accrued
Insurance	$960 accrued	$410 prepaid

Prepare the rates and insurance account to show what would appear in the statement of profit or loss.

> **TIP**
>
> These examples and activities have dealt with expenses to a business. Income accounts can also be accrued and prepaid, these accounts work the opposite to the expense accounts. Accrued income has a debit balance and prepaid income has a credit balance.

WORKED EXAMPLE 3

At Jack's office site he has a second building that he rents out to Luke O'Sullivan.
At 31 March 2021 Luke had paid $35 610 in rent during the year. At the start of the year, Luke owed Jack $1 410 and at the end of the year Luke had made a prepayment of $600.

Prepare the account for Jack to show what will appear in the statement of profit or loss.

Rent income

	Debit	$		Credit	$
2020					
Apr 1	Balance b/d	1 410	Apr–Mar	Bank	35 610
2021					
Mar 31	Statement of profit or loss	33 600			
	Balance c/d	600			
		35 610			35 610
			2021		
			Apr 1	Balance b/d	600

Accrued balances appear on the debit side as in the opening balance and prepaid balances appear on the credit side as in the closing balance. To calculate the amount for the statement of profit or loss, start with the amount received during the year, subtract the amount accrued at the start of the year and subtract the amount prepaid at the end of the year ($35 610 − $1 410 − $600 = $33 600).

4 a At 31 March 2022 Luke had paid $37 890 in rent during the year. At the start of the year, Luke had paid Jack in advance $600 and at the end of the year Luke had an accrued amount of $1 470.

Prepare the account for Jack to show what will appear in the statement of profit or loss.

b At 31 March 2023 Jack extracted the following trial balance.

	$	$
Bank		4 188
Capital at 1 April 2022		117 640
Discounts allowed	1 754	
Discounts received		2 301
Drawings	20 000	
Inventory at 1 April 2022	18 365	
Mortgage (repayable 2031)		118 467

	$	$
Motor expenses	17 437	
Motor vehicles	25 600	
Office equipment	19 240	
Office expenses	26 759	
Premises	160 000	
Purchases	217 044	
Purchases returns		2 243
Rent income		8 712
Sales		320 857
Sales returns	1 709	
Trade payables		11 066
Trade receivables	13 444	
Wages and salaries	64 122	
	585 474	585 474

The following information at 31 March 2023 was also provided:
- Inventory was valued at $20 170
- Office expenses of $1 100 had been paid in advance
- Wages and salaries of $3 280 was owing
- Rental income of $1 450 had been paid in advance

REQUIRED

i Prepare the statement of profit or loss for the year ended 31 March 2023.

ii Prepare the statement of financial position at 31 March 2023.

EXAM-STYLE MULTIPLE CHOICE AND STRUCTURED QUESTIONS

1 A business provided the following information about heat and light expenses for the year ended 31 August 2022.

Accrued at 1 September 2021	$633
Prepaid at 1 September 2021	$781
Bank payments during the year	$6 725
Accrued at 31 August 2022	$439
Prepaid at 31 August 2022	$582

What is the heat and light expense that must appear in the statement of profit or loss for the year ended 31 August 2022?

A $8 282   B $6 720   C $6 730   D $6 634   [1]

CONTINUED

2 The accounts of a business have been prepared, but no adjustments have been made for prepaid expenses at the end of the year. What effect will these omissions have on the accounts?

	Profit for the year	Current assets	Current liabilities
A	overadded	no effect	underadded
B	underadded	no effect	overadded
C	overadded	underadded	no effect
D	underadded	underadded	no effect

[1]

3 Emily O'Brien extracted the following trial balance from her books after she had prepared the trading account section of her statement of profit or loss for the year ended 30 June 2022.

	$	$
Bank	3 925	
Capital at 1 July 2021		131 535
Drawings	31 850	
Gross profit		112 439
Insurance	2 173	
Interest received		885
Inventory at 30 June 2022	22 084	
Motor expenses	12 640	
Non-current assets	97 130	
Office expenses	32 208	
Rent income		5 920
Trade payables		19 885
Trade receivables	41 253	
Wages and salaries	27 401	
	270 664	270 664

Additional information:

- The inventory figure shown here is the closing inventory.
- The following amounts were owing at 30 June 2022: interest received $84 and office expenses $1 086.
- The following amounts had been paid in advance at 30 June 2022: rent income $678 and motor expenses $527.

REQUIRED

a Prepare the statement of profit or loss for the year ended 30 June 2022. [5]

b Prepare the statement of financial position at 30 June 2022. [5]

[Total: 10]

> Chapter 11

Accounting for the depreciation of non-current assets

LEARNING INTENTIONS

In this chapter you will:

- know the difference between capital and revenue expenditure
- understand what depreciation is and why it must be provided for in accounts
- understand the accounting concepts that apply to depreciation
- calculate depreciation by the straight-line and reducing balance methods
- measure the value of non-current assets by the cost model or the revaluation model
- account for the disposal of non-current assets
- prepare financial statements that include depreciation

KEY TERMS

Accumulated depreciation   Capital expenditure   Capitalise/capitalisation   Depreciation   Net book value
Reducing balance depreciation   Residual value   Revaluation method   Revenue expenditure
Straight-line depreciation   Useful life   Warranty

Key skills exercises

Knowledge and understanding

To answer the questions in this chapter, you need to know and understand:

- what the difference is between capital and revenue expenditure
- that depreciation is the loss in value of a non-current asset as a result of age, wear and tear, obsolescence or the passing of time
- provisions for depreciation comply with the matching and prudence principle
- the methods of deprecation: straight-line and reducing balance
- how to measure the value of non-current assets.

You should also be able to apply your knowledge and understanding of depreciation to calculate the different methods and prepare financial statements including depreciation.

CAMBRIDGE INTERNATIONAL AS & A LEVEL ACCOUNTING: WORKBOOK

MINUTEMAN

Haruto owns a courier business in Osaka, Japan, called 'Minuteman'. He owns many motor vehicles for the transportation of his deliveries. Motor vehicles are classified as a non-current asset and lose value over time. Haruto knows that no matter how well he looks after his motor vehicles, services them and repairs them, they will still depreciate on a yearly basis.

When Haruto opened his business, he decided to depreciate his motor vehicles using the straight-line method and according to the consistency concept he has to keep using that method for future accounting years.

Haruto has often wondered how different his profit would have been had he chosen the reducing balance method. He would like to calculate the first three years of one of his motor vehicles' useful life according to the straight-line method and reducing balance method so he can compare the two methods.

Haruto also knows there are two forms of expenditure when dealing with non-current assets, namely capital expenditure and revenue expenditure. He often gets confused between the two and has a few items he would like help in classifying.

1   Haruto purchased a new motor vehicle and needs help classifying which of these items are considered capital expenditure or revenue expenditure. Once the items have been classified, calculate the total cost of each type.

	$
Cost price of the motor vehicle	36 800
Motor vehicle insurance	4 600
Fitting of shelving in the back of the vehicle	9 750
Number plates and delivery	1 040
Servicing the motor vehicle	810
Fuel	390

WORKED EXAMPLE 1

A motor vehicle cost $20 000 and was purchased at the beginning of year 1. The policy is to depreciate vehicles by 25% per annum using the straight-line method.

Calculate the depreciation charge for the first three years. Prepare the journal entries, ledger accounts, extract from the statement of profit or loss and statement of financial position for all three years.

Answer

Year 1

Step 1: Calculate the depreciation charge:

$20 000 × 25% = $5 000

CONTINUED

Step 2: Record a depreciation charge to the general journal at the end of the financial year

General Journal				
Date			Dr	Cr
Year 1			$	$
Dec 31	Statement of profit or loss		5 000	
	Provision for depreciation (vehicles)			5 000
	Depreciation charge of vehicles at the end of the year			

Step 3: Post the entries from the general journal to the nominal ledger accounts and then to the statement or profit or loss and statement of financial position.

The cost of the motor vehicle is recorded in the motor vehicle at cost account:

Motor vehicles at cost account				
		$		$
Year 1	Bank	20 000	Year 1 Balance c/d	20 000
Year 2	Balance b/d	20 000		

Until the motor vehicle is sold, the balance on this account will be transferred to the next year.

The provision for depreciation of motor vehicles account for year 1 is:

Provision for depreciation of motor vehicles account				
		$		$
Year 1	Balance c/d	5 000	Year 1 Statement of profit or loss	5 000
			Year 2 Balance b/d	5 000

Statement of profit or loss for the year ended 31 December year 1		
	Dr	Cr
	$	$
Gross profit		
Expenses		
Depreciation of vehicles	5 000	
Profit for the year		

Statement of financial position at 31 December year 1	Cost	Accumulated depreciation	Net book value
	$	$	$
Non-current assets			
Motor vehicles	20 000	5 000	15 000
Current assets			
Inventory		x	
Bank		x	

CONTINUED

Year 2

Step 1: Calculate the depreciation charge:

Due to the business using the straight-line method the depreciation stays at $5 000 for the year.

Step 2: Make a general journal entry to record the depreciation at the end of year 2.

General Journal			
Date		Dr	Cr
Year 2		$	$
Dec 31	Statement of profit or loss	5 000	
	Provision for depreciation (motor vehicles)		5 000
	Depreciation charge of motor vehicles at the end of the year		

Step 3: Post the entries from the general journal to the nominal ledger accounts and then to the statement of profit or loss and statement of financial position.

Motor vehicles at cost account					
		$			$
Year 1	Bank	20 000	Year 1	Balance c/d	20 000
Year 2	Balance b/d	20 000	Year 2	Balance c/d	20 000
Year 3	Balance b/d	20 000			

Provision for depreciation of motor vehicles account					
		$			$
Year 1	Balance c/d	5 000	Year 1	Statement of profit or loss	5 000
Year 2	Balance c/d	10 000	Year 2	Balance b/d	5 000
				Statement of profit or loss	5 000
		10 000			10 000
			Year 2	Balance b/d	10 000

Statement of profit or loss for the year ended 31 December year 2		
	Dr	Cr
	$	$
Gross profit		
Expenses		
Depreciation of motor vehicles	5 000	
Profit for the year		

11 Accounting for the depreciation of non-current assets AS Level

CONTINUED

Statement of financial position at 31 December year 2			
	Cost	Accumulated depreciation	Net book value
	$	$	$
Non-current assets			
Motor vehicles	20 000	10 000	10 000
Current assets			
Inventory		x	
Bank		x	

> **TIP**
>
> The depreciation amount charged to the statement of profit or loss is for that particular year, whereas the accumulated amount charged to the statement of the financial position is the depreciation for each year of the assets' useful lives to date, added together.

2 Sakura purchased a machine for her business for $46 000. Sakura depreciates machinery at 15% per annum using the reducing balance method.

   a Calculate the annual depreciation charge on machinery for each of the first two years.

   b Prepare the journal entries and ledger accounts for each of the first two years.

   c Prepare extracts from the statement of profit or loss and statement of financial position to show the depreciation charge on machinery for year 2 only.

3 Minato is a mechanic. He has many tools used to repair vehicles. Many of the smaller tools have a low value and he therefore uses the revaluation method to measure the value of these tools.

At 1 May 2020 his tools were valued at $16 700. During the year, he purchased additional tools to the value of $2 160. On 30 April 2021, his tools were revalued at $16 300.

   a Calculate the annual revaluation charge on these tools.

   b Prepare the journal entries and ledger account for the tools.

   c Prepare extracts from the statement of profit or loss and statement of financial position to show the revaluation charge on these tools.

WORKED EXAMPLE 2

Mei owns a textile business. One of her machines, which weaves the threads of the textile together, needs replacing and she disposed of this machine on 1 February 2021. The machine had a net book value of $30 000. She originally bought this machine on 1 February 2019. No depreciation is charged in the year of disposal.

Mei's financial year ends on 31 January. She depreciates her machinery at 20% per annum using the reducing balance method.

Mei's balances on 31 January 2021 were as follows:

	$
Machinery	172 450
Provision for depreciation	56 970

On 1 May 2021 Mei purchased a new machine for $67 240.

Prepare the provision for depreciation of machinery account for the year ended 31 January 2022. Dates are required.

CONTINUED

Answer

Provision for depreciation of machinery					
		$			$
2021			2021		
Feb 1	Disposal	16 875	Feb 1	Balance b/d	56 970
2022			2022		
Jan 31	Balance c/d	67 277	Jan 31	Statement of profit or loss	27 182
		84 152			84 152
			2022		
			Feb 1	Balance b/d	67 277

Disposal workings:

Net book value: $30 000   Depreciation rate: 20% reducing balance method

Year 2 depreciation: $30 000 × 20/80 = 7 500

Year 1 depreciation: ($30 000 + 7 500) × 20/80 = 9 375

Total depreciation: $7 500 + $9 375 = $16 875

Statement of profit or loss workings:

	$
Cost	172 450
Depreciation	56 970
	115 480
Disposal	30 000
	85 480

$85 480 × 20% = $17 096

New machine depreciation: $67 240 × 20% × 9/12 = $10 086

Total depreciation charge to statement of profit or loss: $17 096 + $10 086 = $27 182

---

4 Miu is a sole trader and prepares her statements of financial position to 31 May each year. She depreciates her motor vehicles using the reducing balance method at a rate of 20% per annum. Depreciation is charged monthly.

Miu purchased a motor vehicle on 1 June 2013 for $152 000.

On 1 March 2015, a new motor vehicle was purchased at a cost of $190 000.
The old motor vehicle was part-exchanged at a value of $84 000.

The balance was settled by a bank loan repayable over three years.

REQUIRED

a Prepare the motor vehicles at cost account for the year ended 31 May 2015. [2]

b Prepare the motor vehicle provision for depreciation account for the years ended 31 May 2014 and 31 May 2015. [5]

c Calculate the profit or loss on disposal of the motor vehicle purchased on 1 June 2013. [1]

Cambridge International AS&A Level Accounting (9706) Paper 22, Q3c, June 2016

[Total: 8]

11 Accounting for the depreciation of non-current assets AS Level

EXAM-STYLE MULTIPLE CHOICE AND STRUCTURED QUESTIONS

1 A company experienced the following expenditures on a machine.

		$
Year 1	Purchase of machinery	40 000
Year 2	Servicing of machinery	5 200
Year 3	Purchase of attachment to machine	10 000

Depreciation on machinery is 10% on cost. A full year's depreciation is charged in the year of purchase.
What was the depreciation charge on machinery for year 3?

A $5 000   B $5 520   C $4 708   D $4 200   [1]

2 State three reasons why assets depreciate. [3]

3 Butler operates a small business.
He has provided the following information for non-current assets at 31 July 2016.

$
Plant and machinery
  Cost   195 000
  Provision for depreciation   68 250

During the year ended 31 July 2017, the following transactions took place.
- A machine was sold for $25 000. There was a loss on disposal of $3 000. The machine had been purchased on 28 May 2016.
- A machine was purchased by cheque at a cost of $37 500. The following costs were also incurred for the new machine.

                           $
  Annual insurance   2 825
  Installation expenses   4 500

Plant and machinery is depreciated using the reducing balance method at a rate of 20% per annum.
A full year's depreciation is charged in the year of purchase. No depreciation is charged in the year of disposal.

REQUIRED

a Prepare the following ledger accounts for the year ended 31 July 2017. Dates are **not** required.
   i Plant and machinery at cost. [3]
   ii Provision for depreciation on plant and machinery. [3]

CONTINUED

REQUIRED

b Explain why a business may use the reducing balance method of depreciation for plant and machinery. [3]

Additional information

Butler also purchases loose tools for use in the business.

c Explain **two** accounting treatments for loose tools. [4]

d Explain **one** fundamental accounting concept relating to depreciation.

Adapted from Cambridge International AS&A Level Accounting (9706) Paper 22, Q3, June 2018

[2]

[Total: 15]

Improve this answer

This is a sample answer to **Q3a**.

Plant and machinery at cost			
Debit		Credit	
	$		$
Balance b/d	195 000	Disposal	25 000
Bank	37 500	Balance c/d	207 500
	232 500		232 500
Balance b/d	207 500		

Your challenge

See if you can improve this answer. The working for the bank doesn't seem to have taken the extra costs into consideration and the disposal amount is not using the original cost. A better answer is available online - but write yours out first!

> Chapter 12
Irrecoverable and doubtful debts

LEARNING INTENTIONS

In this chapter you will:

- understand the difference between an irrecoverable debt and a doubtful debt
- learn how to account for irrecoverable debts and irrecoverable debts recovered
- understand how to provide for doubtful debts

KEY TERMS

Allowance for doubtful debts   Doubtful debt   Irrecoverable debt

Key skills exercises

Knowledge and understanding

To answer the questions in this chapter, you need to know and understand:

- an irrecoverable debt is a debt due from a customer that it is expected will never be paid by them
- irrecoverable debts recovered are debts written off that are then paid at a later date
- a doubtful debt is a debt due from a customer where it is uncertain whether or not it will be repaid by them

You should also be able to apply your knowledge and understanding of what an irrecoverable debt and doubtful debt is, account for irrecoverable debts and irrecoverable debts recovered and provide for doubtful debts.

> **Cotton Me**
>
> Cotton Me is an affordable, stylish clothes, accessories and more store in Australia. Cotton Me has a facility whereby customers open accounts with the store and depending on their income they are given a credit limit of how much they may buy on their account. Interest is also charged on the account. The system is based on trust between the store and customer whereby customers may take goods and pay at a later stage. Unfortunately, not all customers end up paying their accounts and some run into financial difficulty and are unable to pay. These accounts are considered bad debts to Cotton Me.

CAMBRIDGE INTERNATIONAL AS & A LEVEL ACCOUNTING: WORKBOOK

WORKED EXAMPLE 1

Oliver Jones is a customer of Cotton Me and has unfortunately run into financial difficulty. He has an account balance of $1 700 and is unable to pay it off. After several months of trying to get Oliver to pay his account, on 31 May 2021 Cotton Me decided to write the debt off as irrecoverable.

Prepare the books to show these transactions.

Answer

To show this in their books it would look as follows:

General Journal			
Date		Dr	Cr
2021		$	$
May 31	Irrecoverable debts	1 700	
	Trade receivables: Oliver Jones		1 700
	Entries to write off irrecoverable debt		

Sales ledger account

Oliver Jones				
Debit		Credit		
	$			$
Balance c/d	1 700	May 31	Irrecoverable debts	1 700

Irrecoverable debts

Oliver Jones			
Debit		Credit	
	$		$
May 31 Oliver Jones	1 700		

A few months later on 28 February 2022, Oliver had enough extra money to partially pay back some of his debt. He paid Cotton Me $900.

Prepare the books to show these transactions.

Answer

The books would show it as follows:

General Journal			
Date		Dr	Cr
2022		$	$
Feb 28	Bank	900	
	Irrecoverable debts recovered		900
	Recovery of $900 of Oliver Jones balance written off in May 2021		

CONTINUED

Oliver Jones

Debit			Credit		
		$			$
	Balance c/d	1 700	May 31	Irrecoverable debts	1 700
2022			2022		
Feb 28	Irrecoverable debts recovered	900	Feb 28	Bank	900

Irrecoverable debt recovered

Debit			Credit		
		$			$
			2022		
			Feb 28	Oliver Jones	900

1 Ava Brown is a customer of Cotton Me. On 27 July 2020 she sent Cotton Me an email explaining she could not pay her debt of $2 400. On 31 July 2020 Cotton Me wrote off her debt as irrecoverable.

On 30 September 2022 Ava managed to pay some of her debt. She made a transfer to Cotton Me for $1 200.

Prepare the journal and ledger entries for the original irrecoverable debt written off as well as the partial debt recovered.

2 Calculate Cotton Me's allowance for irrecoverable debts for 2020, 2021 and 2022 using 3% of the trade receivables amount and complete the table.

Prepare the allowance for doubtful debts account starting with a balance brought down of $894 on 1 January 2020.

Year	Trade receivables	Allowance of doubtful debts	Amount entered on statement of profit or loss	Amount entered on statement of financial position
	$	$	$	$
2020	34 200			
2021	35 700			
2022	31 600			

CAMBRIDGE INTERNATIONAL AS & A LEVEL ACCOUNTING: WORKBOOK

WORKED EXAMPLE 2

Prepare extracts from the statement of profit or loss and statement of financial position for 2017, 2018 and 2019 using the figures from Worked example 1.

Answer

Statement of profit or loss for the year ended 31 December 2017

	Dr $	Cr $
Gross profit		
Expenses		
Allowance for doubtful debts	789	
Profit for the year		

Statement of financial position at 31 December 2017

	Cost $	Accumulated depreciation $	Net book value $
Current assets			
Trade receivables	26 300		
Less allowance for doubtful debts	(789)	25 511	

Statement of profit or loss for the year ended 31 December 2018

	Dr $	Cr $
Gross profit		
Other income		
Decrease in allowance for doubtful debts		141
Expenses		
Profit for the year		

Statement of financial position at 31 December 2018

	Cost $	Accumulated depreciation $	Net book value $
Current assets			
Trade receivables	21 900		
Less allowance for doubtful debts	(648)	21 252	

12 Irrecoverable and doubtful debts AS Level

> **CONTINUED**

Statement of profit or loss for the year ended 31 December 2019		
	Dr	Cr
	$	$
Gross profit		
Expenses		
Increase in allowance for doubtful debts		246
Profit for the year		

Statement of financial position at 31 December 2019			
	Cost	Accumulated depreciation	Net book value
	$	$	$
Current assets			
Trade receivables	29 800		
Less allowance for doubtful debts	(894)		28 906

> **TIP**
>
> The statement of profit or loss only receives the increase or decrease in the allowance for irrecoverable debts each year whereas the statement of financial position shows the full cumulative provision as a deduction from trade receivables.

3 Prepare extracts of the statement of profit or loss and the statement of financial position for 2020, 2021 and 2022 using the figures from **Q2**.

4 A trial balance has been extracted for Cotton Me at 31 December 2023:

	$	$
Administration costs	71 685	
Allowance for doubtful debts		700
Bank		9 280
Business rates	45 630	
Capital at 1 January 2023		164 865
Drawings	75 000	
Equipment at cost	64 000	
Accumulated depreciation on equipment		19 200
Heat and light	13 890	
Inventory at 1 January 2023	65 105	
Irrecoverable debts	11 420	
Land and buildings	270 000	
Mortgage on land and buildings (repayable 2032)		217 500
Office furniture at cost	45 000	
Accumulated depreciation on office furniture		11 250
Purchases	428 990	
Purchases returns		6 545
Sales		765 430
Sales returns	5 980	
Trade payables		26 795
Trade receivables	37 800	
Wages and salaries	87 065	
	1 221 565	1 221 565

Additional information at 31 December 2023:
- Inventory was valued at $78 615.
- An irrecoverable debt of $3 600 had not been recorded at all.
- An unpaid heat and light bill for $4 275 was still outstanding while business rates of $3 510 had been paid in advance.
- Depreciation was to be charged on the following basis:
  - Equipment 30% using the reducing balance method
  - Office furniture 25% using the straight-line method
- The allowance for doubtful debts was to be set at 2.5% of trade receivables.

REQUIRED

a Prepare a statement of profit or loss for the year ended 31 December 2023.

b Prepare a statement of financial position at 31 December 2023.

EXAM-STYLE MULTIPLE CHOICE AND STRUCTURED QUESTIONS

1 The allowance for doubtful debts at 1 January 2022 was $1 780. The allowance is provided for at 4% on the trade receivables. The trade receivables at 31 December 2022 was $18 400. Which amount would appear on the statement of profit or loss for 31 December 2022?

   A $736 expense

   B $736 income

   C $1 044 expense

   D $1 044 income [1]

2 Olivia Taylor's business had trade receivables of $12 380 at 31 December 2016. Allowance for irrecoverable debts was $950 at 1 January 2016. Throughout the year, the business had written off $2 450 as irrecoverable debts. The business provides for depreciation at 5% on trade receivables at each year end.

Which amount for doubtful debts would be included in the statement of profit or loss at 31 December 2016?

   A $453

   B $619

   C $572

   D $331 [1]

[Total: 2]

> Chapter 13
Bank reconciliation statements

LEARNING INTENTIONS

In this chapter you will:

- understand why it is necessary to produce a bank reconciliation statement
- know what a bank reconciliation statement is and how to prepare one
- ensure that the bank balance in the cash book equals the correct balance of cash at the bank
- adjust a trial balance after the cash book has been reconciled to the bank statement
- explain the benefits and limitations of preparing a bank reconciliation statement

KEY TERMS

Bank reconciliation statement   Deposit   Internal control   Omitted items   Unpresented cheques
Uncredited deposits   Segregation of duties   Timing differences   Withdrawal

Key skills exercises

Knowledge and understanding

To answer the questions in this chapter, you need to know and understand:

- a bank reconciliation statement is carried out to ensure the cash book's balance is up to date and to explain the difference between the cash book balance and the bank statement balance

You should also be able to apply your knowledge and understanding of what a bank reconciliation is and why it is used to prepare a bank reconciliation statement.

> **ANNA'S INTERIOR DESIGNING**
>
> Anna is an entrepreneur running an interior designing business in Geneva, Switzerland. Anna uses an accounting firm but she would like to start learning to do her own books. The accountant shows her how to record her cash transactions in the cash book. For the month of April 2021 Anna records all her cash transactions in the cash book and balances it at the end of the month.
>
> Anna receives her bank statement from Banque Geneva and, to her surprise, the bank statement balance and her cash book balance do not agree. Anna goes straight to the accountant for help as she thinks she must have made a mistake.
>
> The accountant explains to Anna that it is quite normal for the two balances not to agree with each other. The accountant tells Anna about a bank reconciliation statement and shows her how to prepare one:

CAMBRIDGE INTERNATIONAL AS & A LEVEL ACCOUNTING: WORKBOOK

- **Step 1**: Compare the entries in the cash book with the bank statements. Tick items that appear in both the cash book *and* the bank statement. Be sure to tick them in both places.
- **Step 2**: Enter in the cash book any items that remain unticked in the bank statement. Tick those in both places. Then calculate the new cash book balance.
- **Step 3**: Prepare the reconciliation statement. Begin with the final balance shown on the bank statement and adjust it for any items that remain unticked in the cash book. The result should equal the balance in the cash book.

WORKED EXAMPLE 1

Cash book for Anna for April 2021

Debit			$		Credit		$
Apr 1	Balance b/d		4 356 ✓	Apr 3	Materials (chq 523)		3 480 ✓
5	Hans		1 080	8	Wages (chq 524)		1 400
11	Lara		630 ✓	14	Stationery (chq 525)		230 ✓
16	Thomas		2 563 ✓	21	Emma (chq 526)		675 ✓
21	Mia		1 387	29	Heat and lights (chq 527)		1 082
30	Peter		493				

Bank statement for Anna for April 2021

Date	Details	Withdrawals $	Deposits $	Balance $	
01.04	Balance b/d			4 356 ✓	
03.04	Cheque 523	3 480 ✓		876	
07.04	Standing order – Business rates	940		64	O/D
11.04	Deposit – Lara		630 ✓	566	
14.04	Cheque 525	230 ✓		336	
16.04	Deposit – Thomas		2 563 ✓	2 899	
21.04	Cheque 526	675 ✓		2 224	
28.04	Bank charges and interest	52		2 172	
30.04	Credit Transfer – Kira		1 340	3 512	

The items not ticked on the bank statement must be added to the updated cash book and the cash book balanced.

CONTINUED

Updated cash book for Anna for Apr 2021

Debit			$	Credit			$
Apr 1	Balance b/d		4 356 ✓	Apr 3	Materials (chq 523)		3 480 ✓
5	Hans		1 080	8	Wages (chq 524)		1 400
11	Lara		630 ✓	14	Stationery (chq 525)		230 ✓
16	Thomas		2 563 ✓	21	Emma (chq 526)		675 ✓
21	Mia		1 387	29	Heat and lights (chq 527)		1 082
30	Peter		493	7	Standing order – Business rates		940
30	Credit transfer – Kira		1 340	28	Bank charges and interest		52
				30	Balance c/d		3 990
			11 849				11 849
May 1	Balance b/d		3 990				

Prepare the bank reconciliation statement.

Answer

Bank reconciliation statement 30 Apr 2021

	Dr $	Cr $
Balance per bank statement		3 512
Add uncleared deposits:		
Name: Hans	1 080	
Mia	1 387	
Peter	493	
	2 960	
Less unpresented cheques:		
Name: Wages	1 400	
Heat and lights	1 082	
	(2 482)	
Balance as per cash book	3 990	

> **TIP**
> Items not ticked on the bank statement are added to the updated cash book. Items not ticked on the cash book are entered in the bank reconciliation statement.

CAMBRIDGE INTERNATIONAL AS & A LEVEL ACCOUNTING: WORKBOOK

1

Cash book for Anna for May 2021

Debit		$	Credit		$
May 1	Balance b/d	3 990	May 4	Insurance (528)	360
6	Luca	2 648	11	Noah (529)	1 493
15	Mila	566	14	Telephone (530)	284
21	David	1 762	19	Sofia (531)	2 341
27	Lena	387	23	Motor vehicle expenses (532)	862
30	Levin	2 094	28	Advertising (533)	472

Bank statement for Anna for May 2021

Date	Details	Withdrawals $	Deposits $	Balance $
01.05	Balance b/d			3 990
04.05	Cheque 528	360		3 630
06.05	Deposit – Luca		2 648	6 278
10.05	Standing order – rent and rates	1 147		5 131
14.05	Cheque 530	284		4 847
19.05	Cheque 531	2 341		2 506
21.05	Deposit – David		1 762	4 268
27.05	Deposit – Lena		387	4 655
28.05	Direct debit – heat and light	634		4 021
28.05	Cheque 533	472		3 549
29.05	Bank charges and interest	125		3 424

REQUIRED

Prepare a bank reconciliation statement for Anna at 31 May 2021.

2

Cash book for Anna for June 2021

Debit		$	Credit		$
Jun 1	Balance b/d	3 729	Jun 2	Telephone (534)	538
3	Elena	364	8	Lara (535)	942
9	Matteo	951	14	Materials (536)	1 652
16	Louis	1 367	23	Marketing (537)	735
16	Liam	218	25	Motor vehicle fuel (538)	438
22	Laura	942	30	Wages (539)	826
29	Hans	156			

Bank statement for Anna for June 2021				
Date	Details	Withdrawals	Deposits	Balance
		$	$	$
01.06	Balance b/d			3 729
02.06	Cheque 534	538		3 191
07.06	Deposit – Elena		364	3 555
08.06	Direct debit – heat and light	1 147		2 408
09.06	Deposit – Matteo		951	3 359
15.06	Cheque 536	1 652		1 707
18.06	Deposit		1 585	3 292
21.06	Standing order – rent and rates	1 762		1 530
23.06	Cheque 537	735		795
28.06	Deposit – Peter		634	1 429
30.06	Cheque 539	826		603
30.06	Bank charges and interest	176		427

TIP

Transactions happening on the same day may be added together in the bank statement as one transaction.

REQUIRED

Prepare a bank reconciliation statement for Anna at 31 June 2021.

3 Prepare a bank reconciliation statement from the following information.

	$
Debit balance as per bank statement	412
Receipts not presented	2 586
Payments not presented	1 375

WORKED EXAMPLE 2

At 31 July 2021 Anna's business had a cash book balance of $80 at the bank. On the same date, the bank statement balance was $650 (credit). When the cash book was compared with the bank statement, the following were found:

- A cheque sent for materials for $1 000 had not been presented for payment.
- A cheque for $220 paid into the bank had not been credited on the bank statement.
- Bank charges of $210 were omitted from the cash book.

REQUIRED

a Calculate the corrected cash book balance at 31 July 2021.

b Prepare a bank reconciliation statement at 31 July 2021.

Answer

a Only one of these transactions affects the cash book: the bank charges of $210.

The corrected cash book balance would be as follows:

Balance of $80 less the bank charges of $210 ($80 − $210 = $130 overdraft)

CONTINUED

b

Bank reconciliation statement 31 July 2021	Dr $	Cr $
Balance per bank statement		650
Add uncleared deposits:		
Unpresented deposit	220	
		220
Less unpresented cheques:		
Materials	1 000	
		(1 000)
Balance as per cash book		(130)

We can now see the two balances agree with each other and therefore they reconcile.

4 At 31 August 2021 Anna's business had a cash book balance of $1 600 at the bank. When the bank statement was received the following were discovered:

- A cheque sent for $425 sent to a supplier had been entered in the cash book as $452.
- A cheque for $375 sent to a supplier had not been presented for payment.
- A cheque for $400 paid into the bank had not been credited in the bank statement.

State the balance on the bank statement at 31 August 2021.

EXAM-STYLE MULTIPLE CHOICE AND STRUCTURED QUESTIONS

1 A bank statement shows a balance of $2 000 (credit).

A payment for $300 for electricity and a receipt for $780 were included in the cash book but have not yet appeared on the bank statement.

Bank charges of $290 had been recorded in the cash book but incorrectly recorded in the bank statement as $209.

What is the cash book balance?

- A $1 601
- B $2 399
- C $399
- D $2 770

[1]

Bank reconciliation statement for Jane at 31 October 2022

Updated cash book:

	$	$
Balance per cash book		3 393
Add: Deposit – Simon	1 730	
Less: Direct debit – Insurance	(846)	
Less: Bank charges and interest	(286)	598
Updated cash book balance		3 991

Bank reconciliation statement at 31 October 2022:

	$	$
Balance per bank statement		2 450
Add: Uncredited deposits		
Sales (11 Oct)	1 473	
Rachel (23 Oct)	375	
Sales (28 Oct)	1 078	2 926
		5 376
Less: Unpresented cheque		
Cheque 879 – Salary		(1 385)
Balance per updated cash book		3 991

Question 2 answer: B $46 915

($45 630 + $5 679 − $3 814 − $580 = $46 915)

> Chapter 14
Control accounts

LEARNING INTENTIONS

In this chapter you will:

- understand what sales and purchases ledger control accounts are and how to prepare them
- reconcile the control accounts with the sales and purchase ledger
- calculate revised profit for the year per draft accounts, after the control and ledger accounts have been reconciled
- revise the current assets and current liabilities in a draft statement of financial position
- explain the benefits and limitations of control accounts

KEY TERMS

Contra (set-off)   Control account   Dishonoured cheques   Error of omission   Error of original entry
Purchases ledger control account   Sales ledger control account

Key skills exercises

Knowledge and understanding

To answer the questions in this chapter, you need to know and understand:

- control accounts contain a summary of the relevant transactions involving that part of the business
- control accounts are mainly used for sales and purchases
- control accounts check the arithmetical accuracy of the bookkeeping
- control accounts provide a total balance to be entered into the trial balance.

You should also be able to use your knowledge and understanding of what control accounts are to reconcile them, calculate revised profit and revise the current assets and current liabilities in a draft statement of financial position.

> **COMFORT HOME FURNISHING**
>
> Comfort Home Furnishing is a furniture business in Fiji. They sell locally made beds and loungers as well as a range of furniture. Their commercial division sells to the hospitality/corporate sector providing bedding and furniture solutions to offices and hotels.
>
> This type of business will have many trade receivables and trade payables. At the end of every month, a sales and purchases control account needs to be created to check the arithmetical accuracy of the bookkeeping and to provide a summary of the total balance for trade payables and trade receivables.
>
> A sales ledger control account is a summary of all trade receivable transactions throughout an accounting year.

14 Control accounts AS Level

WORKED EXAMPLE 1

Prepare a sales ledger control account from the following information for March 2020.

	$
Sales ledger debit balance at 1 March 2020	34 852
Receipts from credit customers	67 359
Sales journal total for March 2020	68 470
Sales returns journal total for March 2020	1 476
Discounts allowed	960
Irrecoverable debts	348
Contras to purchases ledger	641
Returned cheques	273

From this information, the debit side of the sales ledger control account would have the opening balance, sales journal total and returned cheques as all of these amounts increase the trade receivables total. The credit side would have the receipts from customers, sales returns journal total, discounts allowed, irrecoverable debts and contras, as all of these amounts decrease the trade receivables total. The sales ledger control account would look as follows:

Answer

Sales ledger control account

Debit		$	Credit		$
Mar 1	Balance b/d	34 852	Mar 31	Bank	67 359
31	Sales journal	68 470	31	Sales returns journal	1 476
31	Bank (Returned cheque)	273	31	Discount allowed	960
			31	Irrecoverable debt	348
			31	Contra	641
			31	Balance c/d	32 811
		103 595			103 595
Apr 1	Balance b/d	32 811			

We can now see from this information that the total trade receivables at 31 March 2020 are $32 811.

---

1. Prepare a purchases ledger control account from the following information for March 2020.

	$
Purchases ledger credit balance at 1 March 2020	36 412
Payments to credit suppliers	57 490
Purchases journal total for March 2020	49 684
Purchases returns journal total for March 2020	1 431
Discounts received	472
Contras to sales ledger	641
Cancelled cheques	240

2   The following information has been extracted from the books of Vivian Lomani for the month of August 2022.

	$
Sales ledger debit balance at 1 August 2022	23 950
Purchases ledger credit balance at 1 August 2022	29 461
Payments to credit suppliers	47 059
Receipts from credit customers	41 705
Sales journal total for August 2022	36 148
Purchases journal total for August 2022	38 125
Sales returns journal total for August 2022	1 736
Purchases returns journal total for August 2022	1 492
Cash sales total for August 2022	14 638
Cash purchases total for August 2022	18 523
Discounts allowed	658
Discounts received	842
Returned cheque from customer	356
Cancelled cheque to supplier	410
Irrecoverable debts	642
Contras	735

REQUIRED

Prepare a purchases ledger control account and a sales ledger control account at 31 August 2022.

WORKED EXAMPLE 2

Prepare a sales ledger control account with the information extracted from Nikhil's Sports Supplies for November 2022.

	$
Sales ledger debit balance at 1 November 2022	15 843
Sales ledger credit balance at 1 November 2022	630
Sales journal total for November 2022	42 017
Sales returns journal total for November 2022	1 563
Receipts from credit customers	34 752
Returned cheques	354
Irrecoverable debts	520
Discounts allowed	476
Refunds to trade receivables	60
Contras	510
Interest charged on overdue accounts	360
Sales ledger debit balance at 30 November 2022	?
Sales ledger credit balance at 30 November 2022	350

TIP

Decide which entries belong to either the sales ledger control account or purchases ledger control account. Decide if some of the entries don't belong in either of the two ledger accounts.

14 Control accounts AS Level

> **CONTINUED**

Answer

There are a few extra items here compared to the previous example. Namely, refunds to trade receivables and interest charged on overdue accounts, which will both be entered on the debit side of the account.

Sales ledger control account						
Debit				**Credit**		
			$			$
Nov 1		Balance b/d	15 843	Nov 1	Balance b/d	630
	30	Sales journal	42 017	30	Bank	34 752
	30	Bank (returned cheque)	354	30	Sales returns journal	1 563
	30	Bank (refund)	60	30	Discount allowed	476
	30	Interest charges	360	30	Irrecoverable debt	520
	30	Balance c/d	350	30	Contra	510
				30	Balance c/d	20 533
			58 984			58 984
Dec 1		Balance b/d	20 533	Dec 1	Balance b/d	350

3 Prepare a purchases ledger control account with the following information extracted from Nikhil's Sports Supplies for November 2022.

	$
Purchases ledger debit balance at 1 November 2022	420
Purchases ledger credit balance at 1 November 2022	19 634
Purchases journal total for November 2022	32 410
Purchases returns journal total for November 2022	1 372
Payments to credit suppliers	21 683
Cancelled cheques to credit suppliers	367
Discounts received	260
Refunds from trade payables	80
Contras	510
Interest charged on overdue accounts	130
Purchases ledger debit balance at 30 November 2022	390
Purchases ledger credit balance at 30 November 2022	?

4 Lawrence provided the following information at 30 November 2018.

	$
Purchases ledger control account balance	16 970
Sales ledger control account balance	42 350

These did not agree with the list of balances taken from the purchases ledger and sales ledger, respectively. The following items were discovered:

1   A discount received of $280 had been omitted from the books.
2   A credit note for sales returns of $230 had been treated as a sales invoice and entered in the sales journal.
3   An irrecoverable debt of $190 had been written off in the sales ledger. No entry had been made in the control account.
4   A contra entry for $1 070 had been debited twice in the purchases ledger control account.
5   A payment of $120 to a credit supplier had not been recorded.
6   Discount allowed of $70 had been posted to the debit side of both the sales ledger control account and the purchases ledger control account.
7   Lawrence owes Kalim $380 and Kalim owes Lawrence $1 590. They have agreed to offset the balance, on Lawrence's account in Kalim's sales ledger.
8   A customer's dishonoured cheque had been entered in the cash book as $1 560 instead of $1 650.

REQUIRED

a   i   Prepare the corrected purchases ledger control account at 30 November 2018. **[4]**

    ii Prepare the corrected sales ledger control account at 30 November 2018. **[5]**

b   Explain what is meant by the term 'error of commission'. **[2]**

c   Explain the effect on a business of not updating:

    i   customers' accounts in the sales ledger **[2]**

    ii suppliers' accounts in the purchases ledger. **[2]**

Adapted from Cambridge International AS&A Level Accounting (9706) Paper 21, Q2, June 2019

[Total: 15]

EXAM-STYLE MULTIPLE CHOICE AND STRUCTURED QUESTIONS

1   What is the purpose of a business keeping a purchases ledger control account?

    A   cash purchases total
    B   value of goods bought
    C   to help with the preparation of statements of financial position
    D   predict the purchases required for the next year **[1]**

2   Which items will be credited to the sales ledger control account?

    1   interest charges
    2   discount allowed
    3   sales returns
    4   sales journal

    A   1 and 4
    B   2 and 4
    C   1 and 3
    D   2 and 3 **[1]**

CONTINUED

3 Meena did not keep full accounting records. She was advised to keep her books of account using the double entry system.

REQUIRED

a State three benefits a business gains from maintaining a system of double entry book-keeping. [3]

Additional information

Meena now uses the double entry system of book-keeping. At the end of January the total of the balances in the sales ledger was $34 524. However, the balance on the sales ledger control account was $33 205.

On investigation she found the following errors:

1. The sales journal had been undercast by $1 649.
2. A cheque received had been correctly entered in the cash book as $650 but was entered in the sales ledger as $560.
3. An irrecoverable debt, $420, had been written off in the sales ledger but not entered in the control account.
4. A credit note issued for $160 had been completely omitted from the books of account.

REQUIRED

b Prepare a reconciliation between the sales ledger control account and the sales ledger balances at 31 January. [6]

c State **three** reasons why there might be a credit balance on a customer's account in the sales ledger. [3]

Additional information

Meena is considering charging interest on the full account balances of her customers who do not pay promptly.

REQUIRED

d Advise Meena whether or not she should take this course of action. Justify your answer. [3]

Adapted from Cambridge International AS&A Level Accounting (9706) Paper 21, Q3, June 2017

[Total: 15]

Improve this answer

This is a sample answer to **Q3d**.

> Meena should charge interest as she will be making more money from the interest

Your challenge

See if you can improve this answer. The sample answer advises on the course of action Meena should take, but has not provided any justification. A better answer is available online – but write yours out first!

Chapter 15
The correction of errors

LEARNING INTENTIONS

In this chapter you will:

- identify the types of error and their effects on the financial statements
- prepare journal entries to correct errors
- understand the purpose of suspense accounts and how to prepare them
- revise the profit for the year in the draft accounts after errors have been corrected

KEY TERM

Suspense account

Key skills exercises
Knowledge and understanding

To answer the questions in this chapter, you need to know and understand:

- the six errors not affecting the trial balance
- the suspense account is an account opened to record a difference between the debit and credit totals of the trial balance.

You should also be able to use your knowledge and understanding of the errors and the suspense account to prepare journal entries to correct errors, revise the profit for the year after errors have been corrected and revise the net current assets in a draft statement of financial position.

Analysis

To answer the questions in this chapter, you need to be able to:

- analyse financial information to assess the effect of errors on the profit.

> **WELL CATERED**
>
> Shaniqua owns a catering business in Victoria, Seychelles, named 'Well Catered'. She caters for events at hotels, guesthouses, weddings and private functions. She has become too busy to cope with the catering and bookkeeping and has hired an accountant, Ibrahima. Ibrahima prepared a trial balance based on the financial year's books and found the two columns did not agree with each other. As a trained accountant he knew that this means there must be errors and has to figure out what those errors are. Shaniqua asked to have a look at the work he had prepared so far and was shocked to see the two columns of the trial balance did not agree. Ibrahima assured Shaniqua that he would find the errors and get the trial balance to agree.

1 Identify the type of error in each situation.

	Error	Type of error
a	An invoice was received showing a total of credit purchases to the value of $640. The transaction was entered in the purchases journal as $460.	
b	The stationery account was mistotalled as $450 instead of $420. The rent received from a tenant was entered in the rent receivable account as $830 instead of $800.	
c	The purchase of new office furniture was entered into the accounts as purchases.	
d	A cash slip for general expenses to the value of $210 had been omitted from the accounts.	
e	A transaction for wages was entered as follows: debit bank, credit wages.	
f	An invoice for H. Smith's purchase of goods on credit was entered into S. Smith's account.	

WORKED EXAMPLE 1

Ibrahima prepared the trial balance for 30 June 2021 but the totals did not agree. He has posted the difference of $840 (debit) to a suspense account.

Ibrahima has found the following errors:

i   An invoice for purchases of $650 had been entered in the purchases journal as $560.
ii Cash drawings of $400 had been entered correctly in the cash book but had not been entered in the drawings account.
iii The returns inwards journal had been undercast by $120.
iv The payment of rent by cheque, $300, had not been posted from the cash book.
v   The total of the discount received column in the cash book had been undercast by $70.

a   Prepare journal entries to correct these errors. Include narratives for each transaction.
b   Prepare the suspense account.

CONTINUED

Answer

a

General journal			
		$	$
i	Purchases	90	
	Suspense		90
	The correction of purchases of $650 entered as $560		
ii	Drawings	400	
	Suspense		400
	The correction of cash drawings not posted from the cash book to the drawings account		
iii	Returns inwards	120	
	Suspense		120
	The correction of returns inwards account undercast by $120		
iv	Rent expense	300	
	Suspense		300
	The correction of rent expense not posted from the cash book to the rent expense account		
v	Suspense	70	
	Discount received		70
	The correction of the discount received column being undercast by $70 in the cash book		

b

Suspense account				
Debit			Credit	
	$			$
Balance b/d	840	Purchases		90
Discount received	70	Drawings		400
		Returns inwards		120
		Rent expense		300
	910			910

2 The totals of the trial balance on 31 July 2021 did not agree either. The total for the debit column was $45 856 and the credit column was $46 941.

The following errors were discovered:

i The purchases returns journal was incorrectly totalled as $429 and the correct total is $329.

ii Shaniqua took $300 worth of groceries (goods) for personal use. The goods account was credited but no double-entry was made.

iii The payment of wages in cash had been correctly entered in the cash book as $530 but no entry was made in the wages account.

iv Equipment depreciation was overadded by $155.

REQUIRED

a Prepare journal entries to correct these errors. Include narratives for each transaction.

b Prepare the suspense account.

3 Ibrahima prepared the trial balance for 30 September 2021. The totals did not agree. He posted the difference to a suspense account.

Ibrahima found the following errors:

i Stationery, $246, paid for by cash. $246 entered in the stationery account and $346 posted to the cash book.

ii $260 for motor expenses entered into the motor vehicle account.

iii $350 paid for rent expense entered correctly into the cash book but not posted to the nominal ledger.

iv Cash sales of $1 340 had been correctly entered in the cash book, but had been credited to the sales account as $1 530.

v A cheque payment for interest charges had been completely overlooked.

A cheque payment for heat and light of $270 had been debited in the cash book and credited to the heat and light account.

REQUIRED

Prepare the suspense account showing the opening balance.

> **TIP**
>
> Not all errors are entered into the suspense account. From the list of errors shown, decide which ones will be entered into the suspense account and only enter those errors.

WORKED EXAMPLE 2

Ibrahima has prepared the statement of profit or loss for the year ended 31 December 2021. The statement of profit or loss showed a profit of $29 500. The following errors have now been discovered:

i Advertising costs owing of $200 were overlooked when preparing the statement of profit or loss.

ii Discounts allowed of $460 had been incorrectly added to the gross profit.

iii The prepayment for rent had been underadded by $600.

iv Cash sales of $8 900 had been completely omitted from the accounting records.

v No entry was made for depreciation of equipment, $2 100, in the statement of profit or loss.

REQUIRED

Prepare a statement showing the effect of correcting these errors on the draft profit for the year ended 31 December 2021.

CONTINUED

Answer

	Calculation of corrected profit for the year ended 31 December 2021	Increase	Decrease	
		$	$	$
	Profit per draft statement of profit or loss			29 500
Error 1	Increase in advertising expense		200	
Error 2	Increase in expenses, decrease in income		920	
Error 3	Rent expense overadded	600		
Error 4	Increase in sales	8 900		
Error 5	Depreciation overlooked		2 100	
		9 500	3 220	6 280
	Revised profit for the year			35 780

Error 1 decreases the profit as the expenses are increasing.

Error 2 decreases the profit by double the amount as the one transaction cancels the original error and the second transaction is decreasing the expenses as discounts allowed is an expense.

Error 3 increases the profit as too much money was deducted for rent expense.

Error 4 increases the profit as sales is an income that has been overlooked.

Error 5 decreases the profit as depreciation is an expense that was not entered.

---

4   Ibrahima prepared the statement of profit or loss for the year ended 31 December 2023. The statement of profit or loss showed a profit of $41 520. The following errors have now been discovered:

  i   The sales journal had been undercast by $470.

  ii   No entry has been made of goods, cost price $200, withdrawn by Shaniqua for personal use.

  iii The opening inventory of $2 300 had not been entered in the trial balance.

  iv   The total of the discount allowed column in the cash book of $290, had been posted to the credit to the credit of the discount received account as $390.

  v   A purchase invoice of $2 000 had been incorrectly entered in the books as $200.

REQUIRED

Prepare a statement showing the effect of correcting these errors on the draft profit for the year ended 31 December 2023.

EXAM-STYLE MULTIPLE CHOICE AND STRUCTURED QUESTIONS

1   A trial balance does not agree and the bookkeeper finds the following errors:
    i   An insurance invoice for $540 was debited to the wages account.
    ii A bank overdraft of $200 was entered as a debit in the trial balance.
    iii A cash sale of $670 was entered in the sales account as $770; the sale was entered correctly in the cash account.

    The bookkeeper opens a suspense account to correct the errors.
    What is the opening balance in the suspense account?
    A   debit $240
    B   credit $100
    C   debit $270
    D   credit $300 [1]

2   The following errors were discovered after a suspense account was opened:
    i   Discount allowed of $35 had been debited to the discount received account.
    ii $3 400 for electricity had been debited to the heat and light account instead of $4 300.
    iii Motor vehicle repairs were credited to the motor vehicles account, $700.
    iv A cash purchase of goods for resale of $680 had been completely overlooked.

    Which items would be entered in the suspense account?
    A   i and ii
    B   ii and iii
    C   i and iii
    D   iii and iv [1]

3   Contador, a sole trader, has provided the following extract from the trial balance for the year ended 31 March 2015. He does not maintain control accounts as part of his accounting records.

	$
Debit balances	112 375
Credit balances	120 835

    REQUIRED
    a   i   State the use of a suspense account. [1]
        ii State **three** advantages to a business of maintaining a sales ledger control account. [3]

    Additional information
    The following errors have been identified:
    i   The sales journal had been overcast by $26 350.
    ii Motor expenses of $5 270 had been posted to the motor vehicles account. Motor vehicles had been depreciated at 20% per annum.
    iii Interest received of $8 945 had been debited to both the bank account and the interest received account.

CONTINUED

REQUIRED

b Prepare journal entries to correct all of the errors identified. Narratives are **not** required. [8]

c Assess the effect of these errors on the profit for the year. [3]

Cambridge International AS&A Level Accounting (9706) Paper 22, Q3, October 2016

[Total: 15]

Improve this answer

This is a sample answer to **Q3c**.

		Corrected profit	
		Increase $	Decrease $
Error i	Sales		26350
Error ii	Motor expenses		5270
	Depreciation	1054	
Error iii	Interest received	8945	

Your challenge

See if you can improve this answer. Pay particular attention to Error iii, which seems to be the problem. A better answer is available online – but write your own out first!

> Chapter 16
Incomplete records

LEARNING INTENTIONS

In this chapter you will:

- understand why accountants need to be able to apply a range of techniques in order to produce accounts for many small businesses
- calculate profit or loss from statements of affairs
- use control accounts to find missing figures
- deal with transactions involving non-current assets
- prepare the statement of profit or loss and statement of financial position from incomplete records

KEY TERMS

Incomplete records   Receipts and payments account   Single-entry bookkeeping   Statement of affairs

Key skills exercises

Knowledge and understanding

To answer the questions in this chapter, you need to know and understand:

- incomplete records are any method of recording transactions that is not based on the double-entry model
- the different techniques to apply in order to produce final accounts from incomplete records – calculating capital and profit or loss, using control accounts, the receipts and payments account, dealing with non-current assets.

You should also be able to use your knowledge and understanding of the different techniques applied to prepare the statement of profit or loss and statement of financial position.

> **MATEO'S ROCK-CLIMBING EQUIPMENT**
>
> Mateo is a rock-climbing professional living in Chile. He decided to open a rock-climbing equipment shop. Mateo realised that initially he was going to have to invest a large sum of capital for the equipment required to display in his shop, but he was certain he would make his money back quickly. Every month Mateo kept a record of money he was receiving and money he was spending and has a list of his assets and liabilities. At the end of the second year of trading, Mateo was interested in whether or not his business had made a profit. He didn't know how to work this out so he sent all the information he had recorded during the years to an accountant to prepare financial statements for him.

WORKED EXAMPLE 1

Mateo supplied the accountant, Joaquin, with the following list of assets and liabilities.

	1 September 2018	31 August 2019
	$	$
Premises	5 000	5 000
Equipment	3 000	2 700
Amounts owing from clients	150	210
Prepaid expenses	140	160
Balance at bank / (overdraft)	(420)	280
Bank loan	4 000	3 600
Amounts owing to suppliers	260	170
Accrued expenses	110	90

Mateo has drawn $50 each week from the business for personal use.

Joaquin, the accountant, uses a statement of affairs to calculate Mateo's opening and closing capital balances. He lists the assets and totals them and then lists the liabilities and totals them. Finally, he uses the accounting equation to calculate the capital totals.

Statement of affairs				
	1 September 2018		31 August 2019	
	$	$	$	$
Assets				
Premises	5 000		5 000	
Equipment	3 000		2 700	
Amounts owing from clients	150		210	
Prepaid expenses	140		160	
Balance at bank	–		280	
		8 290		8 350
Liabilities				
Less bank overdraft	420		–	
Bank loan	4 000		3 600	
Amounts owing to suppliers	260		170	
Accrued expenses	110		90	
		(4 790)		(3 860)
Capital		3 500		4 490

16 Incomplete records AS Level

CONTINUED

Calculate Mateo's profit.

His profit is as follows:

	$
Closing capital at 31 August 2019	4 490
Add drawings in year to 31 August 2019 (52 × $50)	2 600
	7 090
Deduct opening capital at 1 September 2018	(3 500)
Profit for the year ended 31 August 2019	3 590

TIP

Drawings are added back as these would be part of the profit if Mateo had not taken them for personal use.

1 At 31 August 2021 Mateo supplies Joaquin with the following list of assets and liabilities and asks him to calculate his profit.

	1 September 2020	31 August 2021
	$	$
Premises	5 000	5 000
Equipment	3 500	3 300
Trade receivables	160	150
Prepaid expenses	80	120
Balance at bank	1 047	950
Bank loan	3 200	2 800
Trade payables	320	160
Accrued expenses	140	70

Mateo also informs Joaquin that he was withdrawing $100 per week for personal use.

REQUIRED

Prepare the statement of affairs for 1 September 2020 and 31 August 2021.

Calculate the profit or loss for the year ended 31 August 2021.

WORKED EXAMPLE 2

Back in 2018 when Mateo originally opened his business, he wasn't keeping track of his credit sales and credit purchases. The only information he had regarding trade receivables on 31 August 2019 was as follows:

	$
Opening trade receivables	150
Closing trade receivables	210
Receipts from trade receivables	2 450
Credit sales	?
Discount allowed	340
Irrecoverable debts	180

Prepare the sales ledger control account for 31 August 2019 to calculate the credit sales for the year.

CONTINUED

Answer

Sales ledger control account

Debit		$	Credit		$
Aug 1	Opening balance	150	Aug 31	Bank	2 450
31	Credit sales	3 030		Discount allowed	340
				Irrecoverable debts	180
				Closing balance	210
		3 180			3 180
Sep 1	Balance b/d	210			

Fill in the information given to you in the control account. Balance the side that is 'heavier' and subtract the 'lighter' side's amount from the balance to find the missing figure.

2 Mateo supplied the following information regarding trade payables at 31 August 2019.

	$
Opening trade payables	260
Closing trade payables	170
Payments to trade payables	1 780
Credit purchases	?
Discount received	240
Purchases returns	190

REQUIRED

Prepare the purchases ledger control account for 31 August 2019 using the proforma shown to calculate the credit purchases for the year.

Purchases ledger control account

Debit		$	Credit		$
Aug 31	Bank		Aug 1	Opening balance	
	Discount received		31	Credit purchases	
	Purchases returns				
	Closing balance				
			Sep 1	Balance b/d	

TIP

To find missing figures in the purchases ledger control account, use the same method; items will just be on the opposite side to the sales ledger control account.

TIP

Add the cost of the new equipment to the original cost of equipment when calculating the closing accumulated depreciation.

3 Calculate the depreciation expense and prepare the details that would appear in the non-current assets section of the statement of financial position in the following situations:

Situation 1: Mateo purchased shop fittings to the value of $3 000 on 1 September 2018, which had a net book value of $2 700 on 31 August 2019. On 3 February 2020 he purchased more shop fittings worth $1 100 and at 31 August 2020 his shop fittings had a net book value of $3 300. No shop fittings had been sold during the year.

Situation 2: Mateo purchased shop fittings for $10 750 and this had been depreciated by $1 650 at the start of the year. Depreciation was based on a residual value of $2 500 and a useful life of five years.

Five months into the year, a second batch of shop fittings was bought for $4 600. It was expected to last six years and have a residual value of $1 000. Depreciation on all shop fittings is applied on a monthly basis and uses the straight-line method.

> **TIP**
> Calculate the accumulated depreciation for each batch of equipment separately and then add them together to get the total accumulated depreciation.

4 Santiago did not keep proper books of account but he has provided the following information about his business.

	Balances at 31 August 2020	Balances at 31 August 2021
	$	$
Premises at net book value	96 000	81 000
Equipment at net book value	12 000	18 300
Inventory	12 750	13 200
Trade receivables	11 250	9 300
Prepaid insurance	750	600
Accrued rent	300	150
Loan	8 250	15 000
Trade payables	5 850	7 050

Santiago's bank account transactions for the year ended 31 August 2021 were as follows:

Santiago
Summary bank account for the year ended 31 August 2021

Receipts		Payments	
	$		$
Opening balance	3 450	Trade payables	48 600
Trade receivables	72 150	Insurance	9 000
Loan	7 500	Rent	3 000
		Drawings	12 450
		Purchase of new equipment	9 000
		Loan repayment	750
		Closing balance	300
	83 100		83 100
Balance b/d	300		

> **TIP**
> Remember to calculate and add depreciation as an expense for the statement of profit or loss.

a Calculate the sales for the year ended 31 August 2021.
b Calculate the purchases for the year ended 31 August 2021.
c Calculate the insurance and rent amount for the statement of profit or loss.
d Prepare a statement of profit or loss for the year ended 31 August 2021.
e Prepare a statement of financial position for the year ended 31 August 2021.

> **TIP**
> A statement of affairs needs to be prepared to find the opening capital.

CAMBRIDGE INTERNATIONAL AS & A LEVEL ACCOUNTING: WORKBOOK

EXAM-STYLE MULTIPLE CHOICE AND STRUCTURED QUESTIONS

1 A sole trader did not keep proper accounting records. He has supplied the following information for the year.

	$
Receipts from trade receivables	98 410
Discounts allowed	3 450
Trade receivables opening balance	42 630
Trade receivables closing balance	40 860

What were the credit sales at the year end?

A $103 630

B $93 190

C $96 730

D $100 090 [1]

2 A sole trader deals with cash transactions only and doesn't keep complete accounting records. Which item will not be required to calculate the owner's cash drawings?

A purchases

B non-current assets purchased

C opening capital account

D sales [1]

3 Isidora has not kept a full set of accounting records but has provided the following information relating to the year ended 31 October 2021.

	1 November 2020	31 October 2021
	$	$
Accrued expenses (rent)	1 120	1 200
Bank (Dr)	3 944	5 032
Inventory	17 736	21 136
Motor vehicles (cost $28 000)	21 000	?
Equipment (cost $13 760)	11 904	?
Prepaid expenses (insurance)	2 200	2 464
Trade payables	8 336	7 888
Trade receivables	14 152	15 624

Isidora puts all of her receipts and payments through the business bank account and during the year the following transactions occurred.

CONTINUED

	$	
Cash purchases	43 432	
Cash sales	129 968	
Drawings	????	
Insurance	4 656	
Equipment	7 680	bought on 28 February 2021
Payments to suppliers	78 664	
Receipts from receivables	80 152	
Rent and rates	13 760	
Wages and salaries	26 752	

Discounts given to customers for prompt payment were $1 392 and those received from suppliers were $1 944. There were irrecoverable debts totalling $1 144.

Isidora kept all credit notes received from suppliers – these totalled $3 840 while customers returned goods totalling $2 272.

Depreciation is charged using the straight-line method on the following basis: 20% on motor vehicles and 15% on equipment. Depreciation is charged on a monthly basis.

REQUIRED

a Calculate Isidora's capital at 1 November 2021. [3]
b Prepare the receipts and payments account showing the drawings for the year. [6]
c Prepare the sales ledger control account and the purchases ledger control account showing the credit sales and the credit purchases. [9]
d Prepare the rent and rates and the insurance accounts, showing each expense for the year. [6]
e Calculate the depreciation for the year. [6]

[Total: 30]

> Chapter 17
Incomplete records: Further considerations

LEARNING INTENTIONS

In this chapter you will:

- use the trading account structure to find sales, purchases and inventory values
- use mark-ups and margins to find sales, purchases and inventory values
- use 'dummy inventory figures' to provide a starting point when too much information is missing
- determine inventory loss when the business has suffered a fire or theft
- value inventory in accordance with recognised accounting principles
- learn the advantages and disadvantages of keeping a full double-entry accounting system

KEY TERMS

Cost historic   Cost replacement   Margin   Mark-up   Net realisable value

Key skills exercises

Knowledge and understanding

To answer the questions in this chapter, you need to know and understand:

- how to use the trading account or mark-ups and margins to find sales, purchases and inventory values
- how to provide a starting point when too much information is missing
- how to determine inventory losses due to fire or theft
- how to value inventory at the lower of cost and net realisable value
- the advantages and disadvantages of double-entry bookkeeping.

You should also be able to use your knowledge and understanding to find sales, purchases and inventory values, determining inventory losses, valuing inventory and know what to do when too much information is missing.

> **ANUBIS' VIDEO GAMES**
>
> Anubis from Giza, Egypt, decided to open a Video Game Centre where people could buy or rent games and consoles but also play against each other and against him at the centre. This way, he was doing what he loved and making money from it. Anubis had started small but soon his business became very popular, especially for people aged 15–24 years. Anubis had no accounting background and just kept a cash book and a summary of his stock to sell. Anubis realised after a few years of owning his business he wasn't sure if he had made a profit or not. He decided to send all the paperwork he had of the business's finances to an accountant to see if she could help him get a better understanding of the financial position of his business.

17 Incomplete records: Further considerations AS Level

1 Anubis supplied the accountant with the following information for the years 2019, 2020 and 2021.

	2019 $	2020 $	2021 $
Revenue	41 058	?	85 360
Opening inventory	8 200	5 768	12 490
Purchases	26 310	?	47 520
Closing inventory	?	12 490	?
Cost of sales	28 742	30 170	?
Gross profit	?	23 920	38 470

> **TIP**
> To calculate gross profit, subtract cost of sales from revenue; to calculate revenue, add cost of sales and gross profit; to calculate cost of sales, subtract gross profit from revenue.

REQUIRED

a Prepare the trading account for each of these years for Anubis and use them to find the missing figures.

b Calculate, using the figures calculated in **a** and those given, the margin and mark-up as a percentage (to 1 d.p.).

> **TIP**
> Margin is based on sales and mark-up is based on cost of sales.

WORKED EXAMPLE 1

Anubis supplied the following information, which has been put into a trading account.

	$	$
Revenue		88 000
Less cost of sales:		
Opening inventory	27 630	
Purchases	? [2]	
	? [1]	
Closing inventory	(30 560)	
Cost of sales		?
Gross profit		?

Anubis also informed Rashida, the accountant, that he uses a profit margin of 45%.

Calculate the missing figures.

Answer

First, **calculate** 45% of $88 000 (revenue), which will give you the gross profit figure ($88 000 × 45% = $39 600). Once you have that, you can either work backwards up the trading account or calculate the cost of goods sold as 55% (100 − 45) of $88 000 and then work backwards up the trading account.

Use the percentage 55% × $88 000 = $48 400 to calculate the cost of goods sold or use the revenue less the gross profit to calculate the cost of goods sold ($88 000 − $39 600 = $48 400).

From there, you take the cost of goods sold plus the closing inventory to calculate missing figure [1] ($48 400 + $30 560 = $78 960).

To calculate missing figure [2] use [1] and subtract the opening inventory from it ($78 960 − $27 630 = $51 330).

2 Rashida had the following information available regarding three businesses and needs to find the missing figures for each business.

	Business		
	A	B	C
	$	$	$
Revenue	?	120 000	450 000
Opening inventory	41 700	63 830	94 560
Purchases	?	96 000	?
Closing inventory	53 420	?	118 310
Gross profit	112 000	?	?
Margin	35%	40%	20%

REQUIRED

Produce the trading account for each of the three businesses and use them and your knowledge of margins to find the missing figures.

3 Rashida had the following information available regarding three businesses and needs to find the missing figures for each business.

	Business		
	A	B	C
	$	$	$
Revenue	720 000	960 000	640 000
Opening inventory	31 250	67 340	41 820
Purchases	?	517 000	?
Closing inventory	35 120	?	39 670
Gross profit	?	?	?
Mark-up	50%	60%	25%

REQUIRED

Prepare the trading account for each of the three businesses and use them and your knowledge of mark-ups to find the missing figures.

> **TIP**
>
> Another way to find missing figures is if the mark-up percentage is given to you. It is worked in a similar way to the margin, the difference being that the cost price is now seen as 100% and revenue is seen as 100% + the mark-up percentage.
>
> For example, if you are given that a business has a revenue of $420 000 and their mark-up percentage is 25%, to calculate the cost of goods sold you would take the revenue and divide it by 125% (100% + mark-up percentage). This will give you a cost of goods sold of $336 000. Now you can calculate the gross profit by either subtracting the cost of goods sold from revenue or using 25% of $336 000 ($420 000 − $336 000 = $84 000 or $336 000 × 25% = $84 000).

WORKED EXAMPLE 2

Rashida is given the following information.

	$
Inventory 1 October 2021	4 800
Inventory 30 September 2022	5 300
Revenue for the year	78 650
Rate of inventory turnover is 6 times	

Calculate the opening inventory, cost of sales, purchases and gross profit.

CONTINUED

Answer

First, fill in the information given into a trading account as follows:

	$	$
Revenue		78 650
Less cost of sales:		
Opening inventory	4 800	
Purchases	? [4]	
	? [3]	
Closing inventory	(5 300)	
Cost of sales		? [1]
Gross profit		? [2]

[1] To calculate the cost of sales use the rate of inventory turnover formula:

$$\frac{\text{Cost of sales}}{(\$4\,800 + \$5\,300) \div 2} = 6$$

$$\frac{\text{Cost of sales}}{\$5\,050} = 6$$

Therefore, $\$5\,050 \times 6 = \$30\,300$ (cost of sales).

[2] To calculate the gross profit use revenue less cost of sales ($78 650 − $30 300 = $48 350).

[3] To calculate the total of opening inventory and purchases add cost of sales and closing inventory ($30 300 + $5 300 = $35 600).

[4] To calculate the purchases use the total from [3] and subtract the opening inventory ($35 600 − $4 800 = $30 800).

---

4 Huan owns a business selling electrical goods. He was unable to count his inventory at his year end of 31 March 2016. He counted his entire inventory on 6 April 2016 and valued it at cost, $57 760.

The following information is available:

1 Huan marks up the cost price of all goods by 25% to calculate the selling price.

2 Purchases of inventory between 1 April 2016 and 6 April 2016 amounted to $6 100.

3 Sales between 1 April 2016 and 6 April 2016 amounted to $9 600.

4 Goods with a selling price of $2 100 had been sent to a customer on a sale or return basis on 30 March 2016. The goods had not been sold at 31 March 2016 and had not been included when the inventory was counted.

5 On 4 April 2016, a customer returned goods sold to him on 26 March 2016. The goods had a selling price of $650.

REQUIRED

a Prepare a statement to show Huan the value of inventory to include in the statements of financial position at 31 March 2016. **[5]**

Additional information

The following trial balance has been extracted from the books of account at 31 March 2016.

	Debit $	Credit $
6% Bank loan (repayable 2019)		12 000
Advertising expenses	3 480	
Bank account		4 260
Capital account		145 190
Carriage outwards	810	
Discount allowed	1 250	
Drawings	32 700	
Fixtures and fittings – cost	68 100	
Fixtures and fittings – irrecoverable debts for depreciation		26 500
Insurance	1 090	
Interest paid	950	
Inventory at 1 April 2015	56 800	
Motor expenses	6 460	
Motor vehicles – cost	49 600	
Motor vehicles – irrecoverable debts for depreciation		18 800
Property rental	11 050	
Allowance for irrecoverable debts at 1 April 2015		580
Purchases	239 470	
Returns outwards		410
Revenue		294 200
Other operating expenses	4 690	
Trade payables		21 660
Trade receivables	34 920	
Wages	12 230	
	523 600	523 600

The following information is also available:

1. Interest on the bank loan had been paid up to 31 December 2015.
2. Huan's depreciation policy is as follows:

    Motor vehicles are to be depreciated at 25% per annum using the straight-line method. Depreciation is to be charged on a month-by-month basis.

    Fixtures and fittings are to be depreciated at 15% per annum using the reducing balance method.

3. Huan sold a motor vehicle for $11 000 on 31 March 2016. The vehicle had cost $18 720 on 1 July 2014. No entries for this sale had been made in the books of account.
4. Property rental included a payment of $5 850 covering the period 1 December 2015 to 31 August 2016.

5 Advertising expenses included a charge of $200 relating to advertising planned for September 2016.

6 A customer who had owed Huan $420 at the year end had been declared bankrupt.

7 Huan wishes to maintain a allowance for irrecoverable debts of 2% of trade receivables.

REQUIRED

b Prepare an income statement for Huan for the year ended 31 March 2016. [13]

Additional information

All of Huan's sales and purchases are made on a credit basis. He feels that his accounting records could be improved by preparation of control accounts.

REQUIRED

c State **three** benefits and **one** limitation of preparing a sales ledger control account. [4]

Cambridge International AS&A Level Accounting (9706) Paper 21,
Q1a, b & c, October 2017

[Total: 22]

EXAM-STYLE MULTIPLE CHOICE AND STRUCTURED QUESTIONS

1 A business that doesn't keep complete accounting records and deals in cash transactions only would not require which of the following items to calculate the owner's cash drawings?

   A opening capital account
   B purchases
   C non-current assets purchased
   D sales   [1]

2 A business owner loses some inventory in a burglary. The business owner does not keep complete accounting records. He has the following information available.

Extract of a statement of profit or loss for the month ended 31 May 2021		
	$	$
Revenue		150 000
Opening inventory	24 580	
Purchases	96 420	
	121 000	

The inventory valued at 31 May was $18 500. The business maintains a margin of 35% on sales.

What was the value of the stolen inventory?

   A $6 080
   B $10 500
   C $5 000
   D $7 000   [1]

CONTINUED

3 Francesco is a sole trader who runs a small bicycle distribution business. He does not keep full accounting records.

REQUIRED

a State **two** benefits to a sole trader of keeping full accounting records. [2]

b Explain the accounting treatment at the year-end in the income statement and statement of financial position of:
prepayments
accruals [4]

Additional information

Francesco provided the following information for the year ended 30 April 2017.

	$
Opening inventory	16 250
Total sales	82 500
Total purchases	62 750

Mark-up is 25%.

The normal rate of inventory turnover is 5 times. However, it was discovered at the year-end that some inventory had been stolen. No insurance claim has yet been made for this loss.

REQUIRED

c Prepare an extract from the income statement to show gross profit for the year ended 30 April 2017. Show the value of inventory stolen. [5]

Additional information

The following information has also been provided.

1 Balances on trade receivables, trade payables, expenses prepaid and expenses owing:

	At 1 May 2016	At 30 April 2017
	$	$
Trade receivables	6 875	8 250
Trade payables	5 200	6 350
Expenses prepaid	625	775
Expenses owing	350	425

2 Expenses paid from the bank account amounted to $9 925.
3 Rental income received by credit transfer amounted to $15 700.
4 Balance per bank statement at 30 April 2017 of $4 150 was overdrawn.
5 Unpresented cheques amounted to $850.
6 Uncredited bankings amounted to $1 975.
7 There were no cash transactions. All sales and purchases were on a credit basis.

17 Incomplete records: Further considerations AS Level

CONTINUED

REQUIRED

d Prepare the bank account for the year ended 30 April 2017. Clearly show the **opening** balance. [8]

e Calculate the charge for total expenses which appeared in the income statement for the year ended 30 April 2017. [2]

Adapted from Cambridge International AS&A Level Accounting (9706) Paper 21, Q1 a, b, c, d & e, October 2018

[Total: 21]

Improve this answer

This is a sample answer to **Q3b**.

> Prepayments are deducted from expenses and accruals are added to expenses.

Your challenge

See if you can improve this answer. This answer does not explain the classification of where these will be put in the statement of financial position. Income should also be mentioned. A better answer is available online – but write yours out first!

> Chapter 18
Partnership accounts

LEARNING INTENTIONS

In this chapter you will:

- learn what a partnership is
- learn how profits are shared when there is a partnership agreement
- apply the Partnership Act 1890 when there is no partnership agreement
- prepare partnership capital and current accounts
- prepare the partnership appropriation account
- prepare the statement of profit or loss and statement of financial position for a partnership
- learn the advantages and disadvantages of partnerships

KEY TERMS

Appropriation   Appropriation account   Interest on capital   Interest on drawings   Partners' salary   Partnership
Partnership Act 1890   Partnership agreement

Key skills exercises

Knowledge and understanding

To answer the questions in this chapter, you need to know and understand:

- a partnership is two or more people carrying on a business together with a view to making a profit
- profit sharing with a partnership agreement
- profit sharing without a partnership agreement
- the advantages and disadvantages of a partnership.

You should also be able to use your knowledge and understanding to prepare partnership capital and current accounts, appropriation accounts, statements of profit or loss and statements of financial position.

> **DREAM DESTINATIONS GETAWAYS**
>
> Ariana and Nikau met at the New Zealand School of tourism in Hamilton where they were both studying a Diploma in Tourism and Travel. Once they had both completed their course they decided to go into partnership together starting a travel and tourism business called Dream Destinations Getaways. Both partners would work in the business as they were both qualified and would therefore both earn a salary from the partnership. Ariana was able to contribute more capital than Nikau and therefore had a higher proportion of the profit sharing ratio.

WORKED EXAMPLE 1

Ariana and Nikau made a profit of $62 000 in their first year of business and the partnership agreement specified the following.
- Profits are to be shared 60:40.
- Interest on drawings is to be charged at 5%.
- Interest on capital is to be paid at 9%.
- Ariana is to be paid a salary of $11 000 and Nikau is to be paid a salary of $8 000.

Other information was available:

	Ariana	Nikau
	$	$
Capital account balance	150 000 (credit)	120 000 (credit)
Current account balance	3 400 (credit)	8 600 (debit)
Drawings for the year	9 200	7 300

Prepare the appropriation account and current accounts for the partners.

	$	$
Profit for the year		62 000
Add: Interest on Drawings:		
Ariana (5% x 9 200)	460	
Nikau (5% x 7 300)	365	825
		62 825
Less: Interest on Capital:		
Ariana (9% x 150 000)	13 500	
Nikau (9% x 120 000)	10 800	(24 300)
		38 525
Salaries:		
Ariana	11 000	
Nikau	8 000	(19 000)
Profit available for distribution		19 525
Profit Share (60:40):		
Ariana	(11 715)	
Nikau	(7 810)	(19 525)
		0

CONTINUED

Answer

Current accounts

	Ariana	Nikau		Ariana	Nikau
	$	$		$	$
Opening balance b/d		8 600	Opening balance b/d	3 400	
Drawings	9 200	7 300	Interest on capital	13 500	10 800
Interest on drawings	460	365	Salaries	11 000	8 000
Closing balance c/d	29 955	10 345	Profit share	11 715	7 810
	39 615	26 610		39 615	26 610
			Closing balance b/d	29 955	10 345

TIP

It is important to read the question carefully. A minor mistake of putting the opening balance on the incorrect side can have a major impact on the final outcome.

1 Ariana and Nikau made a profit of $56 000 in their third year of business and the partnership agreement specified the following.

- Profits are to be shared 60:40.
- Interest on drawings is to be charged at 5%.
- Interest on capital is to be paid at 9%.
- Ariana is to be paid a salary of $11 000 and Nikau is to be paid a salary of $8 000.

Other information was available:

	Ariana	Nikau
	$	$
Capital account balance	150 000 (credit)	120 000 (credit)
Current account balance	2 600 (credit)	14 800 (credit)
Drawings for the year	12 700	9 200

TIP

Add money earned from the partners (interest on drawings) to, and subtract money paid to the partners (interest on capital and salaries) from, the profit made to get the final profit or loss to be shared according to the partnership agreement.

REQUIRED

a **i** Calculate the interest on drawings.

  ii Calculate the interest on capital.

  iii Prepare the appropriation account showing how the profit has been divided up between the partners.

b Calculate the current accounts for the partners, showing the entries needed to record the appropriations of the profit.

TIP

The current account includes drawings.

WORKED EXAMPLE 2

Ariana and Nikau had the following balances.

	Ariana	Nikau
	$	$
Capital account	150 000	120 000
Current account	16 842 (credit)	142 (debit)

Prepare the capital section of the statement of financial position.

CONTINUED

Answer

	$	$
Capital and liabilities		
Capital accounts		
Ariana	150 000	
Nikau	120 000	270 000
Current accounts		
Ariana	16 842	
Nikau	(142)	16 700
Total capital		286 700
Current liabilities		
Trade payables		?
Total capital and liabilities		?

The current account balances are taken into account in the capital section. A credit balance in the current account indicates a positive amount invested in the business, a debit balance would suggest a partner's drawings were too large. Debits are shown in brackets and subtracted.

2 The trial balance for Dream Destinations Getaways at 31 August 2021 was as follows:

	$	$
Bank	52 891	
Capital account – Ariana		150 000
Capital account – Nikau		120 000
Current account – Ariana		16 842
Current account – Nikau	142	
Drawings – Ariana	13 800	
Drawings – Nikau	11 400	
Inventory at 1 April 2019	36 780	
Loan from Ariana (repayable 2026)		15 000
Motor expenses	8 750	
Motor vehicles at cost	32 100	
Accumulated depreciation on motor vehicles		6 300
Office equipment at cost	17 600	
Accumulated depreciation on office equipment		7 040
Office expenses	4 560	
Premises	183 629	
Purchases	140 590	
Sales		235 740
Trade payables		11 570
Trade receivables	14 620	
Wages and salaries (employees)	45 630	
	562 492	562 492

Additional information at 31 August 2021

- Inventory was valued at $38 560.
- Motor expenses of $540 were prepaid and office expenses of $120 were accrued.
- Depreciation is to be provided on the following basis: 20% straight-line on office equipment and 30% reducing balance on motor vehicles.
- The loan had a rate of interest of 6%.

The partnership agreement made the following arrangements:

- Interest on drawings was 5%.
- Interest on capital was 9%.
- Ariana was to receive a salary of $11 000 and Nikau was to receive a salary of $8 000.
- Profits were to be shared between Ariana and Nikau in the ratio of 60:40.

REQUIRED

a Prepare a statement of profit or loss for the year ended 31 August 2021.

b Prepare an appropriation account showing that the profit or loss for the year has been shared between the partners in accordance with the partnership agreement.

c Prepare the current accounts for Ariana and Nikau, showing the balances at 31 August 2021.

d Prepare the statement of financial position at 31 August 2021.

> **TIP**
> The statement of profit or loss is calculated in the same way as for a sole trader.

3 Kauri, Tia and Moana are in partnership, sharing profits and losses as follows: Kauri 25%, Tia 25%, Moana 50%. The following trial balance was extracted from the business's books of account at 30 April 2022.

	$	$
Administration expenses	2 400	
Bank	34 600	
Capital accounts		
Kauri		100 000
Tia		70 000
Moana		90 000
Current accounts		
Kauri		6 900
Tia		7 400
Moana	2 100	
Drawings		
Kauri	24 000	
Tia	16 000	
Moana	18 000	
Insurance	16 400	
Inventory at 1 May 2021	63 700	
Loan from Moana (repayable 2026)		20 000

Motor expenses	4 600	
Motor vehicles at cost	57 000	
Accumulated depreciation on motor vehicles		15 300
Equipment at cost	41 000	
Accumulated depreciation on equipment		5 200
Premises	121 000	
Allowance for irrecoverable debts, 1 May 2021		1 400
Purchases	115 000	
Sales		236 000
Trade payables		24 500
Trade receivables	25 200	
Wages and salaries (employees)	35 700	
	576 700	576 700

Additional information

- Inventory at 30 April 2022 was $46 300.
- Insurance is $2 500 prepaid.
- Administration expenses are $630 accrued.
- Depreciation should be provided on motor vehicles at 20% per annum using the straight-line method and equipment at 15% per annum using the reducing balance method.
- Allowance for irrecoverable debts should be maintained at 4% of trade receivables.

The partnership agreement includes the following terms:

- Interest should be charged on drawings at 8% per annum.
- Interest on capital is at 4% per annum.
- Tia is to receive a partnership salary of $35 000 per annum.
- Moana is entitled to interest on her loan at 5% per annum.

REQUIRED

a Prepare a statement of profit or loss for the year ended 30 April 2022.
b Prepare an appropriation account for the year ended 30 April 2022.
c Prepare the partners' current accounts for the year ended 30 April 2022.

EXAM-STYLE MULTIPLE CHOICE AND STRUCTURED QUESTIONS

1 Hana and Ari are partners in a business and share profits in the ratio 3:2.
   Their profit for the year is $110 000.
   The following information is available.

	Hana	Ari
	$	$
Interest on drawings	1 400	1 900
Interest on capital	3 100	2 200
Partnership salary		25 000

   How will the residual profit be shared?

	Hana	Ari
	$	$
A	$52 200	$34 800
B	$49 800	$33 200
C	$82 200	$54 800
D	$64 800	$43 200

   [1]

2 The following information is available for a partnership at 30 June 2021.

	$
Residual profit	15 200
Total drawings	36 000
Total interest on drawings	4 700
Total interest on capital	16 800
Total salaries to partners	32 000

   How much is the profit for the year?

   A $59 300   C $31 300
   B $95 300   D $23 300

   [1]

CONTINUED

3 Cherie and Harry are in partnership.

REQUIRED

a Explain **three** disadvantages of operating as a partnership rather than being in business as a sole trader. [6]

Additional information

The following information was available for the partnership on 30 June 2017.

	$	
Bank overdraft	1 680	
Capital accounts		
Cherie	42 000	
Harry	28 000	
Current accounts balances at 1 July 2016		
Cherie	1 470	credit
Harry	2 430	debit
Drawings		
Cherie	18 300	
Harry	16 820	
Gross profit for the year	40 960	
Inventory at 30 June 2017	25 540	
Loan account		
Cherie	8 000	
Non-current assets		
Cost	64 000	
Provision for depreciation	22 000	
Operating expenses	28 390	
Trade payables	1 170	

The following information is also available.

1 Operating expenses included a payment for rent, $3 450, for three months ended 31 August 2017.

2 Non-current assets are to be depreciated at 20% per annum using the reducing balance method.

3 Inventory at 30 June 2017 was overvalued by $380.

4 Cherie is to receive interest at 8% per annum on her loan to the partnership.
No entries have been made to record the interest for the year ended 30 June 2017.
The balance of her loan account has remained unchanged throughout the year.

CAMBRIDGE INTERNATIONAL AS & A LEVEL ACCOUNTING: WORKBOOK

CONTINUED

REQUIRED

b Prepare the income statement for the year ended 30 June 2017. Start the statement with gross profit for the year of $40 960. [5]

Additional information

- Interest on drawings has been calculated as follows:

	$
Cherie	310
Harry	240

- The partners are to receive interest on their fixed capital account balances at 10% per annum.
- Residual profits and losses are to be shared in proportion to their capital account balances.

REQUIRED

c Prepare the appropriation account for the year ended 30 June 2017. [4]

d Prepare the partners' current accounts for the year ended 30 June 2017. [5]

Current accounts				
Cherie	Harry		Cherie	Harry
$	$		$	$

Adapted from Cambridge International AS&A Level Accounting (9706) Paper 22, Q1a, b, c & d, June 2018

[Total: 20]

Improve this answer

This is a sample answer to **Q3a**.

> Profits are shared between the partners.
> Control is difficult in a partnership.
> Making decisions in a partnership takes a long time.

Your challenge

See if you can improve this answer.

The answer only mentions partnerships. To answer the question fully, a comparison should be made between a partnership and sole trader. A better answer is available online – but write yours out first!

> Chapter 19
Partnership changes

LEARNING INTENTIONS

In this chapter you will:

- account for the revaluation of assets
- account for partnership goodwill
- prepare partnership accounts when a partner joins or leaves the firm
- account for changes partway through an accounting year
- account for the dissolution of a partnership

KEY TERMS

Dissolution of a partnership   Realisation account   Revaluation of assets

Key skills exercises

Knowledge and understanding

To answer the questions in this chapter, you need to know and understand:

- revaluation of assets is adjustments made to the value of the partnership assets to reflect their market value
- goodwill is the excess value of a business over and above the value of items on the statement of financial position
- dissolution of a partnership is the process by which all the assets of the partnership are sold, and liabilities paid, when the partnership ceases trading
- the realisation account is an account prepared when a partnership is ceasing to trade and is used to record the book value of the assets and liabilities and how much is received for them if sold or paid out in respect of liabilities.

You should also be able to use your knowledge and understanding to account for the revaluation of assets and partnership goodwill, prepare partnership accounts when a partner joins or leaves a firm, account for changes partway through an accounting year and account for the dissolution of a partnership.

DREAM DESTINATIONS GETAWAYS

Ariana and Nikau have been in partnership for a few years and are finding the workload is becoming too much for the two of them to cope with. They are considering bringing a new partner into the business and need to get their financial statements in order before they admit a new partner.

1   Ariana and Nikau have realised that some of their assets need to be revalued. They decide to prepare a revaluation account to revalue their assets.

Ariana and Nikau share the profits and losses in the ratio 60:40. Their summarised statement of financial position at 31 August 2020 is as follows:

	$000	$000	
Non-current assets			
Premises	180		Revised valuation $200 000
Motor vehicles	32		Revised valuation $29 000
Office equipment	17		Revised valuation $15 000
		229	
Current assets			
Inventory	36		Revised valuation $33 000
Trade receivables	14		Revised valuation $11 000
		50	
Total assets		279	
Capital and liabilities			
Capital accounts			
Ariana	150		
Nikau	120	270	
Current accounts:			
Ariana	(4)		
Nikau	(6)	(10)	
Non-current liabilities			
Loan from Ariana		15	
Current liabilities			
Trade payables		4	Revised valuation $2 500
Total capital and liabilities		279	

REQUIRED

a   Prepare a revaluation account to show the profit or loss on revaluation.

b   Prepare the partners' capital accounts.

c   Prepare the revised statement of financial position.

Additional information

Ariana and Nikau would like to calculate the value of the goodwill of the business before considering admitting a new partner. Use the information that follows to help them.

TIP

Assets' old values and liabilities' new values are on the debit side of the account; assets' new values and liabilities' old values are on the credit side of the account.

TIP

Profit on revaluation is on the credit side of the account and added to the capital whereas a loss on revaluation is on the debit side of the account and deducted from the capital.

TIP

The new values of assets, capital and liabilities are used in the revised statement.

	$
Premises	200 000
Motor vehicles	29 000
Office equipment	15 000
Inventory	33 000
Trade receivables	11 000
Prepaid expenses	1 200
Cash and bank	52 000
Loan from Ariana	15 000
Trade payables	2 500
Accrued expenses	960

Ariana and Nikau agree that should they decide to sell the business they would like to receive $370 000 for the business.

REQUIRED

d   Calculate the net assets of the business.

e   Calculate the value of the goodwill.

WORKED EXAMPLE 1

Ariana and Nikau have decided that recently Nikau has been putting more effort and time into the business and it is only fair for him to receive an equal share of the profits. They have therefore decided to change their profit sharing ratio from 60:40 to 50:50.

Ariana and Nikau have also decided it is necessary for them to admit a new partner. Between them they can't cope with the amount of work required and it will always be beneficial to the business to have the extra capital being brought into the business. They decide to admit Mikaere into the partnership on 1 November 2020 and the new profit sharing ratio will be 40:40:20 to Ariana:Nikau:Mikaere.

Mikaere contributed $70 000 capital and it was decided at the time of his joining that although the net assets of the business amounted to $325 000, the business was worth $380 000.

At the time, Ariana's capital account was $150 000 and Nikau's capital account was $120 000.

REQUIRED

Prepare the goodwill account, showing the entries required as a result of the change on profit shares.

CONTINUED

Answer

Goodwill = 380 000 − 325 000 = $55 000

Goodwill			
Debit		Credit	
	$		$
Capital – Ariana	27 500	Capital – Ariana	22 000
Capital – Nikau	27 500	Capital – Nikau	22 000
		Capital – Mikaere	11 000
	55 000		55 000

- The goodwill of $55 000 is split 50:50, i.e. the old profit-sharing ratio, and Ariana and Nikau receive $27 500 each on the debit side of the account.

- The goodwill is split 40:40:20, i.e. the new profit sharing ratio, and Ariana receives $22 000, Nikau receives $22 000 and Mikaere receives $11 000 on the credit side of the account.

2   Ariana, Nikau and Mikaere are sharing profits in the ratio 40:40:20. Their capital and current accounts on 28 February 2022 were as follows:

	Capital	Current
	$	$
Ariana	150 000	3 600
Nikau	120 000	(5 200)
Mikaere	70 000	1 200

After a few years, Ariana made the decision that she needed to spend more time at home with her family rather than travelling around on guided tours and has decided to leave the partnership.

Goodwill was agreed at $100 000 and the new profit sharing ratio was to be 60:40, Nikau: Mikaere.

It was decided that Ariana would receive a cheque for $30 000 and the rest would be converted to a loan account.

REQUIRED

Prepare the following accounts to record Ariana's departure:

a   Goodwill.

b   Capital accounts.

c   Current accounts.

d   Ariana loan account.

TIP

Old goodwill is on the credit side; new goodwill is on the debit side.

3   Colin, Darim and Emran are in partnership sharing profits and losses in the ratio 3:2:1. Their statement of financial position at 30 November 2022 was as follows:

	$
Non-current assets (net book value)	
Premises	135 000
Machinery	84 000
Motor vehicles	36 000
	255 000
Current assets	
Inventory	56 000
Trade receivables	48 000
Bank	21 000
	125 000
Total assets	380 000
Capital and liabilities	
Capital accounts	
Colin	120 000
Darim	80 000
Emran	40 000
	240 000
Current accounts	
Colin	56 000
Darim	16 000
Emran	36 000
	108 000
Current liabilities	
Trade payables	32 000
Total capital and liabilities	380 000

Additional information

- Darim retired on 1 December 2022. Colin and Emran continued in partnership sharing profits and losses in the ratio 2:1.
- Goodwill was valued at $48 000. It does not appear in the partnership's statements of financial position.
- Darim took over one of the partnership motor vehicles at a net book value of $8 000.
- The partners agreed to revalue some of the remaining assets as follows:

	$
Premises	180 000
Motor vehicles	25 000
Inventory	52 000
Trade receivables	46 000

- Darim agreed to receive $50 000 as part of the amount owing to him on his retirement. The balance owing to him was to remain in the partnership as a loan to be repaid in 2025.

REQUIRED

a Prepare the revaluation account on Darim's retirement on 1 December 2022.

Additional information

To help fund the payment to Darim on his retirement, Emran paid additional capital into the partnership bank account. After this payment had been made, the balance on Emran's capital account was $65 000.

b Prepare a statement to show how much cash Emran paid into the partnership bank account.

c State three advantages to a sole trader of forming a partnership.

d State three reasons why partnerships maintain separate capital accounts and current accounts for each partner.

WORKED EXAMPLE 2

A few years later, Nikau and Mikaere had a disagreement regarding the running of the business and decided it was time to part ways. They decided to dissolve the partnership.

Nikau and Mikaere share the profits and losses in a ratio of 60:40. Their summarised statement of financial position is as follows:

	$000	$000
Non-current assets		
Premises		210
Office equipment		16
Motor vehicles		23
		249
Current assets		
Inventory	20	
Trade receivables	7	
Bank	7	34
Total assets		283
Capital and liabilities		
Capital accounts		
Nikau	120	
Mikaere	70	190
Current accounts		
Nikau	35	
Mikaere	28	63
Current liabilities		
Trade payables		30
Total capital and liabilities		283

CONTINUED

On the dissolution of the business:

The premises were sold for $170 000 and office equipment was sold for $12 000.

- Mikaere agrees to take one of the vehicles at a value of $13 000. The remaining vehicles are sold for $9 000.
- The inventory is sold for $15 000 and the partners collected $6 000 from the trade receivables.
- They pay their trade payables $22 000.
- The cost of dissolution amounted to $7 000.

REQUIRED

Prepare the realisation account relating to the dissolution of this partnership.

Answer

Realisation account

Debit	$000	Credit	$000
Premises	210	Trade payables	30
Office equipment	16	Bank – premises	170
Motor vehicles	23	Bank – office equipment	12
Inventory	20	Bank – vehicle	9
Trade receivables	7	Bank – inventory	15
Bank – trade payables	22	Bank – trade receivables	6
Bank – cost of dissolution	7	Capital Mikaere – vehicle	13
		Loss on dissolution:	
		Nikau	30
		Mikaere	20
	305		305

- Asset values from the statement of financial position are placed on the debit side of the realisation account.
- Liabilities are placed on the credit side.
- Amounts received from selling the current assets or taken over by a partner and amounts from credit customers are placed on the credit side and amounts paid to credit suppliers are placed on the debit side.
- Cost of dissolution is placed on the debit side.
- Balance the two sides. If the debit side outweighs the credit side, a loss on dissolution is realised. If the credit side outweighs the debit side, a profit on dissolution is realised.

EXAM-STYLE STRUCTURED QUESTIONS

1 Paul and Angela are in partnership sharing profits and losses in the ratio of 3:2, respectively. No separate current accounts are maintained. On 1 May 2017, Rachael was admitted into the partnership.

    a **i** State **two** advantages to existing partners of introducing a new partner. [2]

        ii State **two** disadvantages to existing partners of introducing a new partner. [2]

A summarised statement of financial position at 30 April 2017 before the admission of Rachael is as follows:

	$
Non-current assets	225 000
Cash and cash equivalents	7 450
Other current assets	61 500
	293 950
Capital accounts:	
Paul	145 000
Angela	95 000
Current liabilities	53 950
	293 950

The following information is available:

1 Rachael paid $75 000 as capital into the partnership bank account.
2 Goodwill was valued at $50 000. No goodwill account was to be maintained in the books of account.
3 Non-current assets were revalued at $270 000.
4 Current assets (excluding cash and cash equivalents) were revalued at $40 500.
5 Current liabilities were revalued at $45 950.
6 Paul, Angela and Rachael will share profits and losses in the ratio 5:3:2, respectively.

REQUIRED

    b Calculate the profit or loss from revaluation on 1 May 2017 when Rachael was admitted. Show how this is divided between the partners. [2]

    c Prepare the partners' capital accounts on 1 May 2017 after the admission of Rachael. [5]

    d Explain why an adjustment for goodwill may be made when a new partner joins a business. [2]

    e State **two** factors that may result in the creation of goodwill for a business. [2]

Adapted from Cambridge International AS&A Level Accounting (9706) Paper 22, Q3, March 2018

[Total: 20]

CONTINUED

2 Ahmed and Omar were sole traders in the same trade. They decided to merge their businesses to form a partnership on 1 January 2020.

The books of account of Ahmed and Omar had the following balances of assets and liabilities at 1 January 2020.

	Ahmed $	Omar $
Plant and equipment	203 000	134 000
Motor vehicles	74 000	46 000
Inventories	51 000	36 500
Cash at bank	Nil	28 600
Trade receivables	59 700	53 800
Trade payables	42 500	34 100
Bank overdraft	8 900	Nil

The following were also agreed:

- The values of each sole trader's business at 1 January 2020 were:

	$
Ahmed	400 000
Omar	300 000

The partnership would take over all the assets and liabilities of both businesses at the following values.

	Ahmed $	Omar $
Plant and equipment	230 000	144 000
Motor vehicles	71 000	40 000
Inventories	52 500	34 400
Cash at bank	Nil	28 600
Trade receivables	58 000	52 000
Trade payables	42 500	34 100
Bank overdraft	8 900	Nil

a Calculate the value of goodwill of each of Ahmed's and Omar's businesses. [6]

b Prepare the statement of financial position of the partnership at 1 January 2020 if goodwill is included. [6]

CONTINUED

Additional information

The profit and loss sharing ratio between Ahmed and Omar is 3:2.

Both partners also agreed that goodwill would not be maintained in the books of account.

- c Calculate the capital account balance of each partner after goodwill is eliminated. [2]
- d Explain the meaning of the term 'goodwill'. [3]
- e Explain why the goodwill account is not maintained in the books of the partnership. Support your answer by reference to the accounting concepts. [4]

Additional information

The partners plan to purchase additional equipment costing $80 000. They are considering making loans to the partnership or applying for a bank loan.

- f State one advantage and one disadvantage to the partnership of each option. [4]

[Total: 25]

Improve this answer

This is a sample answer to **Q1ai**.

> Unlimited liability is shared. Losses are shared.

Your challenge

See if you can improve this answer. Is unlimited liability really shared?

A better answer is available online – but write yours out first!

> Chapter 20
Manufacturing accounts

> **LEARNING INTENTIONS**

In this chapter you will:

- prepare a manufacturing account
- calculate the manufacturing profit in the statement of profit or loss
- provide for unrealised profit inventories of finished goods

> **KEY TERMS**

Direct costs   Factory cost of completed goods   Factory manufacturing cost   Factory overheads   Factory profit   Finished goods   Indirect costs   Manufacturing account   Prime cost   Raw materials   Transfer price   Work in progress

Key skills exercises

Knowledge and understanding

To answer the questions in this chapter, you need to know and understand:

- a manufacturing account is used to record the various direct and indirect costs associated with making a product
- a manufacturing account identifies the cost of completed goods
- there are three different classes of inventory: raw materials, work in progress and finished goods
- there is a need to ensure that the finished goods inventory is included in the statement of financial position at cost by deducting any unrealised profit included in it.

You should also be able to apply your knowledge and understanding to prepare a manufacturing account, calculate manufacturing profit in the statement of profit or loss and provide for unrealised profit in inventories of finished goods.

Analysis

To answer the questions in this chapter, you need to be able to:

- analyse financial information and communicate the outcome.

Evaluation

To answer the questions in this chapter, you need to be able to:

- evaluate financial and non-financial information to facilitate effective decision-making.

CHINESE MANUFACTURING

Manufacturing is the biggest industry in China accounting for 46.8% of the country's GDP. China is the world's number one producer of cement, steel and chemical fertilisers. China also has the largest cotton textile output with textile manufacturing accounting for 10% of the country's gross industrial output. China is the third largest producer of cars in the world behind the USA and Japan with annual car exports being estimated at $70 billion.

> **TIP**
> Manufacturing is a continuous process and therefore not all items are completed at the end of the financial period. These items are known as Work in progress inventory. The other two forms of inventory in a manufacturing business are raw materials and finished goods.

Knowledge and understanding

1   Identify which of the following costs are direct and indirect costs of a manufacturing business. Tick the relevant block.

Cost	Direct	Indirect
Administration expenses		
Lease of factory		
Manufacturing labour		
Office salaries		
Insurance and rates		
Cost of raw materials		
Depreciation of machinery		
Commission expense		
Quality control costs		
Factory workers wages		

> **TIP**
> Direct costs are those involved in the actual manufacture of the product. Indirect costs relate to the factory but are not directly associated with the product itself.

WORKED EXAMPLE 1

Wang Wei is a manufacturer. The following has been extracted from his trial balance at 31 May 2021.

	$
Opening inventory: raw materials	24 000
Work in progress	52 000
finished goods	73 000
Factory direct wages	128 000
Factory indirect wages	169 000
Office salaries	75 000
Factory overheads	43 000
Carriage inwards	13 000
Carriage outwards	9 000
Closing inventory: raw materials	36 000
work in progress	49 000
finished goods	87 000
Purchase of raw materials	183 000
Purchase returns of raw materials	14 000
Heat and light	26 000
Sales	670 000

CONTINUED

Additional information

Heat and light is apportioned $\frac{3}{4}$ factory and $\frac{1}{4}$ general office.

REQUIRED

Prepare the manufacturing account for Wang Wei for the year ended 31 May 2021.

Answer

Manufacturing account for Wang Wei for year ended 31 May 2021

	$	$
Opening inventory of raw material		24 000
Add purchases of raw materials	183 000	
Less purchase returns of raw materials	(14 000)	
Carriage inwards	13 000	182 000
Less closing inventory of raw materials		(36 000)
Cost of raw materials consumed		170 000
Direct wages		128 000
Prime cost		298 000
Indirect wages	169 000	
Factory overheads	43 000	
Heat and light (W1)	19 500	231 500
Factory manufacturing cost		529 500
Add: opening work in progress	52 000	
Less: closing work in progress	(49 000)	3 000
Cost of production		532 500

Working

W1: Heat and light

$26 000 ÷ 4 = $6 500

$6 500 × 3 = $19 500

Knowledge and understanding

2 Prepare the trading account for Wang Wei for the year ended 31 May 2021, showing the gross profit.

3 Li Jing is a manufacturer who started trading on 1 November 2018 and has 31 October as her year end. The transfer pricing mark-up has always been 25%. Her inventory figures (including the factory profit) were:

	Opening inventory	Closing inventory
Year ended:	$000	$000
31 October 2019	0	420
31 October 2020	420	470
31 October 2021	470	410

REQUIRED

a Calculate the amount of unrealised profit contained within the inventory values at the end of each year.

b Prepare the provision for unrealised profit account for Li Jing for each of the three years ended 31 October 2019, 31 October 2020 and 31 October 2021.

> **TIP**
> If the unrealised profit has increased from one year to the next, the increased amount is on the credit side of the account. If the unrealised profit has decreased from one year to the next, the decreased amount is on the debit side of the account.

WORKED EXAMPLE 2

Fei Hong is the owner of a manufacturing business.

The following information is available for the year ended 31 December 2020.

	$
Factory machinery – at cost	260 000
Office equipment – at cost	87 000
Provision for depreciation at 1 January 2020	
Factory machinery	140 000
Office equipment	36 000
Inventory at 1 January 2020	
Raw materials	47 000
Work in progress	82 000
Finished goods (at cost)	107 000
Revenue	3 628 000
Purchases of raw materials	396 000
Factory direct wages	423 000
Factory indirect wages	105 000
Office salaries	479 000
Carriage inwards	14 000
Carriage outwards	53 600
Direct expenses	98 000
Factory overheads	418 900
General office expenses	230 000
Insurance and rates	73 000
Rent	380 000
Heat and light	167 000

Cost of production transferred is $1 364 000.

Closing inventory of finished goods is $124 000

REQUIRED

Prepare the trading section of the statement of profit or loss to show the gross profit for the year ended 31 December 2020.

CONTINUED

Answer

Fei Hong statement of profit or loss (trading section) for the year ended 31 December 2020

	$	$
Revenue		3 628 000
Opening inventory of finished goods	107 000	
Cost of production transferred	1 364 000	
	1 471 000	
Closing inventory of finished goods	(124 000)	
Cost of goods sold		(1 347 000)
Gross profit		2 281 000

Knowledge, understanding, analysis and evaluation

4 L plc is a manufacturing business. The total prime cost for the year ended 31 December 2017 was $350 000.

The following selected balances were extracted from the company's books of account at 31 December 2018.

	$000
Indirect wages	100
General expenses	64
Power	36
Factory plant	
Cost	600
Accumulated depreciation at 1 January 2018	150
Inventory	
Work in progress at 1 January 2018	23

The following information is available at 31 December 2018.

1. The prime cost for the year was 10% greater than the previous year.
2. Indirect wages are to be apportioned between the factory and office in the ratio 2:3, respectively.
3. General expenses of $6 000 were prepaid. General expenses are to be apportioned equally between the factory and the office.
4. A power bill of $4 000 remained unpaid. 60% of the total power expense is charged to the factory.
5. The value of work in progress was $31 000.

The following information is also available for the year ended 31 December 2018.

1. A new item of factory plant was acquired on 31 October 2018 at a cost of $30 000.

   This transaction has not been recorded in the books of account.

   Factory plant is depreciated at 25% per annum using the reducing balance method. A full year's depreciation is charged on assets acquired during the year.

2   Goods are transferred to the sales department at a mark-up of 20%.

a   Explain what is meant by:
  i   prime cost [2]
  ii   work in progress. [2]

b   Prepare the manufacturing account for the year ended 31 December 2018. [13]

Additional information

After the draft statement of financial position had been prepared, it was noted that the inventory value of finished goods was $33 000. This was the value at which these goods had been transferred from the manufacturing account.

c   Discuss whether the inventory should have been included at this value. Justify your answer by referring to relevant accounting concepts and appropriate calculations. [8]

Cambridge International AS&A Level Accounting (9706) Paper 32, Q1, June 2019

[Total: 25]

EXAM-STYLE STRUCTURED QUESTIONS

1   Ted is the owner of a manufacturing business.

The following information is available for the year ended 31 December 2016:

	$
Factory machinery – at cost	330 000
Office equipment – at cost	142 000
Provision for depreciation at 1 January 2016	
Factory machinery	276 000
Office equipment	67 000
Inventory at 1 January 2016	
Raw materials	52 000
Work in progress	97 000
Finished goods (at cost)	122 000
Revenue	4 268 000
Purchases of raw materials	484 000
Factory direct wages	626 000
Factory indirect wages	132 000
Office salaries	548 000
Carriage inwards	21 000
Carriage outwards	87 600
Direct expenses	120 000
Factory overheads	510 900
General office expenses	276 000
Insurance and rates	92 000
Rent	440 000
Heat and light	178 000

CONTINUED

Additional information

1. Goods are transferred from the factory at a mark-up of 20%. Increase in provision for unrealised profit at 31 December 2016 amounted to $15 840.

2. Inventory at 31 December 2016:

	$
Raw materials	67 000
Work in progress	102 000
Finished goods	?

3. Non-current assets are depreciated at 15% per annum using the reducing-balance method.

4. At 31 December 2016:

	$
Rent owing	40 000
Insurance and rates prepaid	6 000

   Insurance and rates, rent and heat and light are apportioned ¾ factory and ¼ general office.

5. Production for the year ended 31 December 2016 was 80 000 units.

REQUIRED

a. Explain why a mark-up is added to the factory cost of production. [3]

b. Prepare the manufacturing account for the year ended 31 December 2016. [10]

c. Prepare the trading section of the statement of profit or loss to show the gross profit for the year ended 31 December 2016. [6]

d. Prepare an extract from the statement of financial position to show the value of finished goods inventory at 31 December 2016. [2]

Cambridge International AS&A Level Accounting (9706) Paper 31, Q1a, b, c & d, October 2017

[Total: 21]

CONTINUED

2 M Limited manufactures a single product. The following balances have been extracted from the ledgers for the year ended 31 December 2021.

	Debit $	Credit $
Inventories at cost at 1 January 2021		
Raw materials	10 400	
Work in progress	12 600	
Finished goods at transfer price	14 904	
Purchases of raw materials	146 200	
Carriage inwards	3 160	
Carriage outwards	2 790	
Direct wages	249 400	
Indirect wages	54 650	
Rent	49 000	
Heat, light and power	28 600	
General expenses	12 600	
Office salaries	24 780	
Revenue		742 490
Provision for unrealised profit at 1 January 2021		2 484
Plant and machinery at cost	200 000	
Office equipment at cost	15 000	
Motor vehicles used by salespeople	25 000	
Provision for depreciation:		
Plant and machinery		60 000
Office equipment		4 600
Motor vehicles		5 740

Additional information

- Inventories at 31 December 2021:

	$
Raw materials at cost	11 750
Work in progress at cost	14 670
Finished goods at transfer price	15 750

- Expenses are to be apportioned to the production department as follows:

Rent	4:1
Heat, light and power	4:1
General expenses	3:1

CONTINUED

- Rent has been prepaid by $4 000 at 31 December 2021.
- Heat, light and power expense is in arrears by $3 500 at 31 December 2021.
- Completed goods are transferred at a mark-up on factory cost of 20%.
- Depreciation is to be provided for as follows:

    Plant and machinery 10% per annum on cost

    Motor vehicles 25% per annum on cost

    Office equipment 15% per annum on net book value

REQUIRED

a   Prepare the manufacturing account for the year ended 31 December 2021. [9]

b   Prepare the statement of profit or loss for the year ended 31 December 2021. [10]

c   Explain what is meant by the term transfer price. [2]

Additional information

A total of 10 000 units of the product were manufactured in the year, which is the maximum that can be produced. A supplier has offered to supply the product to M Limited for $60 per unit in the future.

REQUIRED

d   Advise the directors of M Limited whether or not they should accept this offer. Justify your answer on financial grounds. [4]

[Total: 25]

> Chapter 21

An introduction to limited company accounts

LEARNING INTENTIONS

In this chapter you will:

- learn what limited companies are and how they differ from partnerships and sole traders
- learn the UK Companies Act 2006 and some of the legal requirements for companies
- learn the format of financial statements: statement of profit or loss and statement of financial position in line with IAS 1
- learn the types of share capital and reserves
- learn the accounting entries for the issue of shares
- learn the effect of the issue of shares on the statement of financial position of a limited company
- learn what debentures are and how they differ from shares
- prepare a statement of profit or loss and a statement of financial position for a limited company

KEY TERMS

Annual general meeting (AGM)   Capital reserves   Limited company   Limited liability   Private limited company
Public limited company (plc)   Revenue reserves   Share   Share capital   Statement of changes in equity
Unlimited liability

Key skills exercises

Knowledge and understanding

To answer the questions in this chapter, you need to know and understand:

- a limited company is an organisation that is owned by shareholders and that, is regarded as a separate legal entity
- ordinary shareholders are the owners of the company
- debentures are a loan of a fixed amount given to a company
- capital reserves are gains that arise from non-trading activities, such as the revaluation of a company's non-current assets
- revenue reserves are profits made by a company that have not been distributed to shareholders.

You should also be able to use your knowledge and understanding of companies to prepare the accounting entries for the issue of shares, and prepare a statement of profit or loss and statement of financial position for a limited company.

21 An introduction to limited company accounts AS and A Level

GLOBAL IT

Global IT is an IT and software development company that was founded in Buenos Aires, Argentina. Global IT is a publicly listed company on the New York Stock Exchange, with more than 8 300 employees working from 14 different countries. This means that shares for their company are available for the public to buy. Anyone is able to buy shares in the company and then earn dividends from their shares.

Knowledge and understanding

1 A limited company has issued share capital of 400 000 ordinary shares of $1.50 each.

At the financial year end, 31 August 2021, a dividend of $0.08 per share was paid on the ordinary shares.

REQUIRED

Calculate how much the company paid out as dividends during the year ended 31 August 2021.

WORKED EXAMPLE 1

The balances for the shareholders' equity for Global IT on 1 September 2021 were as follows:

	$000
Share capital	23 000
Retained earnings	963
Share premium	680
General reserves	1 500

The events that took place during the year were as follows:

- Shares with a face value of $2 500 000 were issued; cheques for $2 700 000 had been received.
- Profit for the year was $2 634 000.
- There had been a transfer of $550 000 to general reserves.
- Dividends of $1 700 000 had been paid.

Prepare a statement of changes in equity for the year ended 31 August 2022.

Answer

	Share capital	Share premium	General reserve	Retained earnings	Total equity
	$000	$000	$000	$000	$000
Balance at 1 September 2021	23 000	680	1 500	963	26 143
Changes in equity:					
Profit for the year				2 634	2 634
Dividends				(1 700)	(1 700)
Transfer to reserves			550	(550)	0
Issues of shares	2 500	200			2 700
Balance at 31 August 2022	25 500	880	2 050	1 347	29 777

2 The following balances have been extracted from the books of Delfina Ltd at 30 April 2021.

	$	$
Administration expenses	28 000	
Cost of sales	59 400	
Debenture interest	16 000	
Directors' salaries	68 000	
Distribution costs	39 000	
General reserve		140 000
Ordinary shares of $1 each		800 000
Retained earnings		120 000
Revenue		265 000
Share premium		100 000

Additional information

- Administration expenses of $1 400 are prepaid.
- Shares with a face value of $300 000 were issued; cheques for $330 000 had been received.
- Profit for the year was $56 000.
- There had been a transfer of $10 000 to general reserves.
- Dividends of $62 000 had been paid.

REQUIRED

a Prepare a statement of profit or loss for the year ended 30 April 2021.

b Prepare a statement of changes in equity for the year ended 30 April 2021.

TIP

The statement of profit or loss is prepared in the same way as with a sole trader and partnership.

21 An introduction to limited company accounts AS and A Level

WORKED EXAMPLE 2

The following balances had been extracted from the books of Global IT at 30 November 2022.

	Dr	Cr
	$	$
Administration expenses accrued		1 200
Cash and cash equivalents		36 140
Equipment: net book value	124 860	
General reserve		42 000
Insurance prepaid	2 100	
Inventory at 31 October 2021	63 700	
Issued share capital:		
Ordinary shares of $1 each		290 000
Property: net book value	280 380	
Rent expense accrued		2 700
Retained earnings		47 000
Share premium		32 000
Trade payables		20 500
Trade receivables	36 500	
7% debentures 2025–2027		36 000
	507 540	507 540

REQUIRED

Prepare the statement of financial position for Global IT at 30 November 2022.

Answer

Global IT
Statement of financial position at 30 November 2022

	$	$
Non-current assets		
Property		280 380
Equipment		124 860
		405 240
Current assets		
Inventory	63 700	
Trade receivables	36 500	
Other receivables	2 100	102 300
Total assets		507 540

CONTINUED

Equity		
Ordinary shares of $1 each		290 000
Share premium		32 000
General reserve		42 000
Retained earnings		47 000
		411 000
Non-current liabilities		
7% debentures (2025–2027)		36 000
Current liabilities		
Trade payables	20 500	
Other payables	3 900	
Cash and cash equivalents	36 140	60 540
Total equity and liabilities		507 540

3 The following balances has been extracted from the books of Nicolas Limited for 31 October 2021.

	Dr	Cr
	$	$
Administration expenses accrued		3 500
Cash and cash equivalents		25 420
Equipment: net book value	161 320	
General reserve		35 000
Insurance prepaid	2 300	
Inventory at 31 October 2021	68 700	
Issued share capital:		
Ordinary shares of $2 each		330 000
Property: net book value	270 300	
Rent expense accrued		3 100
Retained earnings		42 000
Share premium		37 000
Trade payables		26 500
Trade receivables	34 900	
8% debentures 2025–2027		35 000
	537 520	537 520

REQUIRED

Prepare the statement of financial position for Nicolas Limited at 31 October 2021.

4 The following trial balance has been extracted from Felipe Ltd at 31 May 2021.

	Dr $	Cr $
Administration expenses	648 000	
Cash and cash equivalents		51 000
Distribution costs	540 000	
Finance costs	260 000	
Inventory at 1 June 2020	85 000	
Issued ordinary shares of $0.50 each		800 000
Machinery: cost	246 000	
Machinery: provision for depreciation		162 000
Motor vehicles: cost	230 000	
Motor vehicles: provision for depreciation		114 000
Ordinary shares final dividend paid (2020)	50 000	
Ordinary shares interim dividend paid (2021)	25 000	
Property: cost	1 500 000	
Purchases	1 152 000	
Retained earnings		69 000
Revenue		2 996 000
Share premium		220 000
Trade payables		60 000
Trade receivables	96 000	
9% debenture 2026–2028		360 000
	4 832 000	4 832 000

Additional information

- Inventory at 31 May 2021 was valued at $105 000.
- Depreciation is to be provided as follows:
  - Machinery at 25% per annum using the straight-line method
  - Motor vehicles at 20% per annum using the reducing balance method
- The interest on the 9% debenture has been paid up to 30 November 2021.
- The directors have recommended a final dividend of $0.25 per share.
- During the year, the company issued 150 000 ordinary shares of $0.50 at a premium of $0.20.

REQUIRED

a Prepare a statement of profit or loss for the year ended 31 May 2021.

b Prepare a statement of changes in equity for the year ended 31 May 2021.

c Prepare a statement of financial position at 31 May 2021.

EXAM-STYLE MULTIPLE CHOICE AND STRUCTURED QUESTIONS

1 A company has ordinary shares of $0.75 each. It has issued 120 000 shares. The directors recommend an interim dividend of $0.10 per share. What will be the amount of the interim dividend?

- **A** $3 500
- **B** $6 000
- **C** $12 000
- **D** $7 700

[1]

2 A shareholder sold 2 000 ordinary shares of $1 each in a public limited company for $4 600. What effect will this have on the share capital of the company?

- **A** It will increase by $2 000
- **B** It will remain unchanged
- **C** It will decrease by $4 600
- **D** It will increase by $2 600

[1]

3 The trial balance of Benicio Limited at 30 June 2021 is as follows.

	$000	$000
Freehold premises at cost	1 000	
Provision for depreciation of freehold premises		60
Delivery vehicles at cost	80	
Provision for depreciation of delivery vehicles		28
Office machinery at cost	70	
Provision for depreciation of office machinery		21
Trade receivables	82	
Trade payables		33
Bank balance	67	
12% debentures 2030–2032		100
900 000 ordinary shares of $1		900
General reserve		50
Retained earnings		7
Revenue		1 000
Inventory at 30 June 2020	46	
Purchases	630	
Sales staff wages	79	
Administration wages	36	
Delivery vehicle expenses	38	
Advertising	34	
Office expenses	24	
Debenture interest paid	6	
Interim ordinary dividends paid	7	
	2 199	2 199

CONTINUED

Additional information

- Inventory at 30 June 2021 was valued at $38 000.
- Account is to be taken of the following:
  - accrued expenses at 30 June 2021: delivery vehicle expenses $2 000; office expenses $3 000
  - advertising include $6 000 paid for services to be received after the year end.
- Freehold premises were revalued to $1 200 000 at 30 June 2021. No adjustment for this has been made.
- Depreciation is to be provided as follows for the year ended 30 June 2021:
  - delivery vehicles 25% per annum using the reducing balance method
  - office machinery 10% on cost.
- Debenture interest is payable half-yearly on 1 July and 1 January.
- Tax on the profit for the year is estimated to be $16 000.
- $50 000 is to be transferred to the general reserve.
- The directors have recommended a final dividend of 3% on the ordinary shares.

REQUIRED

a Prepare Benicio Limited's statement of profit or loss for the year ended 30 June 2021 in as much detail as possible. [11]

b Prepare Benicio Limited's statement of changes in equity for the year ended 30 June 2021. [5]

c Prepare Benicio Limited's statement of financial position for the year ended 30 June 2021 in as much detail as possible. [7]

Additional information

The directors are considering expansion plans for the business. This will involve obtaining additional capital. They are considering two options:

i issuing an additional 100 000 ordinary shares of $1 each at a premium of $0.50.

ii issuing a further debenture of $150 000.

REQUIRED

d State two uses of the share premium account. [2]

e Advise the directors which option they should choose to finance the proposed expansion. Justify your answer. [5]

[Total: 30]

Improve this answer

This is a sample answer to **Q3e**.

> The directors should take a further debenture of $150 000. They will need to pay extra interest on the debenture before any dividends to ordinary shareholders but all profit made from the expansion will go to the shareholders. Directors can negotiate a lower interest rate. The directors are still in full control of the company by taking out the loan.

Your challenge

See if you can improve this answer.

This sample answer advises which option should be chosen, but doesn't really explain the reasoning behind the decision. A better answer would compare the two options against each other before going on to explain why the benefits of the chosen option outweigh the alternative.

A better answer is provided online – but write yours out first!

Chapter 22
Limited companies: Further considerations

LEARNING INTENTIONS

In this chapter you will:
- calculate the asset value of ordinary shares in proportion to the shares held by them
- learn what bonus and rights issues are and why companies make them
- understand the difference between liabilities, provisions and undistributed profits
- learn the sources of finance available to limited companies

KEY TERMS

Bonus share issue   Hire purchase   Lease   Rights issue of shares

Key skills exercises

Knowledge and understanding

To answer the questions in this chapter, you need to know and understand:

- bonus issues are issues of free shares to existing shareholders from the accumulated reserves of the company in proportion to the shares held by them
- rights issues are an issue of shares made for cash; shares are offered first to existing shareholders, in proportion to the shares held by them
- liabilities are the amounts owing by a company to trade or other payables
- provisions are created to provide for liabilities that are known to exist
- reserves are undistributed profits
- other sources of finance available to companies are bank overdrafts, bank loans, hire purchase, leasing, trade payables, long-term capital, net current assets, debentures, mortgages and long-term capital.

You should also be able to use your knowledge and understanding to calculate the asset value of ordinary shares and the bookkeeping treatment of bonus and rights issues.

Analysis

To answer the questions in this chapter, you need to be able to:

- analyse financial accounting information and cost and management accounting information
- select, calculate and interpret relevant data and information
- communicate outcomes in the most appropriate form.

22 Limited companies: Further considerations AS and A Level

Evaluation

To answer the questions in this chapter, you need to be able to:

- evaluate financial accounting information and cost and management accounting information to make informed recommendations and decisions
- make judgements and draw conclusions based on financial and non-financial data.

WORKED EXAMPLE 1

The following had been taken from the statement of financial position for Santiago plc at 28 February 2022.

	$
Total assets	560 000
Equity and liabilities	
Equity	
Share capital (ordinary shares of $1 each)	270 000
Share premium	28 000
Revaluation reserve	100 000
General reserves	25 000
Retained earnings	51 000
Total equity	474 000
Non-current liabilities	55 000
Current liabilities	31 000
Total liabilities	86 000
Total liabilities and equity	560 000

REQUIRED

Calculate the asset value per share at 28 February 2022.

Answer

$$\frac{\text{Total equity}}{\text{Number of ordinary shares}}$$

$$\frac{474\,000}{270\,000} = \$1.76 \text{ per share}$$

CAMBRIDGE INTERNATIONAL AS & A LEVEL ACCOUNTING: WORKBOOK

Knowledge and understanding

1 The following had been taken from the statement of financial position for Pedro plc at 31 December 2021.

	$
Total assets	450 000
Equity and liabilities	
Equity	
Share capital (ordinary shares of $1.50 each)	225 000
Share premium	16 000
Revaluation reserve	90 000
General reserves	21 000
Retained earnings	47 000
Total equity	399 000
Non-current liabilities	32 000
Current liabilities	19 000
Total liabilities	51 000
Total liabilities and equity	450 000

REQUIRED

Calculate the asset value per share at 31 December 2021.

WORKED EXAMPLE 2

The following had been taken from the statement of financial position of Emilia Ltd at 31 March 2022.

	$000
Non-current assets	1 340
Net current assets	880
	2 220
Equity	
Share capital (ordinary shares of $1 each)	930
Share premium (capital reserve)	120
Revaluation reserve (capital reserve)	460
General reserve (revenue reserve)	290
Retained earnings (revenue reserve)	420
	2 220

The directors have decided to make a 1-for-5 bonus share issue – this will be carried out using the capital reserves starting with the share premium account.

22 Limited companies: Further considerations AS and A Level

CONTINUED

REQUIRED

Show the journal needed to record the bonus share issue and the statement of financial position after that issue has taken place.

Answer

Bonus issue	$	$
Share premium	120 000	
Revaluation reserve	66 000	
Share capital		186 000

930 000 ÷ 5 = 186 000 bonus shares

Statement of financial position	$000
Non-current assets	1 340
Net current assets	880
	2 220
Equity	
Share capital (ordinary shares of $1 each) ($930 + $186)	1 116
Revaluation reserve ($460 − $66)	394
General reserve	290
Retained earnings	420
	2 220

2 The following had been taken from the statement of financial position of Tomas Ltd at 30 September 2021.

	$000
Non-current assets	945
Net current assets	780
	1 725
Equity	
Share capital (ordinary shares of $0.50 each)	650
Share premium (capital reserve)	100
Revaluation reserve (capital reserve)	550
General reserve (revenue reserve)	75
Retained earnings (revenue reserve)	350
	1 725

- The directors have decided to make a 1-for-4 bonus share issue – this will be carried out using the capital reserves starting with the share premium account.
- The directors have decided to make a 1-for-2 rights issue instead. The shares will be sold for $0.75 each – the current market price is $0.90.

REQUIRED

a Prepare the journal needed to record the bonus share issue and the statement of financial position after that issue has taken place. A total column is required.

b Prepare the journal needed to record the rights share issue and the statement of financial position after that issue has taken place.

Knowledge, understanding, analysis and evaluation

3 The directors of Rebuild Limited are preparing the statements of financial position for the year ended 31 December 2015. The equity section of the statement of financial position at 31 December 2014 was as follows.

	$
Ordinary shares of $2 each, fully paid	240 000
Share premium	8 000
General reserve	40 000
Retained earnings	75 500
	363 500

During the year ended 31 December 2015, the following transactions took place:

March 1	Issued 10 000 ordinary shares at $2.10 each
March 31	Paid final dividend of 3% on all shares in issue at 31 December 2014
December 31	The directors revalued the company premises upwards by $20 000

The profit for the year ended 31 December 2015 was $47 100.

REQUIRED

a Prepare the statement of changes in equity for the year ended 31 December 2015. **[5]**

Additional information

The directors of Rebuild Limited made a bonus issue of ordinary shares on 30 June 2016. The basis of the issue was 1 ordinary share for every 25 ordinary shares held. The company policy is to leave reserves in their most flexible form.

The profit for the 6 months ended 30 June 2016 was $25 000.

REQUIRED

b Prepare the statement of changes in equity for the 6 months ended 30 June 2016. **[4]**

c State the **two** differences between ordinary shares and debentures. **[4]**

Additional information

The following item appears on the statement of financial position of Rebuild Limited at 31 December 2015:

6% debentures (2018–2020) $60 000

REQUIRED

d State the significance of (2018–2020). **[1]**

e State why an issue of debentures does **not** appear in the statement of changes in equity. [1]

Cambridge International AS&A Level Accounting (9706) Paper 22, Q2, October 2016

[Total: 25]

EXAM-STYLE MULTIPLE CHOICE AND STRUCTURED QUESTIONS

1 Benjamin Ltd had an issued share capital of $600 000 made up of ordinary shares of $1 each fully paid. The following transactions took place:
   - A bonus share issue was made on the basis of one ordinary share for every five ordinary shares already held.
   - Later, a rights issue of ordinary shares of one new share for every three already held at a premium of $0.10 per share was made. The issue was fully subscribed.

   By how much will Benjamin Ltd's bank account be increased?

   A $264 000
   B $220 000
   C $82 500
   D $132 000   [1]

2 The following balances were extracted from the books of XY plc on 31 January 2017.

	$
Land and buildings – at cost	700 000
Equipment – at cost	320 000
Motor vehicles – at cost	230 000
Accumulated depreciation	
Land and buildings	100 000
Equipment	186 000
Motor vehicles	96 000
Ordinary shares of $5 each	500 000
Share premium	120 000
Retained earnings at 1 February 2016	125 000
Inventory at 1 February 2016	37 100
Trade receivables	102 000
8% loan	150 000
Allowance for irrecoverable debts	2 100
Revenue	985 000
Purchases	428 000
Administrative expenses	346 000
Distribution costs	144 000
Interim dividend paid	20 000

CONTINUED

Additional information

1. Inventories at 31 January 2017 included 100 units of damaged items. These items, with a unit cost of $80, were all sold on 2 February 2017 for $65 each. At 31 January 2017, all other inventories were valued at cost, $36 000, and had a net realisable value of $85 400.

2. The administrative expenses included an amount of $30 000 for a machine purchased on 1 February 2016. The machine has a useful life of three years and will then be scrapped with nil proceeds. Any costs related to the machine should be charged to the cost of sales.

3. The figure for land and buildings (at cost) includes land that had cost $300 000.

4. During the year, XY plc purchased a motor vehicle that cost $60 000. This was settled by a payment of $40 000 from the bank and the part exchange of an old vehicle. This old vehicle had originally cost $75 000 and had been depreciated by $27 000. Only the bank payment had been recorded in the books of account.

5. Depreciation is to be charged on the following basis:

    Land   not depreciated
    Buildings   straight-line method over 25 years, charged to cost of sales
    Equipment   straight-line method over 5 years, charged to administrative expenses
    Motor vehicles   reducing balance method at 20% per annum, charged to distribution costs.

    The company policy is to charge a full year's depreciation in the year of purchase and none in the year of sale.

6. Trade receivables included an irrecoverable debt of $8 800. An allowance for irrecoverable debts of 4% is to be maintained. These items need to be included in administrative expenses.

7. The loan was obtained on 1 September 2016.

REQUIRED

a   State **two** objectives of the statements of financial position of a limited company. [2]

b   Prepare the statement of profit or loss for the year ended 31 January 2017. [15]

Additional information

In October 2016, XY plc made a bonus issue of 1 ordinary share for every 10 ordinary shares held. No entry had been made in the books of account.

REQUIRED

c   Prepare the statement of changes in equity for the year ended 31 January 2017.
    (A total column is not required.) [4]

Additional information

The directors are considering making a further issue of bonus shares rather than paying a cash dividend.

REQUIRED

d   Advise the directors which course of action they should take. Justify your answer. [4]

Cambridge International AS&A Level Accounting (9706) Paper 31, Q1, June 2017

[Total: 25]

> Chapter 23
Clubs and societies

LEARNING INTENTIONS

In this chapter you will:

- learn the terms used for non-profit making organisations
- prepare ledger accounts for subscriptions, life membership and entry fees
- learn forms of financial statements for non-profit making organisations
- apply the techniques used for incomplete records to prepare accounts for non-profit making organisations

KEY TERMS

Accumulated fund   Deficit of income over expenditure   Donations   Income and expenditure account
Life membership   Receipts and payments account   Subscriptions   Surplus of income over expenditure

Key skills exercises

Knowledge and understanding

To answer the questions in this chapter, you need to know and understand:

- the income and expenditure account takes the place on the statement of profit or loss
- the accumulated fund is used in place of capital account
- the receipts and payments account takes the place of the bank account
- subscriptions take the place of sales as the main source of income.

You should be able to use your knowledge and understanding of non-profit making organisations to prepare ledger accounts for subscriptions, life membership and entry fees; prepare the new forms of financial statements for non-profit making organisations and apply the techniques used for incomplete records to prepare accounts for non-profit making organisations.

Analysis

To answer the questions in this chapter, you need to be able to:

- analyse financial accounting information and cost and management accounting information
- select, calculate and interpret relevant data and information
- communicate outcomes in the most appropriate form.

Evaluation

To answer the questions in this chapter, you need to be able to:

- evaluate financial accounting information and cost and management accounting information to make informed recommendations and decisions
- make judgements and draw conclusions based on financial and non-financial data.

CAMBRIDGE INTERNATIONAL AS & A LEVEL ACCOUNTING: WORKBOOK

Knowledge and understanding

1 Brooklyn Youth Sports Club is a non-profit making organisation. Members each pay an annual subscription of $260. The number of members who had paid their subscriptions in advance or who were in arrears was as follows.

	1 January 2021	31 December 2021
In arrears	5	8
In advance	7	11

During the year ended 31 December 2021, $14 300 was received in subscriptions. Three members were written off as irrecoverable debts.

REQUIRED

Prepare the subscriptions account for the year ended 31 December 2021.

> **TIP**
>
> Subscriptions in arrears from the beginning of the year are entered on the debit side and subscriptions in arrears at the end of the year as the balance c/d on the credit side. Subscriptions in advance at the beginning of the year are entered on the credit side and subscriptions in advance at the end of the year as the balance c/d on the debit side.

WORKED EXAMPLE 1

Youth Basketball of America had the following information available for the year ended 31 July 2022.

	$
Subscriptions received	26 490
Administration	943
Refreshments purchases	7 630
Refreshments staff wages	6 910
Refreshments takings	11 385
Club staff wages	8 750
Sports equipment purchased	3 470
Maintenance	760
Cash balance at 1 August 2021	9 047

The treasurer of the club, was booked off for an operation and during this time proper accounting records were not kept. The cash balance at 31 July 2022 was $7 450.

The treasurer believes that some cash is missing.

Prepare the receipts and payments account for the year ended 31 July 2022 to calculate the amount of cash missing.

CONTINUED

Answer

Receipts and payments account				
Receipts		Payments	
	$		$
Opening balance b/d	9 047	Administration	943
Subscriptions received	26 490	Refreshments purchases	7 630
Refreshments takings	11 385	Refreshments staff wages	6 910
		Club staff wages	8 750
		Sports equipment purchased	3 470
		Maintenance	769
		Missing cash	11 000
		Closing balance c/d	7 450
	46 922		46 922
Closing balance b/d	7 450		

2 Steamboat Springs Winter Sports Club's treasurer had become ill. One of the other club members took over the accounting records. When the treasurer returned, they were convinced some cash was missing.

Steamboat Springs Winter Sports Club had the following information available at 30 April 2021.

	$
Subscriptions received	5 390
Social evening ticket sales	2 470
Social evening costs	1 060
Club staff wages	740
Administration	360
Maintenance	280
Cash balance at 1 May 2020	1 380
Cash balance at 30 April 2021	1 050

REQUIRED

Prepare the receipts and payments account for the year ended 30 April 2021 to calculate the amount of cash missing.

WORKED EXAMPLE 2

Harper Sports Club operates a bar that serves cold food and drinks and a shop that sells sports equipment and clothing at a subsidised price to its members. Inventory for both of these activities was:

	1 June 21	31 May 22
	$	$
Bar inventory	760	930
Shop inventory	2 480	3 160

The receipts and payments account for the year was as follows:

Receipts and payments account			
Receipts		Payments	
	$		$
Opening balance b/d	2 170	Bar purchases	11 430
Subscriptions (general)	42 630	Shop purchases	20 380
Subscriptions (life)	6 300	Dinner dance – catering costs	1 755
Bar income	25 780	Dinner dance – band	475
Shop income	21 300	Quiz – cost of prizes	940
Dinner dance – ticket sales	4 150	Heat & Light	2 170
Quiz income	2 630	Water rates	2 310
		Rent, rates and insurance	5 800
		Motor expenses	6 980
		Wages and salaries (general)	22 470
		Closing balance c/d	30 250
	104 960		104 960
Closing balance b/d	30 250		

REQUIRED

Prepare the bar trading account for the year ended 31 May 2022.

Answer

Bar		
	$	$
Revenue (takings)		25 780
Less cost of sales:		
Opening inventory	760	
Purchases	11 430	
	12 190	
Closing inventory	(930)	(11 260)
Bar profit		14 520

23 Clubs and societies A Level

3   Little League Baseball Club is a non-profit making organisation. Members each pay an annual subscription of $230. The number of members who had paid their subscriptions in advance or in arrears was as follows.

	1 May 2020	30 April 2021
In arrears	29	27
In advance	17	16

During the year ended 30 April 2021, $33 350 was received in subscriptions.

The club offers a life membership option where members can pay $700 – the club has decided that this income should be spread over a five-year period. Twenty-one members took advantage of this option during the year. The balance on the life subscription account at the start of the year was $9 800.

REQUIRED

a Prepare the subscriptions account to show the general subscription income the account transferred to the income and expenditure account.

b Prepare the life subscriptions account to show the life subscriptions income earned by Little League Baseball Club during the year ended 30 April 2021.

Further information

Little League Baseball Club operates a refreshments station that serves cold food and drinks and a shop that sells sports equipment and clothing at a subsidised price to its members. Inventory for both of these activities was:

	1 May 2020	30 April 2021
	$	$
Refreshments inventory	850	740
Shop inventory	3 600	3 070

The receipts and payments account for the year was as follows:

Receipts and payments account			
Receipts		Payments	
	$		$
Opening balance b/d	2 210	Refreshments purchases	10 730
Subscriptions (general)	33 350	Shop purchases	18 650
Subscriptions (life)	14 700	Social evening – catering costs	2 470
Refreshments income	19 560	Social evening – entertainment	630
Shop income	23 480	Quiz – cost of prizes	380
Social evening ticket sales	4 010	Heat & light	740
Quiz income	2 630	Water rates	860
		Rent, rates and insurance	1 250
		Motor expenses	4 630
		Wages and salaries (general)	21 560
		Closing balance c/d	38 040
	99 940		99 940
Closing balance b/d	38 040		

Additional information

- The club owned a number of non-current assets:

Asset	Cost	Accumulated depreciation
Equipment	39 420	11 826
Motor vehicles	24 500	8 820

- Equipment is depreciated at 15% per annum straight-line method
- Motor vehicles are depreciated at 20% per annum reducing balance method.

- Water rates of $640 was owing at 30 April 2021 but $850 of insurance had been prepaid.

REQUIRED

c   Prepare the refreshments trading account and the shop trading account for the year ended 30 April 2021.

d   Prepare the income and expenditure account for Little League Baseball Club for the year ended 30 April 2021.

TIP

Income and expenditure account uses the words 'surplus of income over expenditure' in place of 'profit for the year'. 'Deficit of expenditure over income' is used in place of 'loss for the year'.

Knowledge, understanding, analysis and evaluation

4   A Social Club had the following assets and liabilities at 1 April 2018.

	$
Non-current assets	14 500
Bank overdraft	3 600
Trade payables	2 250
Accrued electricity expenses	1 550
Prepaid insurance	300
Inventory	2 200
Subscriptions in arrears	150
Subscriptions in advance	100

a   Explain what is meant by the term 'accumulated fund'. [2]

b   Calculate the accumulated fund at 1 April 2018. [3]

Additional information

The annual subscription has been unchanged for the past few years. During the year ended 31 March 2019, a total of $13 900 was received from 278 members who paid their annual subscription in full. One member, who owed the club for the previous year's subscription, was unable to pay and this amount was written off.
At 31 March 2019, six members had not paid their annual subscription and one member had paid the following year's subscription in advance.

c   Prepare the subscriptions account for the year ended 31 March 2019. [8]

d   Prepare an extract from the statement of financial position at 31 March 2019 to show how the balances on the subscriptions account are recorded. [4]

Additional information

The annual surplus of income over expenditure has fallen steadily in recent years. The treasurer is considering introducing a life membership scheme to improve this.

He believes that the total life membership should be recorded in full as income in the income and expenditure account when it is received.

e Discuss **two** ways other than a life membership scheme by which the club could increase the future annual surplus. [4]

f Discuss if the treasurer's proposed accounting treatment for life membership is correct. Justify your answer by reference to any relevant accounting concept. [4]

Cambridge International AS&A Level Accounting (9706) Paper 31, Q1, October 2019

[Total: 25]

EXAM-STYLE STRUCTURED QUESTIONS

1 The AB Cricket Club prepares its statements of financial position annually.

REQUIRED

a Identify **three** differences in the terminology used in the statements of financial position of a club compared to a profit-making organisation. [3]

Additional information

The club runs a small snack bar. The following information is available for the year ended 31 December 2016.

- The snack bar takings for the year totalled $52 750.
- The food inventory was valued at $260 at 1 January 2016. This had been reduced by 40% at 31 December 2016.
- All food is purchased from one supplier. The supplier was paid $33 785 during the year.
- At 1 January 2016 the supplier was owed $460. There was $585 owing to the supplier at 31 December 2016.

REQUIRED

b Prepare the snack bar trading account for the year ended 31 December 2016. [6]

Additional information

- The annual subscription per member has remained at $250 for many years.
- There are currently 310 members. There were no resignations or new members joining during 2016.
- At 31 December 2015, there were 7 members who had not paid their 2015 subscription and 2 members who had paid their subscriptions for 2016.
- At 31 December 2016, there were 12 members who had not paid their 2016 subscription and 3 members who had paid their 2017 subscription.

REQUIRED

c Prepare the subscriptions account for the year ended 31 December 2016. [7]

Additional information

The club buildings are in urgent need of repairs. The committee has decided to carry out the required work during 2017. The club is proposing a scheme whereby local businesses are invited to sponsor matches. At 31 December 2016, there was a small debit balance on the bank account.

CONTINUED

REQUIRED

d Identify **four** actions **other than sponsorship** that could be taken by the club to fund the repairs of the buildings. [4]

e State the advantages and disadvantages to the club if the proposed sponsorship is adopted. [5]

Cambridge International AS&A Level Accounting (9706) Paper 32, Q3, March 2017

[Total: 25]

2 The following information is available for a club.

At 1 July 2017

	$
Clubhouse at cost	300 000
Accumulated depreciation on clubhouse	156 000
Equipment at cost	140 000
Accumulated depreciation on equipment	64 000
Subscriptions in arrears	7 000
Subscriptions in advance	3 400
Accumulated fund	194 000

For the year ended 30 June 2018

	$
Operating expenses	192 000
Staff salaries	326 000
Subscriptions received	544 000
Restaurant profit	12 600

At 30 June 2018

	$
Restaurant inventory	23 400
Restaurant trade payables	12 100
Loan from a club member (repayable 2022)	10 000
Cash and cash equivalents	7 700
Subscriptions in arrears	8 200
Subscriptions in advance	2 400

The following information is also available.

- Depreciation is charged as follows: clubhouse at 4% per annum using the straight-line method and equipment at 15% per annum using the reducing balance method.
- Accrued restaurant wages, $3 300, had not been accounted for.
- The loan from the club member was received on 1 January 2018. Interest is to be paid at 10% per annum. No interest has yet been paid.

CONTINUED

a   Prepare the income and expenditure account for the year ended 30 June 2018. [7]

b   State **two** differences between an income and expenditure account and a receipts and payments account. [2]

c   Prepare the statement of financial position at 30 June 2018. [7]

Additional information

At 1 July 2017 the following balances for the restaurant were available.

	$
Inventory	15 700
Trade payables	13 900

d   Calculate the restaurant profit for the year ended 30 June 2018. [4]

Additional information

The club plans to improve the clubhouse next year at a cost of $50 000. The chairman is considering financing the improvement by either members' loans or taking a bank loan.

e   Evaluate whether the club should finance the improvement by members' loans or take a bank loan. Justify your answer. [5]

Cambridge International AS&A Level Accounting (9706) Paper 32, Q1 March 2019

[Total: 25]

Improve this answer

This is a sample answer to **Q2e**.

> The club should ask the members for a loan. Members have a loyalty to the club and will want to improve the clubhouse for their own benefit as well. Members will possibly give it as a donation to the club. Members won't expect interest as they are doing the club a favour.

Your challenge

See if you can improve this answer.

The sample answer is very one-sided and lacks evaluation. A better answer would show this evaluation by weighing up the advantages and disadvantages of both the bank loan and members' loan in order to justify a final decision. A better answer is provided online – but write yours out first!

Chapter 24
Statement of cash flows

LEARNING INTENTIONS

In this chapter you will:

- learn what a statement of cash flows is and why it is an important addition to the annual financial statements of a business
- learn how and why companies are required to include a statement of cash flows in their annual accounts
- prepare a statement of cash flows in line with IAS 7
- prepare a statement of financial position with the aid of a statement of cash flows
- prepare a statement of cash flows for limited companies
- learn the advantages and disadvantages of statements of cash flows

KEY TERMS

Cash   Financing activities   Investing activities   Operating activities

Key skills exercises

Knowledge and understanding

To answer the questions in this chapter, you need to know and understand:

- a statement of cash flows is one that lists the inflows and outflows of cash for a business over a period of time
- a statement of cash flows is important because the money inflow and outflow of a business will be of considerable interest to a wide range of people
- advantages and disadvantages of statements of cash flow.

You should also be able to apply your knowledge and understanding to prepare statements of cash flow for sole traders and partnerships and prepare a statement of financial position.

WORKED EXAMPLE 1

Bingwen Limited has a year end of 31 December and has provided you with the following information.

	2020	2019
	$	$
Operating profit for the year	20 500	18 450
Trade receivables	24 983	27 651
Trade payables	18 537	17 642
Inventories	36 458	34 589
Depreciation charge for the year	13 290	
Interest paid	7 410	9 650
Taxation paid	10 760	13 408

24 Statement of cash flows A Level

CONTINUED

REQUIRED

Prepare a reconciliation of profit from operations to net cash from operating activities for Bingwen Limited for the year ended 31 December 2020.

Answer

	$
Operating profit for the year	20 500
Depreciation	13 290
Increase in inventories	(1 869)
Decrease in trade receivables	2 668
Increase in trade payables	895
Cash from operating activities	35 484

> **TIP**
> Start with the operating profit for the year and add or subtract any changes that have taken place between the two years. Only the differences between the two years' amounts are used in the reconciliation.

Knowledge and understanding

1 Bingwen Limited has provided you with two years' statements of financial position.

The statements of financial position for Bingwen Limited for 31 December 2019 and 2020 were as follows.

	2019			2020		
	Cost	Depreciation	Net book value	Cost	Depreciation	Net book value
	$	$	$	$	$	$
Non-current assets						
Land and buildings	90 000	–	90 000	90 000	–	90 000
Motor vehicles	62 000	25 640	36 360	80 000	32 080	47 920
Machinery	47 000	32 780	14 220	53 000	39 630	13 370
			140 580			151 290
Current assets						
Inventories	34 589			36 458		
Trade receivables	27 651			24 983		
Bank	10 730	72 970		–	61 441	
Current liabilities						
Trade payables	17 642			18 537		
Tax	13 408			10 760		
Bank overdraft	–	(31 050)		2 340	(31 637)	
Net current assets			41 920			29 804
			182 500			181 094
Ordinary shares		100 000			105 000	
Share premium		30 000			32 000	
Retained profits		26 000	156 000		14 094	151 094
Non-current liabilities						
Bank loan			26 500			30 000
			182 500			181 094

161

Dividends paid during the year amounted to $14 236.

The relevant details from the statement of profit or loss were as follows.

Profit from operations	20 500
Interest payable	(7 410)
Profit before tax	13 090
Tax	(10 760)
Profit for the year	2 330

> **TIP**
>
> Take care with cash and cash equivalents – if it falls under current assets it has a positive balance; if it falls under current liabilities it has a negative balance.

REQUIRED

a Prepare a reconciliation of cash generated by operations to net cash from operating activities for Bingwen Limited for the year ended 31 December 2020.

b Prepare a statement of cash flows for Bingwen Limited for the year ended 31 December 2020.

WORKED EXAMPLE 2

Chonglin has provided the following information regarding his company's disposals during the year. Complete the following table by calculating the missing figures about the items that were sold.

	Original cost	Accumulated depreciation	Net book value	Profit or loss	Proceeds
	$	$	$	$	$
Equipment	62 000	49 900			10 360
Machinery		28 400	15 300	Profit 3 700	
Motor vehicles	43 800		9 600		11 200
Office furniture	15 300		3 800	Loss 700	

Answer

	Original cost	Accumulated depreciation	Net book value	Profit or loss	Proceeds
	$	$	$	$	$
Equipment	62 000	49 900	12 100 [1]	Loss 1 740 [2]	10 360
Machinery	43 700 [3]	28 400	15 300	Profit 3 700	19 000 [4]
Motor vehicles	43 800	34 200 [5]	9 600	Profit 1 600 [6]	11 200
Office furniture	15 300	11 500 [7]	3 800	Loss 700	3 100 [8]

Notes

[1] The net book value is the original cost less the accumulated depreciation ($62 000 − $49 900).

[2] Proceeds less net book value determine whether a profit or loss has been made. If the proceeds are less than the net book value, a loss has been made on disposal ($10 360 − $12 100).

[3] Accumulated depreciation plus net book value determines original cost ($28 400 + $15 300).

[4] Net book value plus profit determines proceeds ($15 300 + $3 700).

CONTINUED

[5] Original cost less net book value determines accumulated depreciation ($43 800 − $9 600).

[6] Proceeds less net book value determines profit or loss on disposal ($11 200 − $9 600).

[7] Original cost less net book value determines accumulated depreciation ($15 300 − $3 800).

[8] Net book value less loss determines proceeds ($3 800 − $700).

2 Huang provided the following table, which contains some of the information about the items that were sold.

	Original cost	Accumulated depreciation	Net book value	Profit or loss	Proceeds
	$	$	$	$	$
Equipment	54 200	38 400			12 600
Machinery	41 900		13 050		14 600
Motor vehicles		34 200	8 500	Loss 2 700	
Office furniture	20 700		11 400	Profit 3 700	

REQUIRED

Calculate the missing figures regarding disposals and complete the table.

WORKED EXAMPLE 3

Ada Choi provided the following information:

	2020	2019
	$	$
Non-current assets (net book value)	923 000	869 000

During the year, non-current assets costing $125 000, which had been depreciated by $97 000, were sold and a profit on disposal of $21 000 was made. The value of the buildings had been increased from $200 000 to $350 000 during 2020. Depreciation for the year was $147 000.

REQUIRED

a Calculate the purchases of non-current assets for the year.

CAMBRIDGE INTERNATIONAL AS & A LEVEL ACCOUNTING: WORKBOOK

> **WORKED EXAMPLE 3**
>
> **Answer**
>
> | Non-current assets: | $ | |
> |---|---|---|
> | Opening balance (net book value) | 869 000 | |
> | + Purchases | 79 000 | = 948 000 − 869 000 |
> | | 948 000 | = 923 000 + 147 000 (depreciation) + 28 000 (disposal net book value) − 150 000 (revaluation) |
> | + Revaluations | 150 000 | = 350 000 − 200 000 |
> | − Disposals (net book value) | (28 000) | = 125 000 − 97 000 |
> | − Depreciation expense | (147 000) | |
> | = Closing balance (net book value) | 923 000 | |
>
> **b** Calculate the proceeds arising from the disposals.
>
> **Answer**
>
> Proceeds = $28 000 + $21 000 = $49 000

3 Donghai Limited provided the following information:

	2022	2021
	$	$
Non-current assets (net book value)	1 235 630	952 000

During the year, non-current assets costing $186 000, which had been depreciated by $83 450, were sold and a profit on disposal of $27 500 was made. The value of the buildings had been increased from $340 000 to $520 000 during 2021. Depreciation for the year was $176 300.

REQUIRED
a Calculate the purchases of non-current assets for the year.
b Calculate the proceeds arising from the disposals.

4 The statement of financial position for Changming Limited for 30 September 2020 was as follows.

	Cost	Depreciation	Net book value
Non-current assets	$	$	$
Machinery	135 000	67 000	68 000
Fixtures and fittings	86 000	29 000	57 000
			125 000
Current assets			
Inventories	33 400		
Trade receivables	18 600		52 000
Current liabilities			
Trade payables	17 300		
Bank overdraft	3 900		
Tax	7 300	(28 500)	23 500
			148 500

	$	$	$
Ordinary shares		80 000	
Retained earnings		38 500	
8% debentures		10 000	
Non-current liabilities			
Bank loan		20 000	
			148 500

Additional information

- Machinery costing $30 000, which had been depreciated by $24 300, was sold for $10 000.
- Depreciation on machinery during the year was $23 600.
- Machinery was purchased for $53 000.
- Fixtures and fittings costing $19 000, which had been depreciated by $13 700, was sold for $4 800.
- Depreciation on fixtures and fittings during the year was $11 200.
- Fixtures and fittings were purchased for $17 000.

The relevant details from the statement of profit or loss were as follows.

	$
Operating profit	32 700
Interest payable	(2 800)
Profit before tax	29 900
Tax	(9 600)
Profit for the year	20 300

The following statements were available.

Reconciliation of profit from operations to net cash from operating activities for Changming Limited for the year ended 30 September 2021	
	$
Net cash inflow from operating activities	
Profit from operations	32 700
Depreciation for year	34 800
Gain on disposal of non-current assets	(3 800)
Decrease in respect of inventories	9 000
Decrease in respect of trade receivables	3 700
Increase in respect of trade payables	5 800
Cash generated by operations	82 200
Interest paid	(2 800)
Tax paid	(10 500)
Net cash from operating activities	68 900

Statement of cash flows for Changming Limited for the year ended 30 September 2021

	$	$
Net cash from operating activities		68 900
Investing activities		
Purchases of non-current assets	(70 000)	
Proceeds on disposal of non-current assets	14 800	
Net cash used in investing activities		(55 200)
Financing activities		
Proceeds of share issue	40 000	
Repayment of loan	(7 000)	
Dividends paid	(10 000)	
Net cash from financing activities		23 000
Net increase in cash and cash equivalents		36 700
Cash and cash equivalents at the start of the year		(3 900)
Cash and cash equivalents at the end of the year		32 800

REQUIRED

Prepare the statement of financial position for Changming Limited at 30 September 2021.

EXAM-STYLE STRUCTURED QUESTIONS

1 Bohai, a sole trader, statement of financial position at 31 March 2020 and 2021 are here.

Bohai plc
Statements of financial position at 31 March

	2021			2020		
	Cost	Accumulated depreciation	Net book value	Cost	Accumulated depreciation	Net book value
	$	$	$	$	$	$
Non-current assets						
Land and buildings	60 000		60 000	30 000		30 000
Machinery	55 000	25 000	30 000	39 000	21 000	18 000
	115 000	25 000	90 000	69 000	21 000	48 000
Current assets						
Inventories		16 000			11 000	
Trade and other receivables		12 000			15 000	
Cash and cash equivalents		–			3 000	
			28 000			29 000
Total assets			118 000			77 000

CONTINUED

Equity		
Capital	61 000	52 000
Capital introduced	10 000	–
	71 000	52 000
Profit for the year	50 000	20 000
Drawings	(21 000)	(9 000)
	100 000	61 000
Non-current liabilities		
Long-term loan	8 000	–
Current liabilities		
Trade and other payables	8 000	16 000
Cash and cash equivalents	2 000	–
	10 000	16 000
Total equity and liabilities	118 000	77 000

Income statement (extract) for the year ended 31 March 2021

	$
Profit	25 000
Depreciation of machinery	(5 000)
Profit on disposal of machinery	1 000
Profit on revaluation of land	30 000
Interest paid	(1 000)
Profit for the year	50 000

Bohai tells you that during the year she scrapped some machinery which had cost $6 000. She cannot understand why she has an overdraft at 31 March 2021, despite making a profit for the year, and asks for your help to explain the situation.

REQUIRED

a Prepare a statement of cash flows for Bohai for the year ended 31 March 2021. [5]
b Identify why she has made a profit for the year, yet her bank account is overdrawn. [10]

[Total: 15]

CONTINUED

2 The statement of cash flows of T plc for the year ended 31 December 2018 was as follows:

T plc
Statement of cash flows for the year ended 31 December 2018

	$000	$000
Profit from operations		288
Depreciation – land and buildings	4	
– machinery	84	
– fixtures and fittings	9	97
Profit on disposal of machinery		(12)
Increase in inventory		(46)
Increase in trade receivables		(14)
Decrease in trade payables		(4)
Cash from operations		309
Interest paid		(29)
Taxation paid		(87)
Net cash from operating activities		193
Cash flow from investing activities		
Purchase of non-current assets	(272)	
Proceeds of sale of machinery	42	
Net cash used in investing activities		(230)
Cash flow from financing activities		
Proceeds from rights issue of shares	480	
Dividend paid	(80)	
Repayments of debentures	(200)	
Net cash from financing activities		200
Net increase in cash and cash equivalents		163
Cash and cash equivalents 31 December 2017		(81)
Cash and cash equivalents 31 December 2018		82

Further information relating to the year ended 31 December 2018 was as follows:

1 Balances at 1 January 2018 were

	$000
Land and buildings	
Cost	400
Accumulated depreciation	12
Machinery	
Cost	214
Accumulated depreciation	112

CONTINUED

	$000
Fixtures and fittings	
Cost	82
Accumulated depreciation	17
Ordinary share capital ($1 shares)	500
Retained earnings	105
General reserve	40

2 The cost of the non-current assets purchased was $262 000 for new machinery and $10 000 for fixtures and fittings.

3 The machinery sold during the year had an original cost of $100 000.

4 The rights issue was made at a premium of $0.20 per share.

5 Tax owing amounted to $72 000 at the start of the year and $85 000 at the end of the year.

6 Interest accrued amounted to $10 000 at the start of the year and $2 000 at the end of the year.

7 A transfer to general reserve, $10 000, had been made by the directors.

REQUIRED

a i State why a bonus issue of shares would not be recorded in a statement of cash flows. [1]

   ii Name **one** financial item, other than a bonus issue of shares and a transfer to the general reserve, which would **not** be recorded in a statement of cash flows. [1]

b Prepare the non-current assets schedule for the year ended 31 December 2018 for inclusion in the notes to the statements of financial position of the company. A total column **is** required. [9]

c Prepare the statement of changes in equity for the year ended 31 December 2018. A total column **is** required. [9]

Additional information

The directors are considering publishing a cash budget instead of preparing a statement of cash flows in the future.

d Advise the directors whether or not to proceed with this change. Justify your answer. [5]

Cambridge International AS&A Level Accounting (9706) Paper 32, Q4, March 2019

[Total: 25]

Improve this answer

This is a sample answer to **Q2d**.

> A cash budget is a management tool which deals with the future. If published, a cash budget can be used by competitors. The directors should not publish a cash budget.

Your challenge

See if you can improve this answer. The sample response is correct in saying they should not publish a cash budget, but doesn't explain what a statement of cash flow is and why it should be used. In order to answer fully, both options should be compared against each other and the final choice justified. A better answer is available online – but write yours out first!

Chapter 25
Auditing and stewardship

LEARNING INTENTIONS

In this chapter you will:

- learn the role of the shareholders of a limited company
- learn the role of the directors of a limited company
- learn the contents of directors' reports
- learn the role of the auditors of a limited company
- learn the importance and contents of the auditor's reports
- learn the financial statements and reports that must be published and sent to the shareholders
- learn the reporting standards relating to information that comes to light after the year-end
- learn the reporting standards relating to provisions, contingent assets and contingent liabilities

KEY TERMS

Auditor's report   Directors' report   International accounting standards (IASs)

Key skills exercises

Knowledge and understanding

To answer the questions in this chapter, you need to know and understand:

- the role of shareholders, directors and auditors of a limited company
- the contents of directors' reports and auditor's reports.

You should also be able to apply your knowledge and understanding of published limited accounts to prepare financial statements according to International Accounting Standards.

Analysis

To answer the questions in this chapter, you need to be able to:

- analyse financial accounting information and cost and management accounting information
- select, calculate and interpret relevant data and information
- communicate outcomes in the most appropriate form.

Evaluation

To answer the questions in this chapter, you need to be able to:

- evaluate financial accounting information and cost and management accounting information to make informed recommendations and decisions
- make judgements and draw conclusions based on financial and non-financial data.

Knowledge and understanding

1   a   Identify the two accounting concepts that should be used when preparing statements of financial position.

b Identify the four characteristics that statements of financial position must have.

c Explain why there is a need for International Accounting Standards.

d Identify, as a list, the components of a complete set of statements of financial position identified in IAS 1.

e Explain the difference and how they should be dealt with, between adjusting events and non-adjusting events identified in IAS 10.

WORKED EXAMPLE 1

The following situations affect the financial affairs of Guangli Limited; their year end is 31 May 2021.

State, for each situation, the International Accounting Standard (number and name) that should be applied.

a It was discovered on 17 February 2021 that inventory had been overadded by $53 000 due to a problem with computer software.

b On 22 March 2021, the size of the directors' bonuses was established as $190 000. A provisional figure of $150 000 had been put into the original draft statements.

Answer

a IAS 8 – Accounting policies.

b IAS 10 – Events after the statement of financial position date.

---

2 The following situations affect the financial affairs of Nianzu Limited; their year end is 30 April 2021.

State, for each situation, the International Accounting Standard (number and name) that should be applied.

a The company is being sued by Meilin Ltd for $15 000. By the end of the financial year, a court case decision had not yet been made but it was likely that Meilin Ltd would win the case and receive the amount mentioned.

b The company's statement of financial position at 30 April 2021 included an amount in trade receivables of $12 400 that was owed by Guangli Ltd. On 28 April 2021 the company was informed that Guangli Ltd had been declared bankrupt and they would not be able to pay the amount due.

c The company's statements of financial position must include a statement of changes in equity.

d At the end of the financial year the company's premises were damaged by a fire. Shortly after the statements of financial position were prepared, the insurance company valued the damage.

WORKED EXAMPLE 2

State, for each of the situations stated in Worked example 1, how the situation should be handled in the published statements of financial position of the company, dated 31 May 2021.

Answer

a Overadded inventory should be adjusted under IAS 8 as it would appear to be a (large) material error.

b The directors' bonuses are an adjustable event under IAS 10 as the conditions existed at the year end. The directors were always going to be paid a bonus, it was just the size that was unknown.

3 State, for each of the situations stated in question 2, how the situation should be handled in the published statements of financial position of the company, dated 30 April 2018.

Knowledge, understanding, analysis and evaluation

4 The financial statements of W Limited for the year ended 31 December 2018 are ready to be audited.

The directors have provided the following assets balances from the statement of financial position.

	$
Property, plant and equipment	682 000
Inventory	94 200
Trade receivables	87 400
Other receivables	9 430
Cash and cash equivalents	21 170

The following information is available.

i Included in property, plant and equipment was equipment with a carrying value if $140 000. The fair value of the equipment was $132 000 and the value in use was $136 000.

ii The retained earnings for the year ended 31 December 2018 were $184 000. This is after deducting a proposed final dividend of $12 000.

iii The directors had budgeted to incur $25 000 advertising in 2019. A provision was made for this expenditure.

REQUIRED

a Explain one benefit of auditing. [2]

b Explain to the directors the appropriate accounting treatments for items **i**, **ii** and **iii**, making reference to the relevant International Accounting Standards. (IAS) [7]

Additional information

The following information is also available.

1 A deposit of $3 000 had been paid to a supplier for goods to be delivered in April 2019. This amount had been recorded as purchases.

2 Goods costing $5 400 and with a sales value of $7 000 were sent to a customer on a sale or return basis. The directors had recorded $7 000 as a sale.
At 31 December 2018, the customer had not decided whether to buy the goods.

REQUIRED

c Calculate the revised retained earnings at 31 December 2018 using all the information available. [6]

d Calculate the **corrected** figure for the following items for inclusion in the revised statement of financial position at 31 December 2018. [5]

    i Property, plant and equipment
    ii Inventory
    iii Trade receivables
    iv Other receivables
    iv Total assets

Additional information

At the annual general meeting, some of the shareholders queried that the final dividend proposed by the directors was too low.

e   Advise the directors whether or not they should increase the proposed dividend. Justify your answer by discussing benefits and drawbacks of your advice for **both** the company and the shareholders. [5]

Cambridge International ASAL Accounting (9706) Paper 32, Q3, June 2019

[Total: 25]

EXAM-STYLE STRUCTURED QUESTIONS

1 DG Limited has been trading for several years. The external auditors are about to commence work on the statements of financial position for the year ended 31 December 2017.

The following draft financial information for the year ended 31 December 2017 has been provided by the directors **before** the audit work is started.

	$
Ordinary shares of $1 each	500 000
Share premium	80 000
Retained earnings at 1 January 2017	94 000
Profit for the year	78 000

The directors also provided the following information:

1   The value of inventory at 31 December 2017 was $120 000. As the purchasing cost had decreased, the company had changed its valuation method from First In, First Out (FIFO) to Weighted Average Cost (AVCO). The inventory value would have been $104 000 if FIFO had been used.

2   The profit for the year ended 31 December 2017 was arrived at after charging the following dividends:

	$
Interim dividend paid during the year	75 000
Proposed dividend for the year	82 500

3   A bonus issue of 1 ordinary share for every 10 ordinary shares held was made during the year. No entries had been made in the books of account for this issue. The directors wished to keep the reserves in their most flexible form. This was the only change to share capital during the year.

4   On 1 July 2017, the company had entered into a 3-year tenancy agreement for a new office. The monthly rent was $21 000. A total of $105 000 was paid during the year ended 31 December 2017 and this amount had been charged in the income statement.

REQUIRED

a   Distinguish between the roles of the shareholders and the directors of a limited company. [4]
b   State **one** reason why a sole trader does not require an audit of their statements of financial position. [1]
c   Calculate the adjusted profit for the year ended 31 December 2017. [6]
d   Explain the accounting treatment of information items 1 and 2. [6]
e   Prepare the statement of changes in equity for the year ended 31 December 2017. [4]

Additional information

The directors are trying to obtain a bank loan for expanding the business. The bank has requested the audited statements of financial position for the last three years.

f Advise the directors whether or not the audited statements of financial position provide all the information required in order for the bank to make its decision. Justify your answer. [4]

Cambridge International AS&A Level Accounting (9706) Paper 32, Q4, March 2018

[Total: 25]

2 A new director of R Limited has raised some concerns about their role in the company. He has also questioned the role of the company's auditors.

REQUIRED

a i Explain what is meant by the term 'stewardship'. [2]

   ii State **two** duties of the auditor of a limited company. [2]

Additional information

The directors of R Limited have provided the following information at 31 December 2018.

	$
Ordinary shares of $1 each	200 000
Share premium	20 000
8% Debenture (2025)	150 000
General reserve	54 000
Retained earnings at 1 January 2018	96 000
Debenture interest paid	4 000
Interim dividend paid	6 250
Land and buildings	
cost	450 000
accumulated depreciation	25 000
Plant and machinery	
cost	40 000
accumulated depreciation	15 000
Motor vehicles	
cost	24 000
accumulated depreciation	8 000
Inventory at 31 December 2018	65 000
Trade receivables	42 000
Cash and cash equivalents	37 000
Trade payables	35 000
Profit from operations	65 250

CONTINUED

The 8% debenture (2025) was issued on 1 January 2017.

A bonus issue of shares of 1 ordinary share for every 20 shares held was made on 31 December 2018. This had not yet been recorded in the books of account. The directors wish to keep the reserves in their most flexible form.

A provision for tax of $14 700 is to be made.

The directors have proposed a final dividend of $0.15 per share on all shares in issue at the year end.

b Prepare an extract from the income statement for the year ended 31 December 2018, to show the profit for the year, starting with the profit from operations. [2]

c Prepare the statement of changes in equity for the year ended 31 December 2018. A total column is **not** required. [4]

d Prepare the statement of financial position at 31 December 2018. [6]

Additional information

In February 2019 it was discovered that plant and machinery with a net book value of $15 000 had become obsolete. It could be sold for $8000 with a selling cost of $1200.

The cash flows from the machinery's continued use showed:

	future cash flows	10% discount factor
year 1	$4000	0.909
year 2	$5000	0.826
year 3	$3000	0.751

e Calculate the impairment loss. [4]

Cambridge International AS&A Level Accounting (9706) Paper 31, Q2a, b, c, d & e, October 2019

[Total: 20]

Improve this answer

This is a sample answer to **Q1a**.

> Shareholders entrust the responsibilities of running the company to the directors. Directors manage the day-to-day running of the company.

Your challenge

See if you can improve this answer. The sample answer is correct, but could be expanded on to show a better understanding of the differences between the roles. A better answer is available online – but write yours out first!

Chapter 26
International Accounting Standards

LEARNING INTENTIONS

In this chapter you will:
- learn the accounting standard relating to inventories
- learn the accounting standard relating to property, plant and equipment
- learn the accounting standard relating to the impairment of assets
- learn the accounting standard relating to the presentation of financial statements
- learn the accounting standard relating to the statement of cash flows
- learn the accounting standard relating to accounting policies
- learn the accounting standard relating to events after the reporting period
- learn the accounting standard relating to provisions, contingent liabilities and contingent assets
- learn the accounting standard relating to intangible assets

KEY TERMS

Amortisation   Applied research   Capital expenditure   Development   Purchased goodwill   Pure research

Key skills exercises

Knowledge and understanding

To answer the questions in this chapter, you need to know and understand:
- IAS 2 is the accounting standard relating to inventories
- IAS 16 is the accounting standard relating to property, plant and equipment
- IAS 36 is the accounting standard relating to impairment of assets.

You should also be able to use your knowledge and understanding of the International Accounting Standards to apply the standards to the financial records and statements.

Analysis

To answer the questions in this chapter, you need to be able to:
- analyse financial accounting information and cost and management accounting information
- select, calculate and interpret relevant data and information
- communicate outcomes in the most appropriate form.

Evaluation

To answer the questions in this chapter, you need to be able to:

- evaluate financial accounting information and cost and management accounting information to make informed recommendations and decisions
- make judgements and draw conclusions based on financial and non-financial data.

R6 RETAIL GROUP

R6 Retail Group is a leading Russian retailer.

R6 has inventory consisting of the products they sell in their grocery stores and many big assets owned by the company. Examples of their assets are premises (the actual buildings that the products are sold from), delivery vehicles and machinery.

R6 will have to comply with IAS 2 Inventories and IAS 16 Property, plant and equipment.

Knowledge and understanding

1. R6 bought a delivery vehicle for $163 000 that is expected to have a useful life of 8 years, after which it was expected to be sold for $25 000. The company uses the straight-line method of depreciation.

   After 3 years, the machinery was valued at $90 000 and is thought to have a remaining useful life of 4 years after which it would be sold for $15 000.

   REQUIRED

   a Calculate the initial depreciation expense per year.

   b Calculate the net book value of the machinery at the end of four years after the revaluation review had taken place and the depreciation-related expense for year 4.

   c Calculate the revised depreciation charge per year.

   TIP

   Remember to calculate the impairment and take it into consideration.

WORKED EXAMPLE 1

The following fixed assets appeared in the books of R6 Retail Group on 1 August 2019 (the beginning of the year):

	$	$
Land and buildings at cost	890 000	
Machinery	680 000	
Delivery vehicles	410 000	
Accumulated depreciation on machinery		345 000
Accumulated depreciation on delivery vehicles		156 000

- The company policy for depreciation is to charge 20% straight-line on all machinery owned at the beginning of the year and 25% reducing balance on all delivery vehicles owned at the beginning of the year. Depreciation is to be charged for a full year on assets bought partway through the year.
- During the year, the land and buildings were revalued at $1 050 000. Machinery was bought for $37 000 as were new delivery vehicles costing $21 000.
- During the year, delivery vehicles costing $23 000, which had been depreciated by $18 520, were sold for $7 000. Machinery, which had cost $28 000 and had a net book value at the time of disposal of $8 200, had been part of a trade-in on the new ones (the effective proceeds on disposal were $12 300).

REQUIRED

a Prepare a non-current assets schedule for R6 Retail Group on 31 July 2020 that would be suitable as a note to the statements of financial position.

b Calculate the profit or loss on disposal of each of the two assets sold.

CONTINUED

Answer

a

Non-current assets schedule				
	Land and buildings	Machinery	Delivery vehicles	Total
	$	$	$	$
Cost				
Cost at 1 August 2019	890 000	680 000	410 000	1 980 000
Revaluation	160 000	–	–	160 000
Additions during the year	–	37 000	21 000	58 000
Disposals during the year	–	(28 000)	(23 000)	(51 000)
Cost at 31 July 2020	1 050 000	689 000	408 000	2 147 000
Depreciation				
Accumulated depreciation at 1 Aug 2019	–	345 000	156 000	501 000
Charge during year[W1]	–	137 800	63 000	200 800
Disposals[W2]	–	(19 800)	(18 520)	(38 320)
Accumulated depreciation at 31 July 2020	–	463 000	200 480	663 480
Net book value at 31 July 2020	1 050 000	226 000	207 520	1 483 520
Net book value at 1 August 2019	890 000	335 000	254 000	1 479 000

Workings

W1: Depreciation on machinery = 20% × 689 000 = $137 800

Depreciation on delivery vehicles = 25% × (408 000 − 156 000) = $63 000

W2: Accumulated depreciation on machinery sold = cost − net book value = $28 000 − $8 200 = 19 800

b Profit or loss on disposal of machinery = 12 300 − 8 200 = $4 100 profit

Profit or loss on disposal of delivery vehicles = 7 000 − 4 480 = $2 520 profit

---

2 The following fixed assets appeared in the books of R6 Retail Group on 1 August 2020 (the beginning of the year).

	$	$
Land and buildings at cost	960 000	
Machinery	750 000	
Delivery vehicles	430 000	
Accumulated depreciation on machinery		375 000
Accumulated depreciation on delivery vehicles		129 000

- The company policy for depreciation is to charge 25% straight-line on all machinery owned at the beginning of the year and 30% reducing balance on all delivery vehicles owned at the beginning of the year. Depreciation is to be charged for a full year on assets bought partway through the year.

- During the year, the land and buildings were revalued at $1 210 000. Machinery was bought for $45 000 as were new delivery vehicles costing $26 000.

- During the year, delivery vehicles costing $21 000, which had been depreciated by $17 300, were sold for $5 000. Machinery, which had cost $27 000 and had a net book value at the time of disposal of $7 800, had been part of a trade-in on the new ones (the effective proceeds on disposal were $11 600).

REQUIRED

a Prepare a non-current assets schedule for R6 Retail Group on 31 July 2021 that would be suitable as a note to the statements of financial position.

b Calculate the profit or loss on disposal of each of the two assets sold.

WORKED EXAMPLE 2

R6 Retail Group examined some of its non-current assets with the following results.

	Net book value	Resale value	Benefits from use
	$	$	$
Asset A	96 400	106 300	87 200
Asset B	240 900	186 100	157 500
Asset C	74 000	81 700	34 600

REQUIRED

a Calculate the value of each asset that should be shown in the statements of financial position.

b Calculate the amount of impairment that needs to be applied to each asset and in total.

Answer

	Value in statements of financial position	Impairment required	
	$	$	
Asset A	96 400	0	
Asset B	186 100	54 800	240 900 − 186 100 = $54 800
Asset C	74 000	0	
Total	356 500	54 800	

3 R6 Retail Group examined some more of its non-current assets with the following results.

	Net book value	Resale value	Benefits from use
	$	$	$
Asset D	147 200	105 300	96 800
Asset E	367 400	395 000	284 900
Asset F	48 300	36 100	28 600

REQUIRED

a Prepare the value of each asset that should be shown in the statements of financial position.

b Prepare the amount of impairment that needs to be applied to each asset and in total.

Knowledge, understanding, analysis and evaluation

4 The external auditor of Z Limited has raised some issues relating to the non-current assets.

Information relating to the company's non-current assets at 30 June 2017 and 30 June 2016 is as follows.

	30 June 2017	30 June 2016
	$	$
Non-current assets		
Cost		
Land and buildings	2 400 000	2 400 000
Plant and machinery	540 000	420 000
Motor vehicles	320 000	240 000
Accumulated depreciation		
Land and buildings	192 000	160 000
Plant and machinery	264 000	195 000
Motor vehicles	184 000	150 000

The following information was available.

1. Land and buildings represent the company's office premises. One-third of the value is attributable to buildings and two-thirds to land. On 1 July 2016, land and buildings were revalued at $2 700 000. No accounting entries to record this had been made.

2. A new motor vehicle was purchased for $110 000. This was paid for with a cheque for $80 000 and the part-exchange of an old motor vehicle. The old vehicle had cost $75 000 and had been depreciated by $27 000. The cheque payment had been recorded in the bank account and motor vehicle at cost account. There were no other purchases or disposals of motor vehicles during the year.

3. A customer who owed $23 500 was unable to pay. The directors have agreed to take over one of the customer's machines to the value of $20 000 in full settlement of the debt. The machine was received on 15 May 2017. No record had been made of this arrangement.

4. Depreciation has been charged as follows and included as an expense when calculating the draft profit for the year.

Land	Nil
Buildings	4% per annum on cost
Plant and machinery	20% per annum using the reducing balance method
Motor vehicles	20% per annum using the reducing balance method

A full year's depreciation is charged in the year of purchase and no depreciation in the year of disposal.

The draft profit for the year ended 30 June 2017 was $95 000.

REQUIRED

a Explain **one** benefit of a company's audited financial statements to **each** of the following:

    i shareholders [2]

  ii potential investors [2]

  iii bank. [2]

b Prepare a statement to calculate the adjusted profit for the year ended 30 June 2017, taking into account the additional information 1 to 4. [9]

c Prepare the **motor vehicles column** of the non-current assets schedule as shown in the note to the statements of financial position for the year ended 30 June 2017. [6]

Additional information

The company purchased two plots of land in August 2017: Plot X for $400 000 and Plot Y for $320 000. Plot X has planning permission to build on and is expected to increase in value. Plot Y, however, has been found to have toxic chemicals and is expected to have a lower value.

The directors only want to record the increase in value of Plot X but not the decrease in value of Plot Y.

d Advise the directors whether they can only revalue Plot X but not Plot Y. Support your answer by referring to relevant accounting standard(s). [4]

Cambridge International AS&A Level Accounting (9706) Paper 31, Q3, October 2018

[Total: 25]

EXAM-STYLE STRUCTURED QUESTIONS

1 The trial balance of N plc at 31 December 2017 was as follows:

	$	$
Land and buildings		
cost	600 000	
provision for depreciation 1 January 2017		72 000
Equipment		
cost	278 000	
provision for depreciation 1 January 2017		112 000
Revenue		2 354 000
Purchases	1 322 000	
Administrative expenses	674 000	
Distribution costs	296 000	
Finance charges	9 000	
Inventory 1 January 2017	241 000	
Trade receivables	456 000	
Trade payables		394 000
Cash and cash equivalents	62 000	
Ordinary share capital		600 000
Share premium		140 000
6% debentures (2021)		200 000
Retained earnings		66 000
	3 938 000	3 938 000

CONTINUED

The following information is also available.

1. Revenue included a deposit of $6 000 from a customer for the goods to be delivered in March 2018.
2. Total inventory at 31 December 2017 cost $265 000. Of this, goods costing $24 600 had a net realisable value of $18 800.
3. Land and buildings were acquired in 2008. On 1 January 2017, they were revalued at $720 000 of which two-thirds was allocated to land and one-third to buildings. N plc had not recorded this revaluation.
4. During the year, a new photocopier was purchased for $80 000. The purchase consideration was settled by an exchange for a fully depreciated old photocopier with a trade-in value of $10 000. The old photocopier had been purchased in 2011 for $40 000. The balance of the purchase had been paid by cheque. N plc had recorded only the bank payment transaction.
5. There was no other purchase or sale of non-current assets during the year.
6. Depreciation is to be charged as follows:

Land	Nil
Buildings	over the useful life of 25 years
Equipment	25% per annum on cost

A full year's depreciation is charged in the year of purchase and none in the year of disposal.

All depreciation charged is to be included in administrative expenses.

7. An interim dividend of $30 000 was paid on 1 October 2017 and included in administrative expenses.
8. Interest for three months on the debentures had not been recorded.

REQUIRED

a   Prepare the income statement for the year ended 31 December 2017. [15]

b   Calculate the balance on the revaluation reserve account at 1 January 2017 following the revaluation. [5]

Additional information

There was a water leak in the company's printing room in January 2018. This destroyed the new photocopier which was not insured.

c   State how this should be treated in **both** 2017 financial statements **and** 2018 financial statements. [3]

d   State what is meant by impairment loss in respect of non-current assets. [2]

Cambridge International AS&A Level Accounting (9706) Paper 32, Q2, June 2018

[Total: 25]

CONTINUED

2   The directors of G Limited prepared the following draft statement of financial position at 31 December 2016:

G Limited	
Statement of Financial Position at 31 December 2016	
	$
Non-current assets	642 000
Current assets	
Inventory	78 000
Trade receivables	189 000
Other receivables	3 000
Cash and cash equivalents	54 000
	324 000
Total assets	966 000
Equity and liabilities	
Equity	
Ordinary shares of $1 each	550 000
Retained earnings	235 000
	785 000
Current liabilities	
Trade payables	171 000
Other payables	10 000
	181 000
Total equity and liabilities	966 000

The auditor brings the following items to the attention of the directors:

1   G Limited entered into an 18-month rental agreement for a warehouse on 1 May 2016. The following payments totalling $220 000 were made and charged as an expense in the draft income statement:

$20 000 rental deposit, which is refundable at the end of the lease period; and

$200 000 total rent covering the period from 1 May 2016 to 28 February 2017.

2   After an inspection of G Limited's office premises by the local authority in December 2016, it was found that the fire exits did not meet the safety specifications. A penalty of $27 000 is probable and G Limited will incur a cost of $47 000 to rebuild the fire exits. No accounting entries had been made for this.

3   A customer who owed $12 000 at 31 December 2016 was declared bankrupt on 12 January 2017. It is probable that only 20% of the debt is recoverable. No accounting entries had been made for this.

CONTINUED

REQUIRED

a Prepare the **revised** statement of financial position at 31 December 2016. [10]

b Explain how **each** of items 1 and 2 should be treated in the financial statements. [5]

c Explain the role of an external auditor. [4]

d Explain why the audit report of a limited company is addressed to the company's shareholders and not its directors. [2]

Additional information

G Limited adopted the Weighted Average Cost (AVCO) method to ascertain the value of inventories in 2016. The purchase price has been increasing over recent years. The directors are now considering changing to the First In, First Out (FIFO) method to value inventory in 2017.

REQUIRED

e Advise the directors whether or not the method of valuing inventory should be changed. Justify your answer. [4]

Cambridge International AS&A Level Accounting (9706) Paper 31, Q2, June 2017

[Total: 25]

Improve this answer

This is a sample answer to **Q2e**.

> The directors have to apply the consistency principle. This means that only if the change is required by accounting standards or results in the statements of financial position providing reliable and more relevant information may a change be accepted.

Your challenge

See if you can improve this answer. The sample answer doesn't actually provide the decision asked for. A better answer would give an advised decision and provide the justification for that decision. A better answer can be found online – but write yours out first!

> Chapter 27
Computerised accounting systems

LEARNING INTENTIONS

In this chapter you will:

- understand the need for a business to introduce a computerised accounting system
- discuss the advantages and disadvantages of introducing a computerised accounting system into a business
- understand how a business can transfer its accounting data onto a computerised accounting system
- understand and discuss the ways in which the integrity of the accounting data can be ensured during and after the transfer to a computerised accounting system

KEY TERM

Computerised accounting system

Key skill exercises

Knowledge and understanding

To answer the questions in this chapter, you need to know and understand:

- a computerised accounting system is a set of programs that allow the accounts to be prepared using a computer
- most businesses today make use of a computer system for accounts
- the advantages and disadvantages of the computerised accounting system
- the ways in which the integrity of the accounting data can be ensured during and after the transfer to a computerised accounting system.

HOME GADGETS

Home Gadgets is a company that focuses on producing and distributing home appliances. Their headquarters is in Stockholm, Sweden.

Home Gadgets products include refrigerators, dishwashers, washing machines, cookers, vacuum cleaners, air conditioners and small domestic appliances.

The Home Gadgets Group is spread across many consumer-focused business areas: Europe, North America, Latin America, Asia-Pacific, Middle East and Africa.

It is essential for a company of this size to use computerised accounting systems as all business areas need to be the same to be accurate and give a true and fair view of their financial statements.

WORKED EXAMPLE 1

State an advantage and disadvantage for installing a computerised accounting system from the business point of view with regards to staff.

Answer

Advantages for staff:

- Fewer staff required for the job.

Disadvantages for staff:

- Cost of staff training
- Due to more expertise required by staff to make use of the computerised accounting system you have a higher staff turnover rate.

1   State an advantage and a disadvantage of installing a computerised accounting system from the business point of view with regards to cost.

2   State three steps a business could put in place to ensure the security of a computerised accounting system.

3   State whether each of the following points is an advantage or disadvantage of computerised accounting:

- improved accuracy
- space can be saved
- staff training
- systems crashing
- speed of processing data
- costs
- external risks to the data
- auditing and fraud prevention.

> **TIP**
>
> Restrictions can be put in place to ensure the security of the accounting information.

EXAM-STYLE MULTIPLE CHOICE AND STRUCTURED QUESTIONS

1   The process of introducing a computerised accounting system requires a 10-step process. Put the following three steps in the correct order.

   1 Coding up
   2 Installation
   3 Decide on the date to transfer the balances from the manual system to the computer

   A   Step 3, Step 2, Step 1
   B   Step 2, Step 3, Step 1
   C   Step 2, Step 1, Step 3
   D   Step 1, Step 3, Step 2   [1]

2   Explain the process of transferring a manual accounting system to a computerised accounting system.   [5]

3   Prepare three advantages and three disadvantages of computerised accounting.   [6]

> Chapter 28
Business acquisition and merger

LEARNING INTENTIONS

In this chapter you will:

- learn why business acquisition and merger happens
- understand the difference between the acquisition of a business and a merger of two businesses
- understand the nature and purpose of mergers of different types of business to form a new business entity
- prepare the journal entries to record the merger of two or more sole trader businesses to form a partnership or a limited company
- prepare the journal entries to record the merger of a sole trader's business with an existing partnership to form a new partnership
- learn the acquisition of a sole trader's business or partnership by a limited company
- learn the value of goodwill on the acquisition of a business by another entity
- prepare statements of profit or loss and statements of financial position for the newly formed business entity following the acquisition or merger, for example a limited company acquiring a partnership
- learn the advantages and disadvantages of acquisitions or mergers

KEY TERMS

Inherent goodwill   Merger   Purchased goodwill

Key skills exercises

Knowledge and understanding

To answer the questions in this chapter, you need to know and understand:

- companies merge with or acquire other companies for various reasons, namely efficiency gains, increased expertise, growth, increase supply-chain pricing power, to eliminate competition
- a merger is where two or more independent businesses combine their assets and form a completely new business
- a takeover or acquisition involves the purchase of a smaller company by a much larger one and is less likely to be a mutual decision
- the acquisition of a sole trader's business or partnership by a limited company.

You should also be able to use your knowledge and understanding of purchases and mergers to prepare journal entries, value goodwill and prepare statements of profit or loss and statements of financial position.

Analysis

To answer the questions in this chapter, you need to be able to:
- analyse financial accounting information and cost and management accounting information
- select, calculate and interpret relevant data and information
- communicate outcomes in the most appropriate form.

Evaluation

To answer the questions in this chapter, you need to be able to:
- evaluate financial accounting information to make informed recommendations and decisions
- make judgements and draw conclusions based on financial and non-financial data.

WORKED EXAMPLE 1

Harry and George are partners in a business. They have accepted an offer from Orla Limited to purchase their business. The statements of financial position for both the partnership and the company at 31 December 2021 are as follows.

Harry and George	$000
Non-current assets	
Land and buildings	360
Fixtures and fittings	42
Motor vehicles	58
	460
Current assets	
Inventory	56
Trade receivables	31
Cash and cash equivalents	20
	107
Total assets	567
Capital and liabilities	
Capital accounts	
Harry	230
George	270
	500
Non-current liability	
3% loan from George	40
Current liabilities	
Trade payables	27
Total capital and liabilities	567

Orla Limited	$000
Non-current assets	
Land and buildings	860
Fixtures and fittings	87
Motor vehicles	132
	1 079
Current assets	
Inventory	104
Trade receivables	65
Cash and cash equivalents	93
	262
Total assets	1 341
Equity and liabilities	
Ordinary shares of $0.50 each	1 000
Retained earnings	305
	1 305
Current liabilities	
Trade payables	36
Total equity and liabilities	1 341

CONTINUED

It has been agreed that the partnership assets are to be valued as follows:

	$000
Land and buildings	400
Fixtures and fittings	38
Motor vehicles	55
Inventory	52
Trade receivables	27

Orla Limited has agreed to take over all of the assets and liabilities of the business, with the exception of the partnership bank account and will settle the purchase price as follows:

- a payment of cash, $100 000
- 5% debentures issued to George to ensure that he continues to receive the same amount of interest annually as he has received from the partnership
- the balance to be settled by an issue of 500 000 ordinary shares of $0.50 in Orla Limited, valued at a price of $0.90 per share.

REQUIRED

a   Calculate the value of the debentures that will need to be issued to George.

b   Prepare the journal required to show the valuation of goodwill and the entries that will need to be made in the ledgers of Orla Limited.

c   Prepare the statement of financial position for Orla Limited immediately after the takeover.

Answer

a   George's loan interest = $40 000 × 3% = $1 200

   Value of debentures = $1 200 / 5% = $24 000

b

	$000	$000
Land and buildings	400	
Fixtures and fittings	38	
Motor vehicles	55	
Inventory	52	
Trade receivables	27	
Trade payables		27
Cash and cash equivalents		100
Debenture for George		24
Ordinary share capital ($0.50 each)		250
Share premium account ($0.30 each)		200
Goodwill(W1)	29	
	601	601

Working

W1: Purchase price was 100 + 24 + 250 + 200 = 574
Assets acquired were 400 + 38 + 55 + 52 + 27 − 27 = 545
Goodwill = 574 − 545 = $29 000

CONTINUED

c

	$000
Intangible non-current assets (goodwill)	29
Tangible non-current assets	
Land and buildings (860 + 400)	1 260
Fixtures and fittings (87 + 38)	125
Motor vehicles (132 + 55)	187
	1 601
Current assets	
Inventory (104 + 52)	156
Trade receivables (65 + 27)	92
	248
Total assets	1 849
Equity and liabilities	
Ordinary shares of $0.50 each (1 000 + 250)	1 250
Share premium	200
Retained earnings	305
	1 755
8% debentures (issued to George)	24
Current liabilities	
Trade payables (36 + 27)	63
Cash and cash equivalents (93 – 100)	7
Total equity and liabilities	1 849

Knowledge and understanding

1 Ralph is a sole trader whose business was purchased by Bonnie Limited on 30 September 2020. The statements of financial position of both businesses at that date were as follows.

	Ralph	Bonnie Limited
	$000	$000
Non-current assets		
Premises	230	840
Motor vehicles	96	360
Equipment	47	155
	373	1 355

	$000	$000
Current assets		
Inventory	38	83
Trade receivables	19	41
Cash and cash equivalents	12	72
	69	196
Total assets	442	1 551
Capital and liabilities		
Capital account	417	
Current liabilities		
Trade payables	25	
Total capital and liabilities	442	
Equity and liabilities		
Ordinary shares of $1		865
Share premium		290
Retained earnings		340
		1 495
Current liabilities		
Trade payables		56
Total capital and liabilities		1 551

It was agreed that Ralph's assets should be valued as follows:

	$000
Premises	250
Motor vehicles	90
Equipment	45
Inventory	33
Trade receivables	16
Trade payables	(25)
	409

Bonnie Limited did not acquire Ralph's bank account. The consideration for the sale was $520 000. This consisted of $80 000 in cash and 270 000 ordinary shares of $1 each in Bonnie Limited.

REQUIRED

a Prepare the journal entries in Bonnie Limited's books to record the purchase of Ralph's business.

b Prepare Bonnie Limited's statement of financial position immediately after the acquisition of Ralph's business.

WORKED EXAMPLE 2

Jack and Lyla are partners in a business who share profits equally. They have accepted an offer from Aaron Limited to purchase their business. The statement of financial position for the partnership at 31 December 2020 is as follows:

	$000
Non-current assets	
Land and buildings	50
Motor vehicle	3
Office machinery	20
	73
Current assets	
Inventory	8
Trade receivables	12
	20
Total assets	93
Capital and liabilities	
Capital and current accounts	
Capital – Jack	30
Capital – Lyla	30
Current – Jack	8
Current – Lyla	6
	74
8% loan – Jack	11
Current liabilities	
Trade payables	6
Bank overdraft	2
Total capital and liabilities	93

The partners accept an offer from Aurora Limited for their business. The terms of the sale are as follows:

- Lyla will take over the motor vehicle at its book value.
- Aurora Limited will take over all the remaining assets and liabilities of the business with the exception of the bank overdraft and loan.
- The purchase of the business will be satisfied by the issue to each partner of 50 000 ordinary shares of $1 each issued at a premium of $0.20.
- Aurora Limited will pay $20 000 in cash into the partnership bank account.

28 Business acquisition and merger AS and A Level

> **CONTINUED**
>
> **REQUIRED**
>
> Prepare the realisation account to show the takeover.
>
> **Answer**
>
> | Realisation account | | | |
> |---|---:|---|---:|
> | | $000 | | $000 |
> | Land and building | 50 | Trade payables | 6 |
> | Motor vehicle | 3 | Cash | 20 |
> | Office machinery | 20 | Shares (including premium) | 120 |
> | Inventory | 8 | Capital – Lyla (motor vehicle) | 3 |
> | Trade receivables | 12 | | |
> | Profit on realisation – Jack | 28 | | |
> | Profit on realisation – Lyla | 28 | | |
> | | 149 | | 149 |

TIP

The motor vehicle taken over by Lyla is credited in the realisation account at the agreed amount.

2 Jasper and Edith are partners in a business who share profits in the ratio 5:3. They have accepted an offer from Leo Limited to purchase their business. The statement of financial position for the partnership and the company at 31 July 2020 is as follows:

	$000
Non-current assets	
Premises	250
Office furniture	32
Fixtures and fittings	14
Motor vehicle	33
	329
Current assets	
Inventory	42
Trade receivables	11
	53
Total assets	382
Capital and current accounts	
Capital – Jasper	150
Capital – Edith	90
Current – Jasper	17
Current – Edith	(6)
	251
6% loan – Jasper	80
Current liabilities	
Bank overdraft	32
Trade payables	19
Total capital and liabilities	382

Leo Limited has agreed to take over all of the assets and liabilities of the business, with the exception of the partnership bank account and the motor vehicle that Edith is going to take. The company will settle the purchase price as follows:

- a payment of cash, $70 000.
- Jasper will be issued with 8% debentures that will ensure that he continues to receive the same amount of interest as he did before.
- the balance to be settled by an issue of 400 000 ordinary shares of $0.50 in Leo Limited, valued at a price of $0.65 per share.
- Jasper has indicated that he is happy to be paid out with $20 000 in cash and the rest in shares. Edith is happy with any cash left over plus shares.

REQUIRED

a Calculate the value of debentures that need to be issued by Leo Limited to deal with the loan from Jasper.

b Prepare the entries that need to be made in the following accounts to show the takeover:

- current accounts
- realisation account
- capital accounts
- bank.

Knowledge, understanding and analysis

3 Armfield and Bonetti are sole traders. Their statements of financial position at 31 December 2016 are shown here:

	Armfield	Bonetti
	$	$
Assets		
Non-current assets	85 000	135 000
Current assets		
Inventories	8 000	12 000
Trade receivables	6 000	9 000
Cash and cash equivalents	4 000	5 000
	18 000	26 000
Total assets	103 000	161 000
Capital and liabilities		
Capital accounts	100 000	150 000
Current liabilities		
Trade payables	3 000	11 000
	103 000	161 000

They have decided to merge their two businesses into a partnership on 1 January 2017. All assets and liabilities, with the exception of cash and cash equivalents, were transferred to the new partnership at the following agreed values:

	Armfield	Bonetti
	$	$
Non-current assets	80 000	145 000
Inventories	7 000	11 000
Trade receivables	5 000	8 000
Trade payables	3 000	11 000

REQUIRED

a State the meaning of the term 'capital account'. [2]

b Prepare the capital accounts of Armfield and Bonetti to close their existing businesses. Transfer the balances on their capital accounts to new partnership capital accounts. [6]

Additional information

Each partner will either invest or withdraw cash to achieve a balance of $125 000 to carry forward on their partnership capital account.

REQUIRED

c Prepare the partnership capital accounts showing **each** partner's adjustment for cash. [3]

d Prepare the opening statement of financial position for the partnership at 1 January 2017. [5]

Additional information

Profit for the year ended 31 December 2016 of Armfield was $80 000 and Bonetti was $120 000. The profit for the year of the partnership for the year ending 31 December 2017 is expected to be $200 000. The partners agreed to share the profits and losses equally.

REQUIRED

e Discuss whether or not the merger of the two businesses has been beneficial to each partner. [5]

Additional information

After the first year's successful trading as a partnership the partners were advised to consider incorporating their business. Both partners are close to retirement age and have family.

REQUIRED

f Discuss **two** advantages to the partners of incorporating their business. [4]

Cambridge International AS&A Level Accounting (9706) Paper 31, Q4, October 2017

[Total: 25]

Knowledge, understanding, analysis and evaluation

4 Alfie and Bob have been in partnership sharing profits and losses in the ratio of 3:2.

On 1 January 2018 the partnership business was acquired by G Limited.

The statements of financial position at 31 December 2017 for both businesses were as follows.

	G Limited	Alfie and Bob
	$	$
Assets		
Non-current assets		
Land and buildings	625 000	320 000
Plant and machinery	254 000	178 000
	879 000	498 000
Current assets		
Inventory	142 000	112 000
Trade receivables	251 000	130 000
Cash and cash equivalents	92 000	
	485 000	242 000
Total assets	1 364 000	740 000
Equity and liabilities		
Equity		
Ordinary shares of $5 each	1 000 000	
Capital accounts: Alfie		285 000
Bob		274 000
Retained earnings	194 000	
	1 194 000	559 000
Current liabilities		
Trade payables	170 000	155 000
Bank overdraft	–	26 000
	170 000	181 000
Total equity and liabilities	1 364 000	740 000

The following information is also available.

1. All assets and liabilities of the partnership, except the bank overdraft, were taken over by G Limited at the following values:

	$
Land and buildings	350 000
Plant and machinery	170 000
Inventory	110 000
Trade receivables	125 000
Trade payables	153 000

2. Goodwill of the partnership at 1 January 2018 was valued at twice the value of average profits for the last two years. The profits for the year for 2016 and 2017 were $13 000 and $17 000.

3. The purchase consideration was satisfied with 100 000 ordinary shares in G Limited at $6 per share. The remaining balance was paid in cash.

4. Ordinary shares of G Limited were issued to Alfie and Bob according to their profit sharing ratio.

28 Business acquisition and merger AS and A Level

REQUIRED

a State **one** reason why the assets and liabilities may be revalued when a partnership is sold.

b Calculate for the sale of partnership:
  i the **total** purchase consideration
  ii the amount paid to partners in cash.

c Prepare the statement of financial position of G Limited at 1 January 2018 immediately after the purchase of the partnership.

d Prepare the capital accounts of Alfie and Bob to close the partnership business.

Cambridge International AS&A Level Accounting (9706) Paper 31, Q2a, b, c & d, October 2018

EXAM-STYLE STRUCTURED QUESTIONS

1 Ephraim and Fikriyah are sole traders. They agreed to merge their two businesses into a partnership on 1 October 2017 sharing profits and losses equally.

Ephraim and Fikriyah's statements of financial position at 30 September 2017 were as follows:

	Ephraim	Fikriyah
	$	$
Non-current assets	45 000	110 000
Current assets		
Inventories	7 500	11 500
Trade receivables	9 000	15 500
Cash and cash equivalents	6 500	1 000
	23 000	28 000
Total assets	68 000	138 000
Capital	60 000	120 000
Current liabilities		
Trade payables	8 000	18 000
	68 000	138 000

The agreed valuations for the merger were:

	Ephraim	Fikriyah
	$	$
Non-current assets	55 000	115 000
Inventories	8 000	10 500
Goodwill	10 000	6 000

All other assets and liabilities were transferred at their book value.

Goodwill was **not** to be retained in the books of account.

CONTINUED

REQUIRED

a Prepare the opening statement of financial position for the partnership at 1 October 2017. [13]

Additional information

The average annual profit earned by Ephraim for the past three years was $60 000.

The average annual profit earned by Fikriyah for the past three years was $40 000.

The budgeted profit for the partnership for its first year's trading is expected to be $100 000. In each of the following three years it is expected to be 10% less than the previous year. This is as a result of the increasing competition.

b Discuss the benefits and limitations of the merger to **each** partner. Justify your answer using **both** financial and non-financial factors.

Cambridge International AS&A Level Accounting (9706) Paper 32, Q4, June 2018

[12]

[Total: 25]

2 R Limited has been trading for one year and is considering whether or not to purchase the business of Joe Tu, a sole trader. The draft statements of financial position for both businesses at 31 December 2017 are shown here:

	R Limited	Joe Tu
	$	$
Non-current assets (at net book value)		
Land and buildings	454 000	128 000
Plant and equipment	294 000	30 000
	748 000	158 000
Current assets		
Inventory	98 000	35 000
Trade receivables	123 000	39 000
Cash and cash equivalents	58 000	2 800
	279 000	76 800
Total assets	1 027 000	234 800
Equity and liabilities		
Equity		
Ordinary shares of $1 each	800 000	
Capital at 1 January 2017		160 000
Profit for the year	132 000	19 800
Drawings		(12 000)
	932 000	167 800
Current liabilities		
Trade payables	95 000	67 000
Total equity and liabilities	1 027 000	234 800

28 Business acquisition and merger AS and A Level

CONTINUED

The following information is also available.

Robert and Paul are the only shareholders and directors of R Limited. As part of the purchase agreement, Joe Tu will be appointed as a director of R Limited with an annual director's fee of $30 000, the same amount as Robert and Paul each receive.

The sales revenue and gross margin for both businesses for the year ended 31 December 2017 were:

	R Limited	Joe Tu
Sales revenue	$1 500 000	$250 000
Gross margin	50%	45%

Robert is in favour of buying Joe Tu's business and of him becoming a director. He believes that for the year ended 31 December 2018:

Combined sales revenue can be increased by 20%, earning a gross margin of 50%.
Combined operating expenses, other than directors' fees, can be reduced by 30%.

However, Paul is not happy about buying Joe Tu's business or him becoming a director.

REQUIRED

a i   Prepare a statement to calculate the operating expenses for each business for the year ended 31 December 2017. [4]

   ii Prepare a statement to calculate the expected additional profit R Limited will make for the year ended 31 December 2018 if it buys Joe Tu's business. [4]

Additional information

1 Purchase consideration will be $180 000 payable to Joe Tu by issuing 150 000 ordinary shares of R Limited.
2 R Limited will take over Joe Tu's assets and liabilities, except the bank account, at the following values:

	$
Land and buildings	139 000
Plant and equipment	14 000
Inventory	40 000
Trade receivables	36 000
Trade payables	67 000

3 a   The directors of R Limited will also revalue their own land and buildings upwards by $28 000.
   b   State why a business may revalue its assets when it is being purchased by another business. [1]
   c   Prepare the statement of financial position of R Limited at 31 December 2017 if Joe Tu's business was purchased by it on that date. [11]
   d   Advise Robert and Paul whether or not they should buy Joe Tu's business. Justify your answer by discussing the **non-financial** advantages and disadvantages of this action. [5]

Cambridge International AS&A Level Accounting (9706) Paper 32, Q3, March 2018

[Total: 25]

CONTINUED

Improve this answer

This is a sample answer to **Q4d**.

> Robert and Paul should not buy the business. They will have less control over the business and they might not get on with the directors.

Your challenge

See if you can improve this answer. This answer lacks information on the advantages and only focuses on the disadvantages. To fully answer this question, the advantages should be discussed fully and weighed against the disadvantages so that a justified conclusion can be reached.

A better answer is available online – but write yours out first!

Chapter 29
Ethics and the accountant

LEARNING INTENTIONS

In this chapter you will:

- learn the need for an ethical framework in accounting
- learn the fundamental principles of integrity, objectivity, professional competence and due care, confidentiality and professional behaviour
- learn how the ethical behaviour of accountants and auditors impacts the business and other stakeholders
- learn about some approaches used by organisations to promote ethical behaviour
- learn the social implications of decision making

KEY TERMS

Conflicts of interest   Corporate social responsibility (CSR)   Ethics   Insider trading   Money laundering
Reserved activity   Whistleblowing

Key skills exercises

Knowledge and understanding

To answer the questions in this chapter, you have to know and understand:

- ethics are the moral principles or standards that govern the conduct of a person or organisation
- integrity means being straightforward and honest in the way in which you behave and perform your duties
- showing objectivity is the ability to make impartial and unbiased professional business judgements based on the facts at hand
- an accountant needs to ensure that they have the professional knowledge and skills to ensure that the service provided is both competent and in accordance with the latest legislation and industrial standards
- the ethical behaviour of accountants and auditors impacts the business and other stakeholders
- the social implications of decision-making.

You should also be able to apply your knowledge and understanding of ethics and apply it to situations.

WORKED EXAMPLE 1

State whether the principle of integrity or objectivity is at risk in each of these situations.

Situation 1: A client offers you a thank you gift at the end of a project.

Situation 2: A family member works at a company that has just been assigned to you to work on their books.

Situation 3: You have been assigned to a job; however, you have no experience with this work and have had no training with this area of work.

Answer

Situation 1: Integrity – This might be seen as a bribe and it is necessary to avoid compromising situations.

Situation 2: Objectivity – Familiarity or trust is at risk as someone may be influenced because of a connection with family or friends.

Situation 3: Integrity – Recognising and communicating your personal and professional limitations is at risk as integrity may involve admitting to a manager that you do not have the skills and experience to be able to complete an assignment to a high standard.

1 State, in each of the following situations, whether the principle of integrity or objectivity is at risk.

   Situation 1: You work for an accounting firm that has recently gained a new client. You will more than likely handle this account. You soon find out who the new client is and realise your sister works for the company who is your new client.

   Situation 2: At the end of a successful job, the client has given you a voucher for a weekend away to thank you for your efforts.

   Situation 3: You have been asked to take on a new client; however, you have no experience in the work that is required of you and are not capable of doing so without training.

   Situation 4: Your client has asked you to change a few numbers on the accounts to show a higher profit as they are needing to apply for a loan. The client suggests that should you not comply with the request they will take their business to another firm and inform the partners why.

> **TIP**
>
> Integrity means being straightforward and honest in the way in which you behave and perform your duties. Objectivity is the ability to make impartial and unbiased professional business judgements based on the facts at hand.

WORKED EXAMPLE 2

Explain, in each situation, which risk to objectivity is being displayed and why.

Situation 1: Your religion that you follow is against the consumption of alcohol. You have been assigned to a new client, which is a brewing company.

Situation 2: A client has asked you to change the numbers on the statements of financial position as they are wanting to apply to the bank for a loan. They have suggested that should you not abide by this request they will 'sort' you out.

Answer

Situation 1: Advocacy – Your beliefs may affect your judgement.

Situation 2: Intimidation – There may be a temptation to make a decision because there is an actual warning being made by the client.

2   Explain, in each situation, which risk to objectivity is being displayed and why.

Situation 1: Ekrem is a qualified accountant. Ekrem is currently in negotiations with a potential supplier for a big quantity of goods. Ekrem's contact at the supplier suggests that if Ekrem ensures that his company gets the contract, he will buy Ekrem a new car.

Situation 2: Burhan's religion is against the consumption or association of alcohol. As an accountant, Burhan has been assigned a client from a brewery.

Situation 3: Doruk has been part of a group project at work. One of his colleagues has taken credit for an idea or work that he actually contributed to the project. His colleague has warned that he will hurt him if he tells anyone.

> **TIP**
>
> The risks to objectivity include self-interest, self-review, advocacy, familiarity or trust and intimidation.

3   State, in each of these situations, what you should do (or what information should be disclosed, if any).

Situation 1: A client has not paid their due fees to the accounting firm and their account is now overdue. The firm's credit control manager finds out that you, the client's accountant, are holding money in a separate bank account on behalf of the client to pay their tax. The credit control manager asks you to withdraw money from the account to pay the accounting firm the overdue amount.

Situation 2: You are an accountant at a firm and have gained information about a bid to take over a rival firm. A friend of yours contacts you for advice, as a professional in this industry, as she is considering selling her shares in this rival firm and wants to know whether she should sell or not.

Situation 3: You have a client who sells fridges. The client sells a fridge to a customer and later informs you that the fridge has a faulty cooling system.

EXAM-STYLE STRUCTURED QUESTIONS

1   You receive a call from one of your clients asking about an inheritance tax issue. You have no experience or knowledge about this specific tax issue. What is the most appropriate action? [2]

2   You are working for a client who has offered you shares in their company. Which risks of objectivity are being displayed? Explain your answer. [2]

3   Layla & Jean is an accounting firm. The partners of the firm want to ensure that all of their employees behave ethically and apply the highest professional standards. In order to do this, a set of 'Ethical Guidelines' has been issued to every member of staff who were given some training to ensure that every employee was familiar with the partners' expectations.

   a   State *two* reasons why it is important that the employees at Layla & Jean behave ethically. [2]

   Sheldon is a junior accountant at Layla & Jean and has been assigned to a new client. When Sheldon met with the new client for the first time the client was trying to convince him to make a few changes to the numbers he had supplied to make the books look better. The client offered Sheldon a week away at Magicalland with his family if he agreed to change a few numbers.

   b   Explain how Sheldon might behave unethically in the situation, referring to *two* fundamental ethical principles that would be breached if he does the wrong thing. [3]

   c   Explain what Sheldon should do in this situation. [2]

   d   Explain *one* ethical solution to this problem assuming that Sheldon has taken the action that you recommended in **c**. [2]

   e   Explain *one* other way, apart from issuing guidelines and providing training, that the management at Layla & Jean could try to ensure that their staff behave ethically. [2]

   [Total: 15]

> Chapter 30

Accounting information for stakeholders

LEARNING INTENTIONS

In this chapter you will:

- learn who the stakeholders of a business are
- learn the limitations of financial statements
- analyse and interpret financial statements
- calculate ratios from the financial statements of a business
- use ratios to analyse the performance of a business
- learn the benefits and limitations of using ratios to analyse financial statements

KEY TERM

Stakeholder

Key skills exercises

Knowledge and understanding

To answer the questions in this chapter, you need to know and understand:

- stakeholders are persons or organisations that have a legitimate interest in a business or who can be affected by that business
- the limitations of the published accounts of limited companies when communicating information
- the benefits and limitations of using ratios to analyse financial statements.

You should be able to apply your knowledge and understanding to calculate ratios from the financial statements.

Analysis

To answer the questions in this chapter, you need to be able to:

- analyse financial accounting information
- select, calculate and interpret relevant data and information
- communicate outcomes in the most appropriate form.

30 Accounting information for stakeholders AS Level

Evaluation

To answer the questions in this chapter, you need to be able to:

- evaluate financial accounting information and cost and management accounting information to make informed recommendations and decisions
- make judgements and draw conclusions based on financial and non-financial data.

WORKED EXAMPLE 1

Extracts from the final statements for Freddy Limited for the year ended 30 November 2020 are as follows:

	2020
	$000
Revenue	1 950
Cost of sales	(1 360)
Gross profit	590
Administrative expenses	(314)
Distribution costs	(185)
Operating profit	91
Interest payable	(16)
Profit before tax	75
Tax	(40)
Profit for the year	35
Shareholders' equity	320
Long-term loans	180

REQUIRED

Calculate the following ratios for 2020.

a Gross profit %
b Mark-up %
c Administrative expenses %
d Distribution costs %
e Operating profit %
f Profit for the year %
g Return on capital employed

> **CAMBRIDGE INTERNATIONAL AS & A LEVEL ACCOUNTING: WORKBOOK**

CONTINUED

Answer

		Formula	2020
a	Gross profit %	$\dfrac{\text{Gross profit}}{\text{Revenue}} \times 100$	$\dfrac{590}{1\,950} \times 100 = 30.26\%$
b	Mark-up %	$\dfrac{\text{Gross profit}}{\text{Cost of sales}} \times 100$	$\dfrac{590}{1\,360} \times 100 = 43.38\%$
c	Administrative expenses %	$\dfrac{\text{Administrative expenses}}{\text{Revenue}} \times 100$	$\dfrac{314}{1\,950} \times 100 = 16.10\%$
d	Distribution costs %	$\dfrac{\text{Distribution costs}}{\text{Revenue}} \times 100$	$\dfrac{185}{1\,950} \times 100 = 9.49\%$
e	Operating profit %	$\dfrac{\text{Operating costs}}{\text{Revenue}} \times 100$	$\dfrac{91}{1\,950} \times 100 = 4.67\%$
f	Profit for the year %	$\dfrac{\text{Profit before tax}}{\text{Revenue}} \times 100$	$\dfrac{75}{1\,950} \times 100 = 3.85\%$
g	Return on capital employed %	$\dfrac{\text{Operating profit}}{\text{Capital employed}} \times 100$	$\dfrac{91}{500} \times 100 = 18.2\%$

Knowledge and understanding

1   The following information is a statement of profit or loss that was prepared for Klaas Peeters' business.

Klaas Peeters		
Statement of profit or loss for the year ended 30 June 2020		
	$	$
Revenue		350 000
Opening inventory	58 400	
Purchases	147 200	
	205 600	
Less closing inventory	(46 300)	
Cost of sales		(159 300)
Gross profit		190 700
Less expenses		
Wages	34 000	
Rent	23 000	
Depreciation	18 000	
		(75 000)
Profit for the year		1 156 700

REQUIRED

Calculate the following ratios and state the formula used in each (all answers to 2 decimal places):

a   mark-up

b   gross profit margin

c   inventory turnover period (days and times)

d   profit margin

e   wages as a percentage of revenue

f   rent as a percentage of revenue

g   depreciation as a percentage of revenue.

> **TIP**
>
> Always check if the question is asking for the inventory turnover as the number of times or number of days.

WORKED EXAMPLE 1

The following statement of financial position was prepared for Fleur Verhoeven's business at the year end.

	Cost	Depreciation	Net book value
	$	$	$
Non-current assets	630 000	186 000	444 000
Current assets			
Inventory		48 000	
Trade receivables		9 000	
Other receivables		2 400	
Cash and cash equivalents		10 600	70 000
Total assets			514 000
Capital			
Opening balance		463 000	
Profit for the year		73 300	
		536 300	
Drawings		(43 000)	493 300
Current liabilities			
Trade payables		19 000	
Other payables		1 700	20 700
Total capital and liabilities			514 000

The business had credit sales of $73 000 and credit purchases of $274 000 during the financial year.

REQUIRED

Calculate the following ratios (answers to 2 decimal places):

a   current ratio

b   acid test ratio

c   non-current asset turnover (times)

CONTINUED

d trade receivables turnover (days)

e trade payables turnover (days)

f return on capital employed.

Answer

	Ratio	Formula	Answer
a	current ratio	current assets : current liabilities	70 000 : 20 700 = 3.38 : 1
b	acid test ratio	current assets less inventory : current liabilities	(70 000 – 48 000) : 20 700 = 1.06 : 1
c	non-current assets turnover (times)	$\dfrac{\text{Net revenue}}{\text{Net book value of non-current assets}}$	$\dfrac{73\,000}{444\,000} = 0.16$ times
d	trade receivables turnover (days)	$\dfrac{\text{Trade receivables}}{\text{Credit revenues}} \times 365$	$\dfrac{9\,000}{73\,000} \times 365 = 45$ days
e	trade payables turnover (days)	$\dfrac{\text{Trade payable}}{\text{Credit purchases}} \times 365$	$\dfrac{19\,000}{274\,000} \times 365 = 25.31$ days ≈ 26 days
f	return on capital employed	$\dfrac{\text{Profit before interest}}{\text{Capital employed}} \times 100$	$\dfrac{73\,300}{493\,300} \times 100 = 14.86\%$

2 The following statement of financial position was prepared for Elsje Dupont's business at the year end.

	Cost	Depreciation	Net book value
	$	$	$
Non-current assets	920 000	345 000	575 000
Current assets			
Inventory		61 000	
Trade receivables		12 000	
Other receivables		3 000	
Cash and cash equivalents		11 000	87 000
Total assets			662 000
Capital			
Opening balance		592 000	
Profit for the year		86 000	
		678 000	
Drawings		(43 000)	635 000
Current liabilities			
Trade payables		25 000	
Other payables		2 000	27 000
Total capital and liabilities			662 000

The business had credit sales of $87 000 and credit purchases of $369 000 during the financial year.

REQUIRED

Calculate the following ratios and state the formula used in each (answers to 2 decimal places):

a current ratio

b acid test ratio

c non-current asset turnover (times)

d trade receivables turnover (days)

e trade payables turnover (days)

f return on capital employed.

> **TIP**
>
> The right-hand figure in the ratio should always be expressed as unity or :1.

> **TIP**
>
> Only credit sales and credit purchases are used in the formula for turnover periods.

> **TIP**
>
> Always round ratios that are calculating days to the nearest whole day.

Knowledge, understanding and analysis

3 Extracts from the financial statements for Janssens Limited and Wouters Limited for 2021 were as follows.

	Janssens		Wouters	
	$000	$000	$000	$000
Revenue		1 230		640
Opening inventory	120		56	
Purchases	680		280	
Closing inventory	(96)	704	(45)	291
Gross profit		526		349

	Janssens		Wouters	
	$000	$000	$000	$000
Non-current assets		830		420
Current assets				
Inventory	96		45	
Trade receivables	32		29	
Cash and cash equivalents	27	155	14	88
		985		508
Shareholders' equity				
Share capital	420		300	
Share premium	30		20	
Retained earnings	60	510	40	360
Long-term loans		400		90
Current liabilities				
Trade payables	53		36	
Tax	22	75	22	58
		475		148
Total equity and liabilities		985		508

REQUIRED

a Calculate the following variances:
- Current ratio
- Acid test ratio
- Non-current asset turnover (times)
- Inventory turnover (days)
- Inventory turnover (times)
- Trade receivables turnover (days)
- Trade payables turnover (days).

b Compare the solvency ratios for each company.

c Compare the efficiency ratios for each company.

d Indicate which company might be the best investment.

> **TIP**
> Current ratio benchmark is 2:1 and acid test ratio benchmark is 1:5:1.

> **TIP**
> The benchmark for trade payables and receivables is 30 days.

Knowledge, understanding, analysis and evaluation

4 Razia, a sole trader, started her business on 1 July 2015 selling ladies' clothing. Razia did not keep proper books of account, but was able to provide the following information.

Summary of bank account for the year ended 30 June 2016			
	$		$
Capital introduced	36 340	Payments to trade payables	80 690
Cash banked	78 780	Shop rental	25 200
Balance c/d	4 330	Shop fixtures and fittings	3 600
		Purchase of motor vehicle	5 800
		Motor expenses	3 140
		Light and heat	1 020
	119 450		119 450

Additional information

1 Total revenue for the year was $92 600. All sales were made for cash.

2 Razia kept no record of her cash drawings.

3 The following expenses were paid from cash takings before the money was banked:

	$
General expenses	950
Assistants' wages	2 870

4 Cash in hand at 30 June 2016 was $1 250.

REQUIRED

a Prepare the cash account, showing clearly the value of Razia's drawings for the year. [4]

Additional information

1. All sales made a gross margin of 40%.
2. During the year, Razia had taken goods, $640 at cost price, for her own use.
3. Inventory at 30 June 2016 had been counted and was valued at cost price $31 900. Razia was aware that some goods had been stolen during the year.
4. Razia owed $8 940 to trade suppliers at 30 June 2016.

REQUIRED

b Calculate the value of inventory stolen during the year ended 30 June 2016 at cost price. [4]

Additional information

1. At 30 June 2016, the following expenses were accrued:

	$
Assistants' wages	120
Light and heat	150

2. Non-current assets should be depreciated as follows:

   Shop fixtures and fittings at 15% per annum using the reducing balance method

   Motor vehicle using the straight-line method over five years. The estimated residual value of the motor vehicle after five years is $400.

3. The annual charge for shop rental is $21 600.

REQUIRED

c Prepare the income statement for the year ended 30 June 2016. [8]

d Calculate, to **two** decimal places, the following ratios at 30 June 2016. State the formula used in each case.

   i Current ratio [2]

   ii Liquid (acid test) ratio [2]

e i Name **two** other ratios a business could calculate to explain its liquidity position. [2]

   ii State **two** limitations of using ratio analysis. [2]

Additional information

Razia's brother has suggested that Razia should increase the mark-up on her goods.

REQUIRED

f Advise Razia whether or not she should increase the mark-up on her goods. Justify your answer by discussing advantages and disadvantages of doing this. [6]

Cambridge International AS&A Level Accounting (9706) Paper 22, Q1, March 2017

[Total: 30]

EXAM-STYLE MULTIPLE CHOICE AND STRUCTURED QUESTIONS

1 The financial data relates to two businesses.

	Frans Ltd	Greta Ltd
Current ratio	3.2 : 1	5.3 : 1
Liquid (acid test) ratio	2.5 : 1	1.9 : 1
Trade receivables turnover (days)	50	35
Trade payables turnover (days)	65	75

Which statement about the comparison of the two businesses' performance is correct?

A Greta Ltd has higher profitability
B Frans Ltd has higher profitability
C Frans Ltd has a better credit control system
D Greta Ltd has a better credit control system

[1]

2 The directors of AB Limited provide the following financial information:

Income Statement (extract) for the year ended 30 April 2016

	$
Revenue	300 000
Purchases (80% on credit)	250 000
Expenses	27 000

All sales earned a uniform gross margin of 20%.

Statement of Financial Position at 30 April 2016	
	$
Non-current assets	160 000
Current assets	
Inventory	38 000
Trade receivables	35 000
Cash and cash equivalents	45 000
	118 000
Total assets	278 000
Equity and liabilities	
Equity	
Ordinary share capital of $1 each	170 000
Share premium	5 000
Retained earnings	25 000
	200 000
Current liabilities	
Trade payables	27 000
Other payables	51 000
	78 000
Total equity and liabilities	278 000

CONTINUED

REQUIRED

a   Prepare the income statement for AB Limited for the year ended 30 April 2016 in as much detail as possible. [4]

b   Suggest **two** reasons why the balance on a retained earnings account may be lower than the profit for the year. [2]

c   Calculate the following ratios to two decimal places.

   i   Rate of inventory turnover (to **two** decimal places) [2]
   ii Liquid (acid test) ratio (to **two** decimal places) [2]
   iii Trade payables turnover (days) [2]

Additional information

The following information is available for XY Limited, a competitor of AB Limited.

rate of inventory turnover	8.75 times
Liquid (acid test) ratio	0.85 : 1
trade payables turnover (days)	42 days

REQUIRED

d   Discuss the performance of AB Limited by comparing the ratios calculated in part **c** with those of XY Limited. [6]

Additional information

CD Limited has been asked by both AB Limited and XY Limited to become their supplier. The directors of CD Limited only wish to supply to one of the two companies.

REQUIRED

e   Advise the directors of CD Limited which company they should supply. Give reasons for your answer. [4]

Additional information

The statements of financial position of AB Limited for the year ended 30 April 2017 showed a draft profit for the year of $71 000. A review of the books of account revealed the following errors:

1   A sales invoice for $234 had been recorded as $324.
2   Returns outwards account had been overcast by $100.
3   Inventory of $1 200 had been omitted from closing inventory.

REQUIRED

f   Calculate the revised profit for the year ended 30 April 2017. [4]

g   Explain the difference between a capital reserve and a revenue reserve. [4]

Cambridge International AS&A Level Accounting (9706) Paper 21, Q1, June 2017

[Total: 30]

CAMBRIDGE INTERNATIONAL AS & A LEVEL ACCOUNTING: WORKBOOK

CONTINUED

3 Nibali has provided the following information for the year ended 31 July 2019.

	$
Closing inventory	50 000
Opening inventory	30 000
Revenue	750 000
Trade receivables	65 000
Trade payables	31 850

Cash sales are 10% of total revenue.

Cash purchases are 25% of total purchases.

Gross margin is 20%.

Nibali's standard credit terms with both customers and suppliers are 30 days.

Industry average inventory turnover is 15 days.

REQUIRED

a Calculate:

  i   inventory turnover in days [2]

  ii trade receivables turnover in days [2]

  iii trade payables turnover in days. [3]

b Discuss the liquidity of Nibali's business based on the available information. [5]

c Identify **three** drawbacks for a business of holding too much inventory. [3]

Cambridge International AS&A Level Accounting (9706) Paper 22, Q2, October 2019

[Total: 15]

Improve this answer

This is a sample answer to **Q2g**.

> Capital reserves can't be used to pay dividends but revenue reserves can.
> Revenue and capital reserves belong to the shareholders.

Your challenge

See if you can improve this answer.

The answer provides some comparison between the two terms, but could be expanded on to show a better level of understanding. A better answer is available online – but write yours out first!

Chapter 31
Analysis and communication of accounting information

LEARNING INTENTIONS

In this chapter you will:

- learn what is overtrading and the working capital cycle
- calculate investment ratios
- interpret investment ratios
- draw conclusions about which companies represent a good investment opportunity and which don't

KEY TERMS

Just-in-time   Overtrading

Key skills exercises

Knowledge and understanding

To answer the questions in this chapter, you need to know and understand:

- overtrading is the (rapid) expansion of a business that does not have the financial resources to support such an expansion
- the working capital cycle is inventory turnover + trade receivables turnover − trade payables turnover
- how to draw conclusions about which companies represent a good investment opportunity and which don't.

You should be able to apply your knowledge and understanding to calculate investment ratios.

Analysis

To answer the questions in this chapter, you need to be able to analyse and interpret investment ratios.

Evaluation

To answer the questions in this chapter, you need to be able to:

- evaluate accounting information regarding investment ratios to make informed recommendations and decisions
- make judgements and draw conclusions based on data.

Knowledge, understanding and analysis

1 Extracts from the statements of financial position for Raphaël for the year ended 31 August 2022 were as follows.

	2022	
	$000	$000
Revenue (all on credit)		853
Opening inventories	124	
Purchases (all on credit)	517	
Closing inventories	(96)	(545)
Gross profit		308
Trade receivables		129
Trade payables		65

REQUIRED

a Calculate the inventory turnover, trade receivables turnover and trade payables turnover and use them to calculate the working capital cycle. Round all of your answers to the nearest day.

Suppose that Raphaël introduces a number of measures to improve his working capital cycle management and achieves the following:

Inventory turnover period reduced by 13 days

Trade receivables turnover period reduced by 12 days

Trade payables turnover period increased by 15 days

b Comment on how this is likely to affect his cash flow position.

c Explain two possible problems arising from actions that Raphaël might have taken to achieve these changes.

WORKED EXAMPLE 1

Extracts from the statements of financial position for Camille Limited for the years ended 31 July 2021 and 2022 were as follows:

	2022	2021
	$000	$000
Revenue (sales)	1 470	1 690
Profit from operations	237	215
Finance costs (interest)	64	72
Inventory	71	85
Trade receivables	43	67
Trade payables	31	47
Ordinary share capital	870	630
Share premium	170	210
General reserves	230	300
Retained earnings	460	580
Long-term loans and debentures	650	890

CONTINUED

REQUIRED

a Calculate the net working assets to revenue, interest cover and gearing ratios for Anais Limited for 2020 and 2021.

b Comment on whether each ratio has improved or worsened, in each case giving a reason for the change.

Answer

a and b

	2022	2021
Net working assets to revenue $$\frac{\text{Net working assets}}{\text{Revenue (sales)}} \times 100$$ Net working assets: inventory + trade receivables − trade payables	$\frac{71 + 43 - 31}{1\,470} \times 100 = 5.65\%$	$\frac{85 + 67 - 47}{1\,690} \times 100 = 6.21\%$
	These figures suggest that Camille Limited was making better use of the net working assets at its disposal in 2022. However, we do not know whether the current or acid test ratios have improved as we do not have details of cash, bank or accruals and prepayments.	
Interest cover $$\frac{\text{Profit from operations}}{\text{Interest payable}}$$	$\frac{237}{64} = 3.70$ times	$\frac{215}{72} = 2.99$ times
	These figures indicate that Camille Limited has a better interest cover in 2022 and is now better equipped to meet its interest payments. The main contributor has been an increase in profit from operations.	
Gearing $$\frac{\text{Fixed cost capital}}{\text{Share capital + all reserves + non-current liabilities}}$$	$\frac{650}{870 + 860 + 650} \times 100 = 27.31\%$	$\frac{890}{630 + 1\,090 + 890} \times 100 = 34.10\%$
	The gearing ratio for Camille Limited has improved in 2022 largely due to a share issue and the repayment of some of its loans (or redemption of debentures). Both figures represent fairly low gearing.	

Knowledge, understanding, analysis and evaluation

2 Extracts from the statements of financial position for Anais Limited for the years ended 30 September 2020 and 2021 were as follows.

	2021	2020
	$000	$000
Revenue (sales)	1 980	1 530
Profit from operations	387	296
Finance costs (interest)	75	80
Inventory	88	42
Trade receivables	123	97
Trade payables	69	41
Ordinary share capital	1 040	810
Share premium	250	200
General reserves	280	280
Retained earnings	620	470
Long-term loans and debentures	860	900

REQUIRED

a   Calculate the net working assets to revenue, interest cover and gearing ratios for Anais Limited for 2020 and 2021.

b   Comment on whether each ratio has improved or worsened, in each case giving a reason for the change.

WORKED EXAMPLE 2

The following information was available for Charles Limited and Blanche Limited at 31 October 2022.

	Charles Limited	Blanche Limited
	$000	$000
Profit for the year	257	186
Ordinary share capital	320	170

Additional information

- The share capital of Charles Limited consisted of ordinary shares of $0.50 each where the market price at 31 October 2022 was $1.25. Paid or proposed dividends relating to 2022 amounted to $64 000.
- The share capital of Blanche Limited consisted of ordinary shares of $0.25 each where the market price at 31 October 2022 was $0.75. Paid or proposed dividends relating to 2022 amounted to $53 000.

REQUIRED

Calculate for *both* companies, the following ratios at 31 October 2022:

- earnings per share
- price / earnings ratio
- dividend per share
- dividend yield
- dividend cover

Answer

Charles Limited and Blanche Limited

	Charles Limited	Blanche Limited
Earnings per share $\dfrac{\text{Profit for the year}}{\text{Number of ordinary shares}}$	$\dfrac{257}{640} = \$0.40$ per share	$\dfrac{186}{680} = \$0.27$ per share
Price / earnings ratio $\dfrac{\text{Market price per share}}{\text{Earnings per share}}$	$\dfrac{1.25}{0.40} = 3.13$ times	$\dfrac{0.75}{0.27} = 2.78$ times
Dividend per share $\dfrac{\text{Annual ordinary dividend}}{\text{Number of ordinary shares}}$	$\dfrac{64}{640} = \$0.10$ per share	$\dfrac{53}{680} = \$0.08$ per share
Dividend yield $\dfrac{\text{Dividend per share}}{\text{Market price per share}} \times 100$	$\dfrac{0.10}{1.25} \times 100 = 8\%$	$\dfrac{0.08}{0.75} \times 100 = 10.67\%$

CONTINUED

	Charles Limited	Blanche Limited
Dividend cover		
$\dfrac{\text{Profit for the year}}{\text{Annual ordinary dividend}}$	$\dfrac{257}{64} = 4.02$ times	$\dfrac{186}{53} = 3.51$ times

3 The following information is available for two companies, Hugo Limited and Lola Limited, for the year ended 31 March 2021.

	Hugo Limited	Lola Limited
	$	$
Operating profit	2 360 000	1 546 000
Debenture interest	0	450 000
Tax	879 000	420 000
Preference dividend	220 000	70 000
Ordinary dividends	375 000	340 000
Retained profit for the year	824 000	236 000
Ordinary shares of $1 each	0	3 800 000
Ordinary shares of 50c each	3 820 000	0
7% preference shares	3 860 000	1 200 000
Share premium	1 250 000	2 000 000
Revaluation reserve	470 000	0
Retained earnings	1 630 000	660 000
8% debentures	0	3 200 000
Market price per ordinary share	1.05	2.25

a Calculate the following investment ratios for the two companies:

    i gearing ratio

    ii earnings per share

    iii price / earnings ratio

    iv dividend per share

    v dividend yield

    vi dividend cover.

b Comment on which company presents the best return for its shareholders, using the ratios.

4   The following information has been extracted from the books of account of M plc at 31 December 2016.

	$
Profit for the year	550 000
Ordinary shares ($1)	900 000
6% Preference shares (non-redeemable)	200 000
5% Debentures (2025)	100 000

The market price of one ordinary share at 31 December 2016 was $1.75.

Dividends of $0.08 per ordinary share have been paid during the year ended 31 December 2016.

REQUIRED

a   State **two** advantages of ratio analysis to a user of the financial statements.

b   Calculate the following ratios at 31 December 2016 to **two** decimal places:
   i   earnings per share
   ii   price / earnings ratio
   iii dividend yield
   iv   dividend cover.

Additional information

For the year ended 31 December **2016**:
- The profit for the year was 10% greater than the previous year.
- There had been a share issue of 300 000 ordinary shares.
- The dividend per share had fallen by 20%.

REQUIRED

c   Calculate the same four ratios as in part **b** at 31 December 2015 to two decimal places. The market price of one ordinary share at 31 December 2015 was $1.50.

Additional information

An investor, Bevin, is considering acquiring ordinary shares in M plc. He has been advised that the directors intend to raise extra funds by issuing a further 5% debenture (repayable 2027).

REQUIRED

d   i   Analyse the performance of M plc over the two years 2015 and 2016 using the ratios calculated in parts **b** and **c**.
   ii Advise Bevin whether or not he should make the intended investment. Justify your answer.

Cambridge International AS&A Level Accounting (9706) Paper 31, Q3, October 2017

EXAM-STYLE STRUCTURED QUESTIONS

1 XY Limited produces annual statements of financial position in accordance with International Accounting Standards. Its non-current assets consist of both tangible and intangible assets.

REQUIRED

a Define an intangible asset in accordance with IAS 38. [3]

Additional information

The following are the selected balances from the trial balance produced for the year ended 31 March 2016.

	$
Revenue	680 000
Purchases	378 000
Distribution costs	70 152
Administrative expenses	145 267
Inventories at 1 April 2019	117 257
Allowance for irrecoverable debts	1 569
6% Debenture (2026)	150 000
Trade receivables	87 450
Trade payables	26 550

The directors of XY Limited also provided the following information:

1 The inventories at 31 March 2016 were valued at cost, $108 543. This included a batch of inventory that had been valued at its cost price of $50 000. It can now only be sold for $35 000.

2 The debenture was issued on 1 October 2015 and no interest has been paid at 31 March 2016.

3 The allowance for irrecoverable debts is to be increased to 2% of trade receivables. The increase is to be split equally between distribution costs and administrative expenses.

4 There was an amount of $2 480 outstanding for administrative expenses.

5 There was a prepayment of $3 635 for distribution costs.

6 The tax charge for the year is estimated to be $12 385.

REQUIRED

b Prepare the income statement for XY Limited for the year ended 31 March 2016. [13]

Additional information

All of the company revenues and purchases are operated on a credit basis. The company allows all of its customers 30 days' credit. The company is also allowed 30 days' credit by all of its suppliers.

REQUIRED

c Calculate the working capital cycle (in days). [4]

d Discuss whether or not the liquidity of XY Limited could be improved. Justify your answer. [5]

Cambridge International AS&A Level Accounting (9706) Paper 32, Q1, March 2017

[Total: 25]

CONTINUED

2 Winterbottom plc and Ramsey plc are two similar trading companies that have been successfully trading for many years. Their statements of financial position prepared for internal purposes are shown here:

Income statements for the year ended 30 June 2015

	Winterbottom	Ramsey
	$000	$000
Revenue	6 279	4 527
Cost of sales	(2 075)	(1 254)
Gross profit	4 204	3 273
Depreciation	(1 285)	(720)
Other expenses	(1 227)	(992)
Profit on disposal of non-current assets	28	15
Profit from operations	1 720	1 576
Finance charges	(300)	(180)
Profit before taxation	1 420	1 396
Taxation	(317)	(312)
Retained profit for the year	1 103	1 084

Statements of financial positions at 30 June 2015

	Winterbottom	Ramsey
	$000	$000
Non-current assets	9 864	6 192
Current assets		
Inventories	782	451
Trade receivables	1 362	742
Cash and cash equivalents	135	98
	2 279	1 291
Total assets	12 143	7 483
Equity and liabilities		
Equity		
Ordinary share capital ($1 each)	4 500	2 500
Share premium	200	–
Retained earnings	1 447	1 244
	6 147	3 744
Current liabilities		
Trade payables	679	427
Taxation	317	312
	996	739
Non-current liabilities		
6% Debentures (2024)	5 000	3 000
Total equity and liabilities	12 143	7 483

CONTINUED

Additional information

Neither company has paid an interim dividend during the year ended 30 June 2015.

- The directors of Winterbottom plc propose a dividend of $0.20 per share and those of Ramsey plc $0.35 per share for the year ended 30 June 2015.
- At 30 June 2015, the market value of an ordinary share in Winterbottom plc is $3.50 and in Ramsey plc $2.75.

REQUIRED

a Calculate the following ratios for **both** companies to **two** decimal places. [10]

    i   income gearing
    ii   earnings per share
    iii price / earnings ratio
    iv dividend yield
    v   dividend cover.

Additional information

Alfredo is considering investing in one of the companies but is uncertain which will offer the best return.

Recent industry averages were as follows:

Income gearing 20.25%   Dividend yield 10.45%

Earnings per share $0.33   Dividend cover 1.20 times

Price earnings ratio 12.50

REQUIRED

b Analyse the performance of both companies compared to the industry averages. [10]

c Advise Alfredo which company he should invest in. Justify your answer. [5]

Cambridge International AS&A Level Accounting (9706) Paper 33, Q4, June 2016

[Total: 25]

Improve this answer

This is a sample answer to **Q2c**.

> Alfredo should choose Ramsey. Ramsey's share price is lower and their dividend payment is higher. Meaning you will receive more back than what you would from Winterbottom and pay less to invest in Ramsey than Winterbottom.

Your challenge

See if you can improve this answer. In order to answer this question fully, the two companies should be compared against each other. The data from the ratios in part a should be referenced to help justify the final decision.

A better answer is available online – but write yours out first!

Part 3
Cost and management accounting

> # Chapter 32
> # Costing of materials and labour

LEARNING INTENTIONS

In this chapter you will:

- understand the difference between financial and management accounting
- know what unit costs are
- analyse costs into direct and indirect costs
- record and value direct and indirect materials using FIFO and AVCO methods
- record and value direct and indirect labour

KEY TERMS

Average cost (AVCO)   Bonus payment   Cost accounting   Cost unit   First in, first out (FIFO)   Just-in-time (JIT)   Management accounting   Overtime payment   Overtime premium   Periodic inventory   Perpetual inventory   Piece rate

Key skills exercises

Knowledge and understanding

To answer the questions in this chapter, you need to know and understand:

- financial accounting is the recording and reporting of historical information
- management accounting is the process of preparing financial information that can be used by managers as a basis for making decisions that will affect the future performance of the business
- cost units are the unit of output of a business to which costs can be charged
- FIFO is a method of inventory valuation that assumes that the first items to be purchased will be the first to be used in production and sold
- AVCO is a method of inventory valuation that uses a weighted average to calculate the value of inventory each time new inventory is purchased
- Just-in-time is a system of manufacturing that uses the principle that supplies should be received exactly when they are needed in the production process and do not need to be stored by the business beforehand.

You should be able to apply your knowledge and understanding to record and value direct and indirect materials using FIFO and AVCO methods, and record and value direct and indirect labour.

Analysis

To answer the questions in this chapter, you need to be able to analyse costs into direct and indirect costs.

WORKED EXAMPLE 1

Gert sells one product. He had no inventory at the start of July. He provides the following information for the month of July.

Date	Purchases	Price per unit	Sales
Jul 3	16	$640	
9			5
16	10	$680	
19			6
23			8
30	8	$720	

REQUIRED

Calculate the quantity and value of the inventory throughout July using FIFO.

Answer

Date	Receipts		Issues		Inventory	
	Units	Price per unit	Units	Value ($)	Units	Value ($)
July 3	16	640			16	16 × 640 = 10 240
9			5	5 × 640 = 3 200	11	11 × 640 = 7 040
16	10	680			21	11 × 640 = 7 040
						10 × 680 = 6 800
						Total = 13 840
19			6	6 × 640 = 3 840	15	5 × 640 = 3 200
						10 × 680 = 6 800
						Total = 10 000
23			8	5 × 640 = 3 200	7	7 × 680 = 4 760
				3 × 680 = 2 040		
				Total = 5 240		
30	8	720			15	7 × 680 = 4 760
						8 × 720 = 5 760
						Total = 10 520

WORKED EXAMPLE 2

Calculate, using Gert's information from Worked example 1, the quantity and value of the inventory throughout July using AVCO.

Answer

Date	Receipts		Issues		Inventory	
	Units	Price per unit	Units	Value ($)	Units	Value ($)
July 3	16	640			16	16 × 640 = 10 240
9			5	5 × 640 = 3 200	11	11 × 640 = 7 040
16	10	680			21	(7 040 + 6 800) ÷ 21 = 659.05
						21 × 659.05 = 13 840.05
19			6	6 × 659.05 = 3 954.30	15	15 × 659.05 = 9 885.75
23			8	8 × 659.05 = 5 272.40	7	7 × 659.05 = 4 613.35
30	8	720			15	(4 613.35 + 5 760) ÷ 15 = 691.56
						15 × 691.56 = 10 373.40

Knowledge, understanding and analysis

1 Bertus sells one product. He had no inventory at the start of February. He provides the following information for the month of February.

Date	Purchases	Price per unit	Sales
Feb 2	120	25	
8			35
13			42
20	100	28	
26			56
28	80	29	

REQUIRED

a Calculate the quantity and value of the inventory throughout February using each of the following methods:

   i   FIFO

   ii AVCO.

b State which method gives the higher inventory valuation at the end of February. Explain why this occurs.

2 Jacques began business in year 1 and stopped trading at the end of year 3. The following information is given for each of the three years.

> **TIP**
>
> FIFO assumes that the first items to be bought will be the first to be used in production or sold. This leaves the remaining inventory as the most recently purchased items at the most recent purchase prices.

> **TIP**
>
> AVCO does not make any assumption about which purchases are used or sold first. Instead, a new average value is calculated each time a new delivery of inventory is received.

	Year 1	Year 2	Year 3
	$	$	$
Revenue	2 400	3 200	3 700
Purchases	1 100	1 300	1 000
Closing inventory:			
Using FIFO	100	120	110
Using AVCO	90	110	100

a Calculate the gross profit for each of the three years using:

   i FIFO

   ii AVCO.

b Explain which method resulted in the highest gross profit at the end of year 1.

3

Worker's name	Hourly rate	Hours worked	Units produced
Anja	$7.40	48	620
Adriaan	$8.60	52	750
Katrien	$7.90	54	680

A company pays its workers for a 45-hour week. The company pays time and a half for every extra hour worked above 45 hours.

The company also pays a bonus of $1 per unit for production over 600 units per week. Each worker is guaranteed a minimum wage of $420 per week.

REQUIRED

Calculate the weekly wage for each of the workers.

4 Indicate whether the following are direct or indirect costs. The first one has been done as an example.

	Direct costs	Indirect costs
cleaning materials		✓
carriage inwards		
factory managers salary		
rent		
royalties		
depreciation		
licence fees		
production materials		
heating and lighting		
machinery lubricating oil		
production workers wages		
cleaners salaries		

EXAM-STYLE MULTIPLE CHOICE AND STRUCTURED QUESTIONS

1 The following information is available for the inventory of a business.

Jan 1 opening inventory of 130 units at $28 per unit
 9 sales of 43 units
 14 purchased 70 units at $30 per unit
 21 sales of 97 units
 29 purchased 50 units at $31 per unit

The business uses the AVCO method of valuing inventory. What is the value of the inventory at 31 January?

A $3 350.00
B $3 410.00
C $3 316.75
D $3 283.50 [1]

2 A business values its inventory using the FIFO method. The following transactions took place.

Date		Units
April 3	opening inventory	500 at $360 each
15	purchases	300 at $380 each
28	sales	600 at $520 each

What was the value of the closing inventory at the end of April?

A $104 000
B $76 000
C $73 500
D $72 000 [1]

3 Elsje's business had an inventory of 400 units at $12 each at 31 August. She sells her product at $18 per unit. The following information is available for September.

Date	Quantity received	Price per unit ($)	Sales quantity
Sept 6	130	13	
10			220
19	140	14	
23			250

REQUIRED

a Calculate the value of the inventory at the end of September using the AVCO method on a perpetual basis. [10]

b Calculate the gross profit for September. [5]

[Total: 15]

Chapter 33
Absorption costing

LEARNING INTENTIONS

In this chapter you will:
- understand unit costs and cost centres
- allocate and apportion overheads
- calculate overhead absorption rates
- analyse under-absorption and over-absorption of overheads
- use absorption cost data to support selling price decisions
- explain the usefulness of using absorption costing

KEY TERMS

Absorption costing   Allocation of costs   Apportionment of costs   Cost centre   Over-absorption
Overhead absorption rate (OAR)   Production cost centres   Service cost centres   Under-absorption   Unit cost

Key skills exercises

Knowledge and understanding

To answer the questions in this chapter, you need to know and understand:
- unit costs are the average cost of producing one unit of a product or service
- a cost centre is any part of a business to which costs may be attributed, such as a department
- absorption costing is a method of calculating the cost of making one unit of a product that involves apportioning overheads into cost units
- allocation of costs is charging overheads directly to the cost centre(s) that can be identified with them
- apportionment of costs is the process of charging costs that can't be identified with specific cost centres using a suitable basis.

You should be able to apply your knowledge and understanding to allocate and apportion overheads and calculate overhead absorption rates.

Analysis

To answer the questions in this chapter, you need to be able to analyse the under-absorption and over-absorption of overheads.

Evaluation

To answer the questions in this chapter, you need to be able to:
- evaluate accounting information regarding absorption costing to make informed recommendations and decisions
- make judgements and draw conclusions based on financial and non-financial data.

WORKED EXAMPLE 1

Petra Limited has the following information available regarding their production department.

	Machining department	Assembly department
Direct machine hours	35 000	5 000
Direct labour hours	20 000	25 000
Cost of machinery	280 000	56 000
Floor area (square metres)	28 000	12 000

The factory overheads for the year were:

	$
Heating and light	21 000
Rent	18 000
Machinery insurance	30 000
Depreciation	63 000

REQUIRED

Prepare an overhead apportionment table apportioning the factory overheads to the appropriate departments.

Answer

Overhead apportionment for Petra Limited				
Overhead	Basis	Ratio	Machining	Assembly
		Machining : Assembly	$	$
Heating and light	Floor area	7 : 3	14 700	6 300
Rent	Floor area	7 : 3	12 600	5 400
Machinery insurance	Cost of machinery	5 : 1	25 000	5 000
Depreciation	Cost of machinery	5 : 1	52 500	10 500
			104 800	27 200

Ratio workings

Floor area   Machining : Assembly
                28 000 : 12 000   (divide both ratios by the same number till they are as small as can be, in this
                    7 : 3   example divide both sides by 4 000)

Cost of machinery   Machining : Assembly
                           280 000 : 56 000   (divide both ratios by the same number till they are as small as can be, in this
                           5 : 1   example divide both sides by 56 000)

Department costs

Heating and light $21 000 ÷ 10 (ratio of 7 : 3 added together) = $2 100
                        Machining: $2 100 × 7 = $14 700
                        Assembly: $2 100 × 3 = $6 300

Rent $18 000 ÷ 10 (ratio of 7 : 3 added together) = $1 800
                        Machining: $1 800 × 7 = $12 600
                        Assembly: $1 800 × 3 = $5 400

> **CONTINUED**
>
> Machinery insurance $30 000 ÷ 6 (ratio of 5 : 1 added together) = $5 000
>   Machining: $5 000 × 5 = $25 000
>   Assembly: $5 000 × 1 = $5 000
>
> Depreciation $63 000 ÷ 6 (ratio of 5 : 1 added together) = $10 500
>   Machining: $10 500 × 5 = $52 500
>   Assembly: $10 500 × 1 = $10 500

Knowledge and understanding

1 Heinz Limited has the following information available regarding their production department.

	Machining department	Cutting department
Direct machine hours	42 000	15 000
Direct labour hours	26 000	38 000
Cost of machinery	320 000	80 000
Floor area (square metres)	36 000	15 000

The factory overheads for the year were:

	$
Heating and light	20 400
Factory maintenance	17 000
Machinery insurance	15 000
Depreciation	65 000
Machinery repairs	35 000

REQUIRED

Prepare an overhead apportionment table apportioning the factory overheads to the appropriate departments.

> **WORKED EXAMPLE 2**
>
> Wash Ltd makes washing machines and has two departments, machining and finishing. The machining department uses more direct machine hours and the finishing department uses more direct labour hours. The total overheads for July is $339 000 and split by each department as follows:
>
> | Machining department: | $265 000 |
> |---|---|
> | Finishing department: | $74 000 |
>
> The machining department has 12 500 machine hours and the finishing department has 10 000 labour hours.
>
> Each washing machine takes 4 hours of machine time in the machining department and 1½ hours of labour in the finishing department, at a rate of $12 per hour, to manufacture.
>
> Each washing machine uses $450 worth of material.

> **CONTINUED**
>
> **REQUIRED**
>
> a Calculate the amount of overhead absorbed by *each* department.
>
> b Calculate the unit cost.
>
> **Answer**
>
> a The overhead absorbed per department is:
>
>   i   Machining department: $\dfrac{265\,000}{12\,500} = \$21.20$ per machine hour
>
>   ii Finishing department: $\dfrac{74\,000}{10\,000} = \$7.40$ per labour hour
>
> b
>
> | | Washing machine |
> |---|---|
> | Direct materials | $450.00 |
> | Direct labour (1½ hours × $12 per hour) | $18.00 |
> | Machining department overheads ($21.20 × 4) | $84.80 |
> | Finishing department overheads ($7.40 × 1½) | $11.10 |
> | Full cost | $563.90 |

2 Shirt Ltd makes shirts and has two departments, cutting and finishing. The cutting department uses more direct machine hours and the finishing department uses more direct labour hours. The total overheads figure for October is $124 000 and split by each department as follows:

Cutting department:	$76 000
Finishing department:	$48 000

The cutting department has 8 000 machine hours and the finishing department has 12 000 labour hours.

Each shirt takes ½ an hour of machine hours in the cutting department and 3 hours of labour in the finishing department, at a rate of $9 per hour, to manufacture.

Each shirt uses 1.2 metres of material at $25 per metre.

REQUIRED

a Calculate the amount of overhead absorbed by *each* department.

b Calculate the unit cost.

Knowledge, understanding and analysis

3 Klaus Limited uses machine hours to calculate its overhead absorption rate. It has provided the following information about its overhead expenditure.

	Six months to 30 June	Six months to 31 December
	$	$
Budgeted overhead	240 000	270 000
Budgeted machine hours	12 000	12 000
Actual overhead	255 000	283 000
Actual machine hours	11 800	12 200

REQUIRED

Calculate the under-absorption or over-absorption of overhead in both periods. State in each case whether the overhead was under- or over-absorbed.

Knowledge, understanding, analysis and evaluation

4 Aramis operates a manufacturing business. He has been advised that he should use absorption costing in his factory.

REQUIRED

a Explain two drawbacks for a business of using a budgeted overhead absorption rate. [4]

Additional information

Aramis's factory comprises three departments – drilling, finishing and maintenance. The maintenance department costs consist of maintenance engineers' wages. The manufacturing process is machine intensive. The overheads of the drilling and finishing departments are made up of allocated costs and an apportioned share of the maintenance department.

The following budgeted information for the six months ended 31 March is available.

	Drilling	Finishing	Maintenance
Allocated costs	$435 720	$748 900	$208 000
Use of maintenance	38%	62%	
Machine hours	27 530	32 270	

REQUIRED

b i Allocate the maintenance department overhead costs to the drilling and finishing departments. [2]

ii Calculate, to **two** decimal places, a budgeted overhead absorption rate for the drilling and finishing departments. [2]

Additional information

The following information relates to maintenance engineers' wages during the six-month period:

Total hours worked   7 500

Total basic hours worked   6 800

Workers are paid a basic rate of $30 per hour. Overtime is paid at 1.5 times the basic rate.

REQUIRED

c Calculate the total actual wages for the maintenance engineers for the six-month period. [3]

Additional information

In addition to the actual maintenance wages, the following **actual** information for the six months ended 31 March has been made available:

	Drilling	Finishing
Total overhead costs	$427 360	$713 630
Machine hours	25 110	31 976

REQUIRED

d Calculate the over or under-absorption of production overheads for **each** department for the six-month period. [8]

*Cambridge International AS&A Level Accounting (9706) Paper 22,
Q4a, b, c & d, October 2019*

[Total: 19]

EXAM-STYLE MULTIPLE CHOICE AND STRUCTURED QUESTIONS

1 A business absorbs overheads based on labour hours.
   During May 2021 it had the following results.

Budgeted overheads	$40 320
Budgeted labour hours	1 680
Actual overheads	$42 300
Actual labour hours	2 200

Which statement is correct?

A Overheads were under-absorbed by $10 500
B Overheads were under-absorbed by $1 980
C Overheads were over-absorbed by $10 500
D Overheads were over-absorbed by $1 980 [1]

2 A manufacturing business has the following information.

Budgeted factory overheads	$151 200
Budgeted machine hours	36 000
Actual factory overheads	$174 800
Actual machine hours	38 000

What is the overhead absorption rate per machine hour?

A $3.98   C $4.20
B $4.60   D $4.86 [1]

CONTINUED

3 Bruna Limited is a manufacturing company. It operates three production departments and two service departments. The costs are allocated to each department as follows:

	Production departments			Service departments	
	Machining	Assembly	Finishing	Stores	Canteen
	$	$	$	$	$
Indirect labour	253 000	290 000	340 100	52 000	78 000
Other indirect overhead costs	205 000	90 000	225 000	88 000	92 000

The service departments' costs are allocated to the production departments as follows:

Stores in proportion to the number of stores requisitions.

Canteen in proportion to the number of employees.

The following information is available:

	Machining	Assembly	Finishing
Direct labour hours	15 000	60 000	40 000
Machine hours	45 000	30 000	25 000
Number of employees	5	6	9
Number of stores requisitions	6 300	4 500	7 200

REQUIRED

a Calculate, to **two** decimal places, a suitable overhead absorption rate for **each** of the **three** production departments. [13]

Additional information

Bruna Limited has been approached by a customer to quote for one of their products. This will require the following:

Direct materials   20 kilos at $5 per kilo

Direct labour   10 hours at $9 per hour

Direct labour hours and machine hours required in each department will be:

	Machining	Assembly	Finishing
Direct labour hours	5	3	2
Machine time	2 hours	30 minutes	20 minutes

It is the company's practice to achieve a gross margin of 40% on all its products.

REQUIRED

b Calculate the total price to quote to the customer. [7]

Additional information

The directors are considering changing from departmental overhead absorption rates to one factory-wide rate.

CONTINUED

REQUIRED

c Advise the directors whether or not they should make this change. Justify your answer. [4]

d Explain how over absorption **and** under absorption of overheads can affect the profit of a manufacturing business. [6]

Cambridge International AS&A Level Accounting (9706) Paper 22, Q4, June 2016

[Total: 30]

Improve this answer

This is a sample answer to **Q3c**.

> One factory-wide rate is easier and cheaper to calculate than overhead absorption rates. It is however less accurate.

Your challenge

See if you can improve this answer. Some level of justification has been given here, but the answer lacks detail, along with a final decision.

A better answer is available online – but write yours out first!

Chapter 34
Unit, job and batch costing

LEARNING INTENTIONS

In this chapter you will:

- know the difference between continuous and specific order operations
- understand unit, job and batch costing methods
- apply unit, job or batch costing principles, manufacturing and service businesses
- prepare costing statements and price quotations

KEY TERMS

Batch costing   Job costing   Unit costing

Key skills exercises

Knowledge and understanding

To answer the questions in this chapter, you need to know and understand:

- continuous operations are typically those in which a single type of good is produced and the cost units are identical
- specific order operations are those that are performed in response to special orders received from customers and may be classified according to whether the operations consist of individual jobs, or the production of batches of identical units for a customer
- unit costing is the costing method to find the cost of a single cost unit
- job costing is a costing method that calculates the cost of meeting a specific customer order or job
- batch costing is a costing method to find the cost of a batch of items produced.

You should also be able to apply your knowledge and understanding of unit, job or batch costing principles to manufacturing and service businesses.

Analysis

To answer the questions in this chapter, you need to be able to:

- analyse financial accounting information and cost and management accounting information
- select, calculate and interpret relevant data and information
- communicate outcomes in the most appropriate form.

Evaluation

To answer the questions in this chapter, you need to be able to:

- evaluate financial information regarding costing methods to make informed recommendations and decisions
- make judgements and draw conclusions based on financial and non-financial data.

GARMENTS GALORE

Garments Galore is a clothing manufacturer in Bangkok, Thailand. Garments Galore manufactures polo shirts and t-shirts. Garments Galore also offers custom-made polo shirts to their clients' specifications.

There are lots of things that go into the pricing of a single piece of clothing. Purchasing of raw materials, cost of dyeing, knitting, printing, cost of trims and accessories used, transport cost, packaging, banking charges and overheads are all included in the price.

Garments Galore makes use of unit, job and batch costing. They have ready-made polo shirts and t-shirts that customers can buy from them at a unit cost. They also offer custom-made polo shirts where customers can request their specifications; job costing is used for these custom-made polo shirts. Garments Galore would make use of batch costing if a customer were to order a large quantity of the same shirt.

Knowledge and understanding

1 Garments Galore produces a single type of t-shirt. The following information is for the business for one year:

Number of t-shirts produced	6 000
Direct labour	$15 000
Direct materials	$12 000
Indirect expenses	$30 000

REQUIRED

Calculate the unit cost of producing one t-shirt.

WORKED EXAMPLE 1

Boon-Nam owns a flooring business named 'Carpet Man Flooring'. He has been asked by a customer to give a quote on putting carpets into their house.

Boon-Nam adds 30% to the total cost of each job to provide profit for the business.

Boon-Nam estimates the materials will cost $43 per square metre and the job requires 50 square metres. The job will take 40 hours in total and the work will be divided equally between two employees at a rate of $18 per hour. The overhead absorption rate is $3.50 per labour hour taken on the job.

REQUIRED

a Calculate the total cost for the job.

Answer

	Estimated costs
	$
Direct materials (50 × $43)	2 150
Direct labour (40 hours × $18)	720
Overhead (40 hours × $3.50)	140
Total cost	3 010

CONTINUED

b Calculate the final price Boon-Nam should quote the customer.

Answer

Total cost	3010
Add profit (30% of cost)	903
Quoted price	3913

Knowledge, understanding, analysis and evaluation

2 Garments Galore has the option to offer custom-made polo shirts. They have been asked by a customer, Chaiya, to make a custom-made polo shirt. Garments Galore estimates that the project will require 6 hours of their time, which they charge at $10 per hour. Overheads are recovered at the rate of $4 per labour hour. Material is expected to cost $36 and Garments Galore aims to set their prices at 25% above the cost of a job.

a Prepare a statement to show the amount Garments Galore will charge for this job.

Additional information

The customer has looked at Garments Galore's quote. Chaiya has offered them a fee of $125 for the work instead.

REQUIRED

b Advise Garments Galore whether they should accept the work. Justify your answer.

WORKED EXAMPLE 2

Buppha Saetang is opening a new business. He would like to have 10 000 identical business cards printed to hand out to people advertising his business. He approaches a printing company, Phongwarin Print, to give him a quote on the cost of these 10 000 business cards. Buppha Saetang places the order at a negotiated price of $35 000 for the 10 000 business cards.

Phongwarin Print has the following information available:

Designing:	OAR $25 per labour hour
Printing:	OAR $40 per direct machine hour

The budgeted costs incurred in the production of 10 000 business cards were:

Direct materials	$14 000
Direct labour:	
Designing	25 hours at $12 per hour
Printing	40 hours at $15 per hour

A total of 58 machine hours were required in the printing department for the printing of the business cards.

Phongwarin Print charges its administration expenses at 40% on the total cost of production.

CONTINUED

REQUIRED

a Calculate the cost of producing the batch.

b Calculate the profit from producing the batch.

Answer

The batch cost, cost per business card and profit per business card are calculated as follows:

	Costs for batch of 10 000 business cards	$	$
	Direct materials		14 000
	Direct labour:		
	Designing (25 × $12)	300	
	Printing (40 × $15)	600	900
	Prime cost		14 900
	Production overheads:		
	Designing (25 × $25)	625	
	Printing (58 × $40)	2 320	2 945
	Cost of production		17 845
	Add administration costs		7 138
a	Total cost of batch of 10 000 business cards		24 983
b	Profit		10 017
	Price		35 000

Knowledge and understanding

3 Garments Galore has received a request for a quote for 150 polo shirts for a golf tournament being held at Panya Indra Golf Club.

Garments Galore has two production departments:

Cutting	OAR $3 per direct labour hour
Finishing	OAR $2 per direct labour hour

The budgeted costs incurred in the production of 150 polo shirts were:

Direct materials	$6 000
Direct labour:	
Cutting	300 hours at $3 per hour
Finishing	450 hours at $3 per hour

A mark-up on cost of 25% is required for all sales.

REQUIRED

a Calculate the cost of manufacturing the batch of 150 polo shirts.

b Calculate the price that should be quoted for the batch of 150 polo shirts.

c Calculate the cost of one polo shirt.

EXAM-STYLE MULTIPLE CHOICE AND STRUCTURED QUESTIONS

1 A manufacturer of gloves produces 20 000 pairs each month. It has the following information available for a month.

Sales revenue	$1 300 000
Direct materials	$260 000
Direct labour	$210 000
Overheads	$650 000

What is the unit cost?

A $65

B $45.50

C $43

D $56 [1]

2 Which of the following should use job costing?

A painting the walls of a house

B designing a set of shirts for a football team

C a pallet of bricks for a building

D manufacturing a school bag for a school [1]

3 Anna has a manufacturing business with two production departments and two service departments. She makes circuit boards for electronic games using batch costing.

REQUIRED

a Explain what is meant by 'batch costing'. [2]

Additional information

The following budgeted annual data for Anna is available:

	Production departments		Service departments	
	Assembly	Machining	Stores	Canteen
Overheads	$36 000	$50 000	$6 250	$2 500
Direct labour hours	6 000	3 500	–	–
Machine hours	2 500	5 500	–	–

The following information is also available:

	Assembly	Machining	Stores
Number of orders	800	1 200	–
Use of canteen	65%	25%	10%

CONTINUED

REQUIRED

b Re-apportion the service departments' costs to the production departments using a suitable basis for each. [3]

	Assembly	Machining	Stores	Canteen
	$	$	$	$
Allocated overheads	36 000	50 000	6 250	2 500
Re-apportionment of canteen				
Subtotal				
Re-apportionment of stores				
Total				

c Calculate a suitable overhead absorption rate for **each** production department to **two** decimal places. [4]

Additional information

A typical order for a batch of 1 000 circuit boards requires the following:

Direct materials $48 000

Direct labour
    Assembly department   500 hours at $12 per hour
    Machining department   300 hours at $8 per hour

Machine hours
    Assembly department   210 hours
    Machining department   500 hours

Selling and administration costs $7 000

REQUIRED

d Calculate, to **two** decimal places, the total cost per circuit board based on a batch of 1 000 units. [6]

Additional information

Sally, a customer, asked for a quote for an order for 75 circuit boards. Anna calculates the selling price to give a profit margin of 60%.

REQUIRED

e Prepare a quote showing the total selling price. [3]

Additional information

Sally considered the quoted price and has asked for a discount of 5%.

REQUIRED

f Advise Anna whether or not she should allow Sally the discount. Justify your answer. [5]

Cambridge International AS&A Level Accounting (9706) Paper 21, Q4a, b, c, d, & e, October 2017

[Total: 23]

CONTINUED

Improve this answer

This is a sample answer to **Q1f**.

> Anna would still be making a profit on the sale, even with the discount. If Anna doesn't give the discount she may lose the order and the potential of a repeat customer. Anna should allow Sally the discount.

Your challenge

See if you can improve this answer.

The sample answer does give a decision and provides some brief justification, but further explanation could be added to show deeper understanding. A better answer is available online – but write yours out first!

> Chapter 35
Marginal costing

LEARNING INTENTIONS

In this chapter you will:

- understand the behaviour of variable, semi-variable, fixed and stepped costs
- use and calculate contribution, the contribution to sales ratio and marginal costs
- understand and calculate break-even point and margin of safety
- interpret and analyse break-even information
- evaluate cost-volume-profit data
- evaluate pricing and other management decisions using marginal costing
- make recommendations on business decisions using marginal costing and non-financial information
- use sensitivity analysis to assess break-even and profits
- prepare costing and profit statements using marginal costing
- reconcile reported profits using marginal costing and absorption costing
- understand the uses and limitations of cost-volume-profit analysis and marginal costing

KEY TERMS

Break-even chart   Break-even point   Contribution per unit   Contribution to sales ratio (C/S ratio)   Fixed costs
Limiting factor   Margin of safety   Marginal cost   Marginal cost of production   Marginal cost of sales
Positive contribution   Profit/volume chart   Semi-variable costs   Variable costs

Key skills exercises

Knowledge and understanding

To answer the questions in this chapter, you need to know and understand:

- variable costs vary in direct proportion to changes in the level of output
- fixed costs remain unchanged within a certain level of activity or output
- stepped costs are fixed costs that are only fixed within certain limits and will increase to a higher level when that limit is reached
- semi-variable costs contain both an element of a variable and fixed cost within it
- marginal cost is the cost of making one extra unit of output
- contribution per unit is the difference between the selling price and variable cost of a unit of output
- break-even point is the point at which a business makes neither profit nor loss
- margin of safety is the difference between budgeted or actual output and the break-even quantity
- the uses and limitations of cost-volume-profit analysis and marginal costing.

You should also be able to apply your knowledge and understanding to calculate contribution, the contribution to sales ratio and marginal costs, the break-even point and margin of safety, and prepare cost and profit statements using marginal costing and reconciling reported profits using marginal costing and absorption costing.

Analysis

To answer the questions in this chapter, you need to be able to interpret and analyse break-even information and use the sensitivity analysis to assess break-even and profits.

Evaluation

To answer the questions in this chapter, you need to be able to evaluate cost-volume-profit data and pricing and other management decisions using marginal costing and non-financial information.

> **SPRAY TANNING**
>
> In Portugal, tanning is becoming very popular. There has been a rise in spray tanning salons and products. If people don't want to go through the natural process of tanning, spray tanning is their best option. Spray tanning is a temporary bronzing service provided at salons and spas or products that can be bought to be used at home by yourself.
>
> Spray tanning is done in a booth in a beauty spa or by yourself at home using a spray tanning product.
>
> A beauty shop will have fixed costs in the form of rent and depreciation of non-current assets. It would have variable costs in the form of electricity and beauty products, as these items are dependent on the number of clients seen at the shop.
>
> Stepped costs could come in the form of a salary and commission to an employee working at the shop. An employee could earn a certain salary until they reach a certain target of products sold in a month or money brought into the shop in a month and then the employee might step into a different salary bracket. The salary is fixed until the employee reaches the target and then steps into the next salary bracket.
>
> A form of a semi-variable cost would be a telephone account. The telephone rental is fixed for the employee but the cost of the calls is variable depending on how many calls are made.

WORKED EXAMPLE 1

The costs of producing 500 bottles of a spray tanning solution are shown here.

	$
Direct materials	10 000
Direct labour	25 000
Direct expenses	5 000
Variable overheads	9 000
Fixed overheads	31 000

The business aims for a profit that is 25% of total cost.

REQUIRED

Calculate the following:

i   prime cost
ii marginal cost of production
iii profit
iv sales revenue
v   selling price
vi contribution per unit

CONTINUED

Answer

		Per 500 units	Per 100 unit	Per unit
		$	$	$
	Variable costs			
	Direct materials	10 000	2 000	20
	Direct labour	25 000	5 000	50
	Direct expenses	5 000	1 000	10
i	Prime cost	40 000	8 000	80
	Variable overheads	9 000	1 800	18
ii	Marginal cost of production	49 000	9 800	98
	Fixed overheads	31 000		
	Total cost of production	80 000	16 000	160
iii	Profit (25% of total cost)	20 000	4 000	40
vi	Contribution (v – ii)	51 000	10 200	102
iv	Sales revenue / v Selling price	100 000	20 000	200

Knowledge and understanding

1 The costs of producing 250 units of a product are shown here.

	$
Direct materials	6 000
Direct labour	12 000
Direct expenses	3 000
Variable overheads	14 000
Fixed overheads	25 000

The business aims for a profit that is 30% of total cost.

REQUIRED

Calculate the following:

i prime cost
ii marginal cost of production
iii profit
iv sales revenue
v selling price
vi contribution per unit.

WORKED EXAMPLE 2

The following information relates to the production of the spray tanning solution.

	$
Selling price per litre	100
Marginal cost per litre	70
Total of fixed costs	84 000

The business currently produces and sells 5 000 litres.

CONTINUED

REQUIRED

Calculate:

a the break-even quantity

b the margin of safety

c the break-even revenue.

Answer

a **Step 1**: Calculate the contribution per unit (in this case litres are the units)

The contribution per litre is $(100 − 70) = $30.

Step 2: Divide the fixed costs by the contribution per litre to find the break-even point

Break-even point $\dfrac{\$84\,000}{30}$ = 2 800 litres

b Margin of safety = 5 000 − 2 800 = 2 200 litres

c The revenue at which the product will break even is 2 800 litres × $100 (selling price per unit) = $280 000.

Note: If we had not already calculated the break-even output then the answer to part **c** may also be found by using the contribution to sales ratio as shown here.

The contribution to sales ratio is:

Contribution per $ of selling price = $30 ÷ 100 = 30%.

This is used to calculate the break-even point in revenue, as follows:

$\dfrac{\text{Total fixed costs of } \$84\,000}{\text{Contribution per \$ of selling price 30\% or 0.3}}$ = $280 000

---

2 Spray Tanning Limited supplies the following information for the production of 15 000 products:

	$
Direct materials	45 000
Direct labour	37 500
Other direct expenses	15 000
Variable selling expenses	30 000

Fixed expenses total $74 000. The products sell for $16 each.

Spray Tanning Limited has received the following quotations for the supply of the products:

Tropical Island Tanning Co.	$6 000 per 1 000 products
Caribbean Island Tanning Co.	$6 800 per 1 000 products

REQUIRED

a Calculate the effect on profit and the break-even point of the quotations of:

  i   Tropical Island Tanning Co.

  ii Carinnean Island Tanning Co.

  if either was awarded the contract to supply the products to Spray Tanning Limited.

b State whether Spray Tanning Limited should continue to produce the products or whether it should buy them, and if so, from whom. Support your answer with figures.

Knowledge, understanding, analysis and evaluation

3 W Limited operates a system of marginal costing. The company makes two products, Product A and Product B. The directors provided the following budgeted information for a year.

	Product A	Product B
Production and sales (units)	10 000	6 000
	$	$
Allocated fixed overheads	130 000	120 000
Per unit		
selling price	60	80
direct material	14	16
direct labour	15	21
variable overheads	10	15

REQUIRED

a Prepare a statement for the year to show:

the budgeted **total** contribution for **each** product

the budgeted **total** profit for **each** product

the budgeted **total** profit. [8]

> **TIP**
>
> Contribution = Selling price less variable costs.

Additional information

Included in the allocated fixed overheads is rental of machinery at a cost of $100 000 a year. This cost is allocated 75% to Product A and 25% to Product B.

The directors are now considering two options.

Option 1: Continue with the existing machinery rental on the same terms.

Option 2: Taking out a new rental agreement for new machinery. The new rental agreement would consist of a fixed fee of $28 000 a year plus $4 for each unit produced. The fixed fee would be split across the products in the same proportions as under the current agreement.

REQUIRED

b Complete the following table to show the effect of Option 2. [9]

	Product A	Product B	Total
Revised unit contribution			
Revised allocated total fixed overheads, total for the year			
Revised budgeted profit for the year			

c Advise the directors which option they should choose. Justify your answer using **both** financial and non-financial factors. [7]

d Explain how unit contribution can be used by a business manufacturing multiple products when there is a shortage of production materials. [4]

e State **two** other uses of marginal costing to a business. [2]

Cambridge International AS&A Level Accounting (9706) Paper 22, Q4, March 2019

[Total: 30]

4 Ravi manufactures two products, Exe and Wye. Each product has allocated fixed costs. Figure WB35.1 shows budgeted information for Exe.

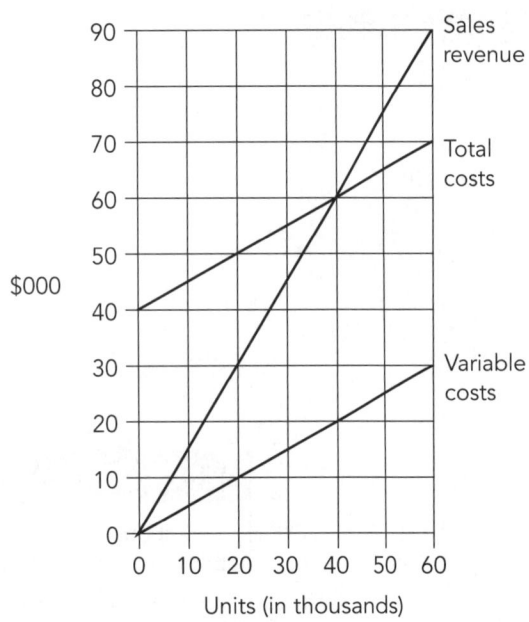

REQUIRED

a Identify the following values **in dollars** from the chart

  i   Break-even point [1]
  ii Allocated fixed costs [1]
  iii Margin of safety [1]
  iv Profit [1]

Additional information

The following budgeted information is available for Wye:

Sales (units)	105 000
	$
Sales revenue	315 000
Direct labour (0.5 hours × $4 per hour)	210 000
Direct materials (0.25 kilos × $2 per kilo)	52 500
Allocated fixed costs	34 500

Ravi is concerned that the budgeted profit for Wye is not very high. He believes the following changes could increase the profit but will have no effect on sales volume.

1 Increase the selling price per unit by 5%.
2 Use skilled labour, which will increase the cost per hour by 5%.
3 Use better quality material, which will increase the cost per kilo by 2%.
4 Increase the advertising cost by $6 000.
5 Offer the sales team a bonus of 2% of the sales revenue earned from all sales above 80 000 units.

REQUIRED

b Calculate, for product Wye **only**, the effect of these changes on the budgeted **total** profit for 105 000 units. [10]

c Calculate, for product Wye **only**, the effect of these changes on the budgeted break-even point in dollars. [5]

d Calculate, for product Wye **only**, the effect of these changes on the budgeted margin of safety in units. [2]

e Recommend whether or not Ravi should proceed with these changes. Justify your answer. [5]

Cambridge International AS&A Level Accounting (9706) Paper 21, Q4a, b, c, d & e, June 2019

[Total: 26]

EXAM-STYLE MULTIPLE CHOICE AND STRUCTURED QUESTIONS

1 Which statement about a positive margin of safety is correct?
   A Sales are less than what was budgeted
   B Sales are greater than what was budgeted
   C Sales are less than the break-even point
   D Sales are greater than the break-even point [1]

2 A company has the following information.

   Sales and production   50 000

	$
Total fixed costs	200 000
Total costs	600 000
Total sales	1 000 000

   What is the contribution to sales ratio?

   A 60%   B 20%   C 40%   D 80%   [1]

CONTINUED

3 K Limited has two production departments. Department A produces bicycles and Department B produces scooters.

The company splits the costs of its maintenance department across the two production departments on the basis of stores requisitions.

REQUIRED

a i Name the accounting term that describes the splitting of a service department's costs based on stores requisitions. [1]

ii Explain how the cost of direct materials is charged to each production department. [2]

Additional information

K Limited provided the following budgeted information for January 2018.

	Department A	Department B
Production (units)	1 000	1 200
Total production costs	$	$
Direct materials	16 000	26 000
Direct labour	18 000	21 000
Indirect materials	4 000	3 000
Maintenance department costs	4 500	7 000
Factory rent	10 000	8 000
Depreciation of factory machinery	10 500	19 000
	63 000	84 000

The selling and distribution costs for January were budgeted to be $33 000 and the administrative expenses for January were budgeted to be $66 000. These were to be split between the two departments on the basis of units produced.

The budgeted selling prices were calculated using a mark-up of 25% on **total cost**.

REQUIRED

b State the bases that the company may have used to split each of the following costs between the two departments.

   i factory rent [1]

   ii depreciation of factory machinery. [1]

c Calculate the inventory value of **one** bicycle produced by Department A

   i using marginal costing [1]

   ii using absorption costing. [1]

d i Calculate the budgeted profit for **one** bicycle. [4]

   ii Calculate the budgeted profit for **one** scooter. [4]

Additional information

The sales director has suggested that the company should reduce production of bicycles by 500 a month and increase production of scooters by 500 a month.

CONTINUED

REQUIRED

e Advise the directors whether or not they should proceed with this suggestion. Justify your answer using both financial and non-financial factors. [7]

Additional information

K Limited pays its production workers $9 an hour.

In January 2018, **actual** results for Department A showed the following.

hours worked   2 100
total overheads $76 200

REQUIRED

f Calculate the overhead absorption rate per direct labour hour for Department A. [3]

g Calculate the under-absorption or over-absorption of overheads for Department A in January 2018. [5]

Cambridge International AS&A Level Accounting (9706) Paper 22, Q4, March 2018

[Total: 30]

Improve this answer

This is a sample answer to **Q3e**.

> The selling price per scooter and budgeted profit per scooter are both higher than the bicycle. This suggestion would increase the profit. The directors should proceed with the suggestion.

Your challenge

See if you can improve this answer.

The sample answer only mentions financial factors, whereas the question asks for non-financial factors to be considered too. Both factors should be discussed equally in order to fully justify the decision being advised.

A better answer is available online – but write yours out first!

Chapter 36
Activity based costing

LEARNING INTENTIONS

In this chapter you will:

- understand cost pools and cost drivers
- use activity based costing to allocate overheads to products
- calculate total cost, selling price and profit using activity based costing
- know the uses and limitations of activity based costing
- evaluate management decisions using activity based costing information

KEY TERMS

Activity based costing (ABC)   Cost driver   Cost pool

Key skills exercises

Knowledge and understanding

To answer the questions in this chapter, you need to know and understand:

- activity based costing is a method for calculating unit cost that absorbs costs into individual products by focusing on the activities that cause a cost to occur
- a cost pool is the total of all the costs associated with a particular activity
- a cost driver is the activity that directly results in a specific cost being incurred
- uses and limitations of activity-based costing.

You should also be able to apply your knowledge and understanding of activity-based costing to allocate overheads to products, calculate the total cost, selling price and profit.

Analysis

To answer the questions in this chapter, you need to be able to:

- analyse financial accounting information and cost and management accounting information
- select, calculate and interpret relevant data and information
- communicate outcomes in the most appropriate form.

Evaluation

To answer the questions in this chapter, you need to be able to evaluate management decisions using activity based costing information.

SODA-POP COMPANY

The Soda-pop Company is a beverage corporation headquartered in Atlanta, Georgia. The Soda-pop Company manufactures, retails and markets beverage concentrates and syrups. Soda-pop is a carbonated soft drink. Soda-pop is sold in over 200 countries across five operating regions.

Soda-pop uses activity based costing to evaluate the differences between its specialty, regionalised products that may not be offered on the global market and its bigger, world-wide products.

Knowledge and understanding

1 Soda-pop produces two types of lemonade, Crazy Lemons and Crazy Lemons Light. The budgeted data for three months is here.

	Crazy Lemons	Crazy Lemons Light
Production in units	10 000	4 000
Direct materials ($)	12 000	10 000
Direct labour ($)	7 000	2 000
Number of quality checks	50	40
Labour hours spent on maintenance	30	20

Total factory overheads:
- $1 500 for machine maintenance
- $1 800 for quality control

REQUIRED

a Calculate the total cost and the cost per unit for each product using ABC (see Worked example 1 for Crazy Lemons).

b Calculate the selling price of each type of lemonade if Soda-pop is aiming for a 55% mark-up on factory cost.

WORKED EXAMPLE 1

Machine maintenance costs: $\frac{\$1\,500}{50} = \$30$ per hour

Quality control costs: $\frac{\$1\,800}{90} = \$20$ per check

Apportionment of each activity to Crazy Lemons and Crazy Lemons Light (using Crazy Lemons as the example):

		Crazy Lemons	Crazy Lemons Light
		$	$
Machine maintenance	30 × $30	900	
Quality control	50 × $20	1 000	
Allocated overheads		1 900	

CONTINUED

	Total cost of 10 000 Crazy Lemons	Total cost of 4 000 Crazy Lemons Lights
	$	$
Overhead cost	1 900	
Direct cost	19 000	
Cost	20 900	

$$\text{Cost per Crazy Lemons} = \frac{\$20\,900}{10\,000} \text{ units} = \$2.09$$

2 Soda-pop produces two coffees, Aroma Mocha and Lava Java. Aroma Mocha is more expensive to produce and has a higher selling price. The following budgeted details are available for one month.

	Aroma Mocha	Lava Java
Units of production and sales	8 000	14 000
Selling price per unit	$15	$12
Direct materials and labour per unit	$3	$1
Direct labour hours per unit	2	1
Number of machine set-ups	90	60
Machine hours	26 000	24 000
Number of orders packed	9 000	7 000

Budgeted factory overheads:

	$
Machine set-up	75 000
Machine running time	25 000
Packing costs	20 000
Total factory overheads	120 000

REQUIRED

a Calculate the following using absorption costing:
  i   the budgeted overhead absorption rate using direct labour hours
  ii the budgeted profit per unit.

b Calculate the following using activity-based costing:
  i   the absorption rate for each cost driver
  ii   the total overhead allocated to product A and product B
  iii the budgeted profit per unit.

c Compare the overheads and profit per unit and explain reasons for any differences.

WORKED EXAMPLE 2

Step 1: Identify the cost drivers for each activity.

Activity	Cost driver
Machine set-up	Number of times machine set up
Machine running time	
Packing costs	

Step 2: Calculate the cost driver rates using the formula:

$$\frac{\text{Cost pool value}}{\text{Number of uses of the cost driver}}$$

Cost driver	Cost	Total number of uses of the cost driver	Cost driver rate
	$		$
Number of machine set-ups	75 000	150 (90 + 60)	500
Machine hours			
Packing costs			

Knowledge, understanding and analysis

3 B Limited produces two products – Premier and Standard. The budgeted cost information for the month of June 2019 is as follows:

	Premier	Standard
Units produced and sold	500	800
Direct materials per unit	$80	$50
Direct labour hourly rate	$30	$25
Direct labour hours per unit	3	2

Budgeted fixed overheads $480 000 for 2019 are allocated to products based on 40 000 budgeted total direct labour hours.

a Calculate the cost per unit for **each** product using absorption costing. [3]

Additional information

A newly recruited management accountant suggests that B Limited should adopt activity based costing (ABC). He has provided an analysis of fixed overheads as follows:

	Cost	Cost driver	Annual quantity
	$		
Materials requisition	90 000	Number of material requisitions	75
Machine set-up	240 000	Number of set-ups	60
Inspection	150 000	Number of inspection hours	5 000
	480 000		

Budgeted use of cost driver for each product for June 2019 is as follows:

	Premier	Standard
Number of material requisitions	2	6
Number of set-ups	2	3
Number of inspection hours	120	320

b Explain the meaning of the term 'cost driver'. [2]

c State **two** advantages and **three** disadvantages of ABC. [5]

d Calculate the cost per unit for **each** product if ABC is adopted. [8]

Additional information

The selling price of **each** product is cost plus 40%.

e i Calculate the selling price of each product using absorption costing. [2]

ii Calculate the selling price of each product using ABC. [2]

iii Calculate, using suitable calculations, why your answers in **i** and **ii** are different. [3]

Cambridge International AS&A Level Accounting (9706) Paper 32, Q5, March 2019

[Total: 25]

Knowledge, understanding, analysis and evaluation

4 Ahmed manufactures two products. He has recently started using Activity Based Costing (ABC) for allocating the overhead costs to these products. The budgeted data for one month is available as follows:

	Product X	Product Y
Demand (units)	10 000	14 000
Number of orders	20	60
Number of production runs	12	36
	Per unit	Per unit
Direct labour hours	0.75	1.5
Machine hours	2.5	0.5
Direct costs ($)	100	50
Total factory overhead costs	$	
Machine maintenance costs	264 000	
Ordering costs	54 000	
Production run costs	24 000	
	342 000	

REQUIRED

a Calculate the **full** cost per unit for Product X and Product Y using ABC. [10]

Additional information

Ahmed previously used direct labour hours as a basis to charge overheads to each product.

REQUIRED

b Calculate the overhead charged to each product using the direct labour hour rate. [3]

c   Explain the effect that changing the method has had on the overhead cost of each product. [4]

Additional information

A customer requires 50 units of Product X and has offered to pay Ahmed a total of $8 450 for them. Ahmed uses 40% mark-up on all his products.

REQUIRED

d   Recommend whether or not Ahmed should accept the offer. Justify your decision using appropriate calculations and considering **both** financial and non-financial factors. [6]

e   State **two** reasons why a business may use ABC for allocating overhead costs. [2]

Cambridge International AS&A Level Accounting (9706) Paper 31, Q6, June 2017

[Total: 25]

EXAM-STYLE STRUCTURED QUESTIONS

1   Chetna runs a business printing logos on sweatshirts. The sweatshirts come in two types, Standard and Superior. The selling price is set at cost plus 30%.

The following information is available for the year.

	Standard	Superior
Number of sweatshirts sold	22 500	9 000
Purchase cost per sweatshirt	$5	$8
Printing materials per sweatshirt	$0.50	$0.50
Labour time to print each sweatshirt	5 minutes	5 minutes

Overheads were as follows:

	$
Machine set up costs	18 900
Other production overheads	5 850
Selling and administration	17 250
Total	42 000

REQUIRED

a   Calculate an overhead absorption rate based on labour hours. [2]

Additional information

Staff printing the logos are paid $10 an hour.

REQUIRED:

b   i   Calculate the total cost allocated to each type of sweatshirt. [4]

    ii Calculate the selling price for **each** sweatshirt. [2]

CONTINUED

Additional information

Chetna has suggested that it would be better to allocate the machine set up cost to each product based on the number of times the machine is set up. The machine has to be set up each time there is a different logo.

During the year the machine was set up 600 times for Standard sweatshirts and 975 times for Superior sweatshirts. Other overheads are still allocated on the basis of labour hours.

REQUIRED

c   i   Calculate the total costs allocated to **each** type of sweatshirt when machine set up costs are allocated using the number of set up times. [4]

     ii   Calculate the revised selling price for **each** type of sweatshirt. [2]

     iii   Calculate the change in selling price for **each** type of sweatshirt. [2]

d   Explain **three** differences between activity based costing and absorption costing. [6]

e   Advise Chetna which method she should use. Justify your answer. [3]

Cambridge International AS&A Level Accounting (9706) Paper 33, Q5, June 2016

[Total: 25]

2   Jumal Limited manufactures two products, Alpha and Beta.

The following budgeted information is available.

	Alpha	Beta
Production and sales (units)	1 000	5 000
Machine hours	5 000	25 000
Direct materials (cost per unit)	$80	$48
Direct labour (cost per unit)	$150	$60

Fixed production overhead is $540 000 and is allocated to the products by machine hours.

REQUIRED

a   Calculate for each product:

     i   total budgeted production cost [2]

     ii   budgeted unit cost. [2]

Additional information

The directors of Jumal Limited will add 50% on to the total production cost to set the selling price for each product.

REQUIRED

b   Calculate the unit selling price of **each** product. [2]

CONTINUED

Additional information

Meena is a management accountant newly recruited by Jumal Limited. She suggests that the company should adopt activity based costing to allocate production overheads. She has identified that the production comprises four major activities. The cost of each activity and the activities consumed by each product are as follows:

	Production overheads $	Alpha	Beta
Machine set-up	110 000	12 times	8 times
Machine maintenance	180 000	90 maintenance hours	110 maintenance hours
Materials handling	90 000	20 deliveries	10 deliveries
Product inspection	160 000	200 inspection hours	120 inspection hours
	540 000		

REQUIRED

c   State **one** benefit of adopting activity based costing. [1]

d   Prepare a table to show the allocation of the **total** budgeted production overheads between Alpha and Beta if Jumal Limited changes to activity based costing. [4]

e   Calculate the budgeted unit cost and budgeted unit selling price of Alpha and Beta if activity based costing is adopted. [5]

f   Discuss the factors the directors of a business should consider before possibly changing the selling price. [6]

g   Recommend whether or not the directors of Jumal Limited should change the selling price of the products. Justify your answer. [3]

Cambridge International AS&A Level Accounting (9706) Paper 32, Q5, March 2016

[Total: 25]

Improve this answer

This is a sample answer to **Q2f**.

> The directors should consider the cost price of the product and what impact the change would have on the profit being made.

Your challenge

See if you can improve this answer.

The sample answer is very brief and does not mention the competitors or the impact this change will have on the customer. These points should be raised as part of a more detailed discussion. A better answer is available online – but write yours out first!

Chapter 37
Budgeting and budgetary control

LEARNING INTENTIONS

In this chapter you will:

- understand the need for budgets
- identify and apply limiting factors to decide the order to prepare budgets
- prepare budgets for sales, production, purchases, labour, trade receivables, trade payables and cash
- understand and prepare the master budget
- evaluate the advantages and disadvantages of budgetary control and using spreadsheets to prepare budgets
- understand the benefits of flexible budgeting

KEY TERMS

Budget   Zero-based budgeting   Incremental budgeting   Master budget   Top-down budgets
Bottom-up budgets   Fixed budget   Flexible budget

Key skills exercises

Knowledge and understanding

To answer the questions in this chapter, you need to know and understand:

- a budget is a plan of future activity, expressed in financial terms
- limiting factors are circumstances that restrict the activities of a business
- limiting factors must be identified before deciding the order in which departmental budgets such as sales and production are prepared
- a master budget is the budgeted statement of profit or loss and the budgeted statement of financial position together
- a fixed budget is a budget that is not changed when sales, or some other activity, increases or decreases
- a flexible budget is a budget that is changed to reflect changes in activity levels.

You should also be able to apply your knowledge and understanding of budgeting to prepare budgets for sales, production, purchases, labour, trade receivables, trade payables and cash, apply limiting factors to prepare budgets, prepare the master budget and use spreadsheets to prepare budgets.

Analysis

To answer the questions in this chapter, you need to be able to analyse financial and non-financial information regarding budgets to communicate the outcomes.

Evaluation

To answer the questions in this chapter, you need to be able to evaluate the advantages and disadvantages of budgetary control and using spreadsheets to prepare budgets.

> **PASTASCIUTTA FOOD COMPANY**
>
> Pastasciutta is an Italian family-owned food company. It is present in more than 100 countries, making it an international group.
>
> Pastasciutta is a world leader in the pasta and ready-to-use sauces market in continental Europe and a world leader in bakery products in Italy. Pastasciutta also produces crispbread and is a world leader in this market in Scandinavia.
>
> Pastasciutta's headquarters is based in Parma, Italy.
>
> It is important for Pastasciutta to budget as without budgeting a company of their size could run into financial problems if they were to overspend and start running at a loss rather than a profit. Budgeting is important for Pastasciutta to make sure that all their branches throughout the world are on track and keeping to their allocated budgets to ensure the success of the business and help it to keep growing.

WORKED EXAMPLE 1

Pastasciutta's sales budget for cannelloni in unit packets for four months ending 30 June is as follows.

March 10 200; April 10 500; May 10 400; June 10 300

The price per unit will be $3 for the two months to 30 April. The price will be increased to $3.50 from 1 May.

REQUIRED

Prepare Pastasciutta's sales budget for this product for the four months ending 30 June.

Answer

	March	April	May	June	Total
Units	10 200	10 500	10 400	10 300	41 400
Price	$3	$3	$3.50	$3.50	
Sales	$30 600	$31 500	$36 400	$36 050	$134 550

Knowledge and understanding

1. Marco's sales budget for cement bags in units for three months ending 30 September is as follows.

   July 21 000; August 22 400; September 23 600

   The price per unit will be $5.50 for the two months to 31 August. The price will be increased to $6 from 1 September.

   REQUIRED

   Prepare Marco's sales budget for this product for the three months ending 30 September.

CAMBRIDGE INTERNATIONAL AS & A LEVEL ACCOUNTING: WORKBOOK

WORKED EXAMPLE 2

Pastasciutta's sales in July were $23 000 and in August were $25 000.

Of the total sales, 40% are on a cash basis. Of the remainder, 50% are to credit customers who pay within one month and receive a cash discount of 2%. The remaining 10% of credit customers pay within two months.

TIP

Remember to take the price increase into account after the two months.

REQUIRED

Prepare Pastasciutta's trade receivables budget for September to December.

Answer

Set out next are the workings required to prepare the trade receivables budget for the period from September to December. Notice that the workings start at the previous July. This is because as we have seen that some of the money from July's sales isn't received until September.

Working						
	July	August	September	October	November	December
	$	$	$	$	$	$
Sales for the month	23 000	25 000	27 000	26 000	24 000	28 000
Cash sales	9 200	10 000	10 800	10 400	9 600	11 200
Credit sales	13 800	15 000	16 200	15 600	14 400	16 800
Cash received one month after sale(W1)		11 270	12 250	13 230	12 740	11 760
Discount(W2)		230	250	270	260	240
Cash received two months after sale(W3)			2 300	2 500	2 700	2 600

Workings

W1: The balance of cash received after one month is 50% of the total sales made the previous month less a 2% cash discount. For example, in August, Pastasciutta receives cash from 50% of July's sales less 2% cash discounts: $11 270 ($23 000 × 50% × 98%).

W2: The discount figure is 2% of 50% of the sales for the previous month. Thus, in August the discount is $230 ($23 000 × 50% × 2%).

W3: The balance of cash received after two months is 10% of the total sales made two months before. Thus, in September Pastasciutta will receive $2 300 (10% of July's sales of $23 000).

Trade receivables budget for the period September to December				
	September	October	November	December
	$	$	$	$
Opening trade receivables(W1)	17 300	18 700	18 300	17 000
Add credit sales for the month	16 200	15 600	14 400	16 800
Less cash received(W2)	14 550	15 730	15 440	14 360
Less discounts allowed	250	270	260	240
Closing trade receivables	18 700	18 300	17 000	19 200

37 Budgeting and budgetary control A Level

CONTINUED

Workings

W1: Opening balance in September is the total of the credit sales from August ($15 000) plus 10% of sales July that are still to be paid ($2 300). All other opening balances are the closing balances of the previous month; so, October's opening balance is September's closing balance etc.

W2: Cash received is the total of cash received after one month of sales plus the cash received after two months of sales. These figures are calculated in the working. For example, for September: $14 550 ($12 250 + $2 300).

The layout of the trade receivables budget starts with the opening balance of trade receivables at the start of the month. The total credit sales for the month are added on to that figure. The cash received in the month and the discount allowed in that month are then deducted. The result is the closing figure for trade receivables. This is carried forward and forms the opening balance at the start of the next month.

2 Valentina's sales are:

February	March	April	May	June	July
$16 000	$17 500	$18 600	$17 300	$16 200	$19 800

Of the total sales, 50% are on a cash basis. Of the remainder, 40% are to credit customers who pay within one month and receive a cash discount of 5%. The remaining 10% of credit customers pay within two months.

REQUIRED

Prepare Valentina's trade receivables budget for April to July.

3 Purchases budget for Alessandro Limited for November to March.

	November	December	January	February	March
No. of units	2 500	3 200	2 800	2 900	3 100
Material required (kg)	10 000	12 800	11 200	11 600	12 400
Purchases	$35 000	$44 800	$39 200	$40 600	$43 400

Expenditure budget for Alessandro Limited for January to April.

	January	February	March	April
	$	$	$	$
Purchases	35 000	44 800	39 200	40 600
Wages	12 000	12 000	12 000	12 000
General expenses	5 000	6 000	7 800	6 400
Loan interest	–	–	300	–
Dividend	–	–	2 000	–
Total expenditure	52 000	62 800	61 300	59 000

Alessandro Limited pays for its raw materials two months after the month of purchase.

REQUIRED

Prepare a trade payables budget for the period January to March.

Knowledge, understanding, analysis and evaluation

4 Sunil is preparing the annual budgets for his manufacturing business.

REQUIRED

a Explain what is meant by a master budget. [2]

Additional information

The finished goods inventory held at 1 January 2017 is expected to be 200 units. This is expected to increase by 20 units each month until 31 March 2017.

Unit sales from December 2016 to April 2017 are expected to be:

December	January	February	March	April
350	370	410	380	430

REQUIRED

b Prepare a production budget for **each** of the four months from January to April 2017. [4]

Additional information

- Goods will be sold on credit with a selling price of $30 per unit. One third is expected to be received in the month of sale with the balance being received in the following month.

- Other income will arise from the interest received on an investment of $50 000 at 4% per annum. Interest will be received quarterly starting 1 January 2017.

- Unit product costs are expected to be as follows:

	$
Direct materials	7
Direct labour	5
Overheads	6
	18

- Direct materials will be purchased to meet the current month's production. Half the amount due will be paid by cash in the month of production and the balance will be paid in the following month. The number of units produced in December 2016 is expected to be 340.

- Direct labour will be paid in the month that the cost is incurred.

- Four-fifths of the overheads will be paid in the month in which they are incurred with the balance being paid in the following month.

- Some new equipment is expected to be acquired on 1 January 2017 at a cost of $12 000. A 50% deposit will be paid on delivery, with the remainder being paid on 1 April 2017. This equipment will be depreciated at 10% using the straight-line method.

- The bank account balance at 1 January 2017 is expected to be overdrawn by $10 450.

37 Budgeting and budgetary control A Level

REQUIRED

c Prepare a cash budget for **each** of the three months from January to March 2017. [10]

d Analyse the options available to Sunil to avoid using a bank overdraft. [6]

e Advise Sunil whether or not he should apply for a loan rather than maintain an overdraft. Justify your answer. [3]

> **TIP**
> Remember to use all sources of receipts, not just revenue.

Cambridge International AS &A Level Accounting (9706) Paper 33, Q6, October 2016

[Total: 25]

5 Luca Limited manufactures a single product. The budgeted information for September 2021 is as follows:

Sales and production	8000 units
Direct materials (per unit)	4 kilos at $6 per kilo
Direct labour (per unit)	3 hours at $22 per hour

The total fixed overheads absorbed on the basis of direct labour hours were $192 000. The actual sales and production for September 2021 was 7500 units.

REQUIRED

a State two reasons why a business prepares a flexed budget.

b Prepare a statement to show the total flexed budgeted production costs for September 2021.

c State two advantages and two disadvantages of budgetary control.

EXAM-STYLE STRUCTURED QUESTIONS

1 Hyung Min manufactures glass vases.

Each vase passes through three production departments: casting, polishing and finishing.

Hyung Min had the following budgeted information for the year ending 31 January 2018.

1 All vases produced were expected to be sold. The selling price would be $60.25 each.
2 The fixed overheads were expected to be $240 000 per annum and are absorbed on the basis of production labour hours.
3 The business is open for 50 weeks a year and each employee works for 40 hours a week.
4 The production costs per vase were expected to be:

	Casting department	Polishing department	Finishing department
Materials	25 grams at $8 per 100 grams	0	25 grams at $16 per 100 grams
Labour	40 minutes at $12 per hour	15 minutes at $8 per hour	2 hours at $14 per hour

5 A total of 24 000 vases were budgeted to be produced and sold for the year ending 31 January 2018.

CONTINUED

REQUIRED

a Explain what is meant by the term 'budgetary control'. [2]

b Prepare the labour budget for the year ending 31 January 2018. Show the number of labour hours, the number of employees and the annual labour cost for each department. [9]

c Analyse the benefits to Hyung Min of using budgetary control in order to achieve his target profit. [6]

Cambridge International AS&A Level Accounting (9706) Paper 32, Q5a, b & c, March 2018

[Total: 17]

Improve this answer

This is a sample answer to **Q1c**.

> Budgetary control motivates staff to reach targets but if the targets are too high it can demotivate staff. Budgetary control helps with decision-making but sometimes staff can feel restricted and not be as creative when budgets are restricting decisions. Budgetary control helps to achieve the target profit.

Your challenge

See if you can improve this answer. The sample answer strays from the question by including information about limitations. The question specifically asks for benefits and so the answer could be improved by discussing the benefits only in greater detail. A better answer is available online – but write yours out first!

2 Marco has been asked by his bank manager to produce a cash budget, budgeted income statement and budgeted statement of financial position for his next three months' trading ending October 2021.

His statement of financial position at 1 August 2021 is as follows:

	$000
Non-current assets	40
Current assets	
Inventory	8
Trade receivables	16
	24
Total assets	64
Capital and liabilities	
Capital account balance	29
Non-current liability	
10% bank loan	15
Current liabilities	
Trade payables	14
Bank overdraft	6
	20
Total capital and liabilities	64

CONTINUED

Additional information

Marco has prepared the following budgeted data for the next three months ending 31 October 2021:

- Budgeted sales and purchases for the next three months are as follows.

Month	Budgeted sales	Budgeted purchases
	$	$
August	15 000	12 000
September	18 000	13 000
October	19 000	13 500

- Customers will pay 80% of the money in the month following the sale and the other 20% in the second month after the sale. However, at 31 July, only July receivables were outstanding.
- Suppliers for purchases will be paid in full in the month following purchase.
- Monthly overheads are $8 000 and will be paid in full in the month.
- Marco takes monthly drawings of $6 000.
- In October, Marco intends to purchase a new delivery vehicle. This will cost $10 000. A 50% deposit will be paid in October. The balance will be added to the outstanding bank loan. No depreciation will be charged on the vehicle in October.
- Non-current assets are depreciated on a month-by-month basis at 10% per annum using the straight-line method.
- Interest on the bank loan will be paid in November 2021.
- At 31 October 2021, inventory is expected to be $7 000.

REQUIRED

a Prepare Marco's cash budget for the three months ending 31 October 2021. [8]
b Prepare a budgeted statement of profit or loss for the three months ended 31 October 2021. [6]
c State two advantages and two disadvantages of a business preparing budgets. [4]
d Evaluate Marco's cash budget and budgeted statement of profit or loss for the three months ending 31 October 2021. Advise Marco of any actions you think he should take in respect of them. [7]

[Total: 25]

> Chapter 38
Standard costing

LEARNING INTENTIONS

In this chapter you will:

- understand standard costing and how to set standards
- discuss the advantages and disadvantages of standard costing
- prepare a flexible budget
- calculate variances for sales, materials, labour and fixed overheads
- reconcile standard costs with actual costs and budgeted profit with actual profit
- analyse actual costs and revenue against standards using variances
- assess the use of standard costing to improve business performance

KEY TERMS

Adverse variance   Favourable variance   Flexible budget   Standard cost   Standard costing   Variance

Key skills exercises

Knowledge and understanding

To answer the questions in this chapter, you need to know and understand:

- standard costing is an accounting system that compares actual costs against standard costs; the comparison helps managers to assess and control costs and take action where needed
- the main type of standards are ideal standards, current standards and attainable standards
- the advantages and disadvantages of standard costing.

You should also be able to apply your knowledge and understanding of standard costing to prepare a flexible budget; calculate variances for sales, materials, labour and fixed overheads; and reconcile standard costs with actual costs and budgeted profit with actual profit.

Analysis

To answer the questions in this chapter, you need to be able to analyse actual costs and revenue against standards using variances.

Evaluation

To answer the questions in this chapter, you need to be able to assess the use of standard costing to improve business performance.

38 Standard costing A Level

WATCHES 4 ME

Watches 4 Me was started in Athens, Greece, in 2013. They are a watch designing and manufacturing company who supply businesses around the world. It is important for a company like Watches 4 Me to make use of standard costing. In their first couple of years, it would have been especially important to compare the standard costs with the actual costs to make sure they were making the optimal profit, making use of the best suppliers and making the best use of labour hours available. By comparing costs, they calculate variances that allow them to be able to improve in areas that are not doing as well as they should.

WORKED EXAMPLE 1

Watches 4 Me uses standard costing for its watches. Estimated production and sales volumes for a year are 5 000 watches. Standard costing information for the watches is as follows.

Details per unit	Watches
Selling price	$450
Direct materials	$100
Direct labour	10 hours at $20 per hour

Total budgeted fixed overheads for the year is $100 000. Fixed overheads are absorbed on the basis of direct labour hours.

REQUIRED

Prepare the budgeted profit statement for the year.

Answer

The standard direct labour cost to make the watches for the year will be:

	Total standard hours	Total standard wage cost(W1)
	$	$
5 000 watches: 10 hours at $20 per hour	50 000	1 000 000
Total standard hours and wages cost of production	50 000	1 000 000

Working

W1: The total for each product is the total time taken × $20.

The standard material costs of production are as follows:

	Total standard material cost
	$
5 000 watches: $100 per unit	500 000
Total standard quantity and cost of material for production	500 000

Budgeted fixed overheads are $100 000. They are absorbed on the basis of direct labour hours, therefore the standard overhead absorption rate is $2 ($100 000 ÷ 50 000 hours).

CONTINUED

	Watches	Total
	$	$
Revenue	2 250 000	2 250 000
Direct materials	(500 000)	(500 000)
Direct labour	(1 000 000)	(1 000 000)
Fixed overhead (at $2(W1) per direct labour hour)	(100 000)	(100 000)
Budgeted profit	650 000	650 000

Working

W1: OAR = $\dfrac{\$100\,000}{50\,000 \text{ hours}} = \$2$

Knowledge and understanding

1 A company makes denim jackets in three different sizes: small, medium and large. The estimated production and sales volumes for a year are 1 000 size small, 2 000 size medium and 1 500 size large denim jackets.

Standard costing information for the denim jackets is as follows.

Details per unit (standard cost)	Denim jacket: small	Denim jacket: medium	Denim jacket: large
Selling price	$175	$185	$195
Direct materials	3 metres at $10 per metre	3.5 metres at $10 per metre	4 metres at $10 per metre
Direct labour	4 hours at $6 per hour	4 hours at $6 per hour	4 hours at $6 per hour

Total budgeted fixed overheads for the year are $360 000. Fixed overheads are absorbed on the basis of direct labour hours.

REQUIRED

Prepare the budgeted profit statement for the year.

WORKED EXAMPLE 2

Watches 4 Me makes watches. The following budgeted information is available for January.

	Standard
Number of units produced and sold:	450
Per unit:	
Selling price per unit	$450
Cost of material per watch	$100
Direct labour (hours)	10
Labour rate per hour	$20

The following actual information is available for January:

- Sales were 490 units at $470 each.
- Direct materials had a total cost of $51 450.
- 4 900 direct labour hours were used at $22 per hour.

CONTINUED

REQUIRED

Calculate for Watches 4 Me for January:

a   the sales volume variance
b   the sales price variance
c   the direct materials price variance
d   the direct labour efficiency variance
e   the direct labour rate variance
f   a statement reconciling the labour efficiency and rate variances with the total direct labour variance.

Answer

a   the sales volume variance
    $(470 \times \$450) - (450 \times \$450) = \$9\,000$ favourable

b   the sales price variance
    $(\$470 - \$450) \times 490 = \$9\,800$ favourable

c   the direct materials price variance
    $(\$100 - \$105(W1)) = \$5$ adverse

    Working
    W1: $\$51\,450 / 490 = \$105$

d   the direct labour efficiency variance
    $(4\,500(W2) - 4\,900) \times \$20 = \$8\,000$ adverse

    Working
    W2: $10 \times 450 = 4\,500$

e   the direct labour rate variance
    $(\$20 - \$22) \times 4\,900 = \$9\,800$ adverse

f   A statement reconciling labour rate and efficiency variances with the total direct labour variance.

	$	
Direct labour rate variance	(9 800)	adverse
Direct labour efficiency variance	(8 000)	adverse
Direct labour variance [(450 × 10 × $20) – $107 800]	17 800	adverse

2 Watches 4 Me's budget for the production of 100 000 watches in the year ending 31 December was as follows:

	$
Variable expenses:	
Direct materials	20 000
Direct labour	15 000
Production expenses	6 000
	41 000
Fixed expenses:	
Production expenses	13 000
Administration	29 000
	83 000

The actual output for the year ended 31 December was 110 000 watches.

REQUIRED

a Prepare a flexed budget for the production of 110 000 watches.

Watches 4 Me has prepared the following budgets for the production of clocks:

	6 000 clocks	8 000 clocks
	$	$
Direct materials	15 000	20 000
Direct labour	36 000	48 000
Production overheads	25 000	31 000
Selling and distribution	24 000	28 000
Administration	80 000	80 000
	180 000	207 000

REQUIRED

b Prepare a flexed budget for the production of 9 000 clocks.

3 Denim Limited makes one design of denim jeans. The following budgeted information is available for March.

	Standard
Number of units produced and sold:	20 000
Per unit:	
Selling price per unit	$220
Direct materials (metres)	3
Cost of material per metre	$24
Direct labour (hours)	5
Labour rate per hour	$15

The following actual information is available for March:

- Sales were 23 000 units at $210 each.
- 69 000 metres of materials were used at a total cost of $1 587 000.
- 115 000 direct labour hours were used at $16 per hour.

REQUIRED

Calculate for Denim Limited for March:

a the sales volume variance
b the sales price variance
c the direct materials usage variance
d the direct materials price variance
e a statement reconciling the material usage and price variances with the total direct materials variance
f the direct labour efficiency variance
g the direct labour rate variance
h a statement reconciling the labour efficiency and rate variances with the total direct labour variance.

> **TIP**
> Remember to flex the budget before calculating the variances.

> **TIP**
> Label if variances are favourable or adverse and show them with either brackets or without.

Knowledge, understanding, analysis and evaluation

4 C Limited produces tables. Each table requires the following:

raw materials	3 metres of wood at $80 per metre
direct labour	12 hours at $30 per hour
fixed production	overhead $10 per direct labour hour

Budgeted production is 5 000 tables.

Actual production was 4 800.

Actual production costs were:

		$
direct materials	15 360 metres	1 190 400
direct labour	55 200 hours	1 766 400
fixed production overhead		579 600

All tables produced were sold.

REQUIRED

a State **two** limitations of a standard costing system. [2]

b Calculate the following variances:

  i   direct materials price
  ii direct materials usage
  iii direct labour rate
  iv direct labour efficiency
  v   fixed overhead expenditure
  vi fixed overhead volume.
  [12]

c Prepare a statement reconciling the budgeted cost of producing 4 800 tables with the actual cost. [8]

Additional information

The directors are considering using higher quality wood and increasing the selling price.

d Advise the directors whether or not they should make these changes. Justify your answer. **[3]**

Cambridge International AS&A Level Accounting (9706) Paper 32, Q6, June 2018

[Total: 25]

Knowledge, understanding and analysis

5 EF plc manufactures a single product. No inventories of materials or finished goods are maintained.

The following budgeted information is available for March:

Production and sales	1 000 units
Unit revenue and costs	
Selling price	$150
Direct material	4 kilos at $6 per kilo
Direct labour	6 hours at $10 per hour
Variable overhead	$2 per direct labour hour
Fixed overhead	$14 per unit

In March, the company actually made and sold 800 units.

REQUIRED

a State **two** reasons why a business prepares a flexed budget. **[2]**

b Prepare a statement to show the budgeted profit for the month of March. **[6]**

Additional information

The actual cost of direct labour in March was $50 176. Staff had been paid at the rate of $9.80 per hour.

REQUIRED

c Calculate the following variances for March:
   i direct labour rate **[2]**
   ii direct labour efficiency **[2]**
   iii total direct labour **[1]**

> **TIP**
>
> Don't include the sales volume variance in your reconciling statement of the budget profit with the actual profit.

Additional information

In April the staff continued to be paid at $9.80 per hour. The variances for April were calculated as follows:

direct labour rate	$1 620 favourable
direct labour efficiency	$18 000 adverse

REQUIRED

d Calculate
   i the number of hours actually worked in April **[2]**
   ii the number of units actually made and sold in April. **[5]**

38 Standard costing A Level

e   Suggest **two** possible reasons why the efficiency variance was adverse in April. [2]

Additional information

The management of the company is evaluating a plan to retrain the existing workers to improve their efficiency.

REQUIRED

f   Discuss the disadvantages to EF plc if they proceed with this plan. [3]

Cambridge International AS&A Level Accounting (9706) Paper 31, Q5, June 2017

[Total: 25]

EXAM-STYLE STRUCTURED QUESTIONS

1   Ella uses flexible budgets as part of her budgetary control system.
    The following information is available for the year ended 31 March 2019.

	Fixed budget activity level		Actual activity level
Units	1 000	3 000	2 500
	$	$	$
Sales	25 000	75 000	63 000
Direct labour	5 000	15 000	12 800
Direct material	6 000	18 000	14 500
Semi-variable overheads	4 000	7 500	7 250
Fixed costs	5 000	5 000	5 200
Profit	5 000	29 500	23 250

REQUIRED

a   State **two** advantages to a business of using a budgetary control system. [2]

b   Calculate the flexed budgeted profit for the year ended 31 March 2019. [8]

c   Prepare a statement, showing the relevant variances, to reconcile the flexed budget profit with the actual profit. [6]

Additional information

For the month of April 2019, Ella's business showed a favourable total direct material variance and an adverse total direct labour variance.

d   Suggest what may have caused the:
    i   favourable total direct material variance [2]
    ii adverse total direct labour variance. [2]

e   Advise Ella whether or not she should continue to flex the budgeted data. Justify your answer. [5]

Cambridge International AS&A Level Accounting (9706) Paper 32, Q6, June 2019

[Total: 25]

CONTINUED

2 Oscar runs a manufacturing business and operates a standard costing system. The following information relates to the year ended 31 March 2019.

	Budgeted	Actual
Production (units)	7 500	7 300
Material usage	6 kilos per unit	42 500 kilos
Material cost	$5 per kilo	$230 000
Labour usage	4 hours per unit	32 000 hours
Labour cost	$8 per hour	$236 000

REQUIRED

a State **two** disadvantages of operating a standard costing system. [2]

b Calculate the following variances:
  i material price [2]
  ii material usage [2]
  iii labour rate [2]
  iv labour efficiency [2]
  v total labour. [1]

c Identify **one** possible reason for **each** of the following variances calculated in part **b**:
  i material price variance   iii labour rate variance
  ii material usage variance   iv labour efficiency variance. [4]

d Prepare a statement to reconcile for actual production the standard labour and material costs with the actual costs. [8]

Additional information

Oscar has not changed his standard costs for three years.

e Advise Oscar whether or not he should change his standard costs. Justify your answer. [2]

Cambridge International AS&A Level Accounting (9706) Paper 31, Q6, October 2019

[Total: 25]

Improve this answer

This is a sample answer to **Q1e**.

> Flexing budgets can be time consuming, an expert might be needed to work it out which will incur an extra cost. Managers may not like having to recalculate their budgets all the time.

Your challenge

See if you can improve this answer.

The sample answer does not give a decision. A better understanding of flexing budgets could be demonstrated through a more detailed response, which is then justified. A better answer is available online – but write yours out first!

Chapter 39
Investment appraisal

LEARNING INTENTIONS

In this chapter you will:

- understand what investment appraisal is
- calculate and use accounting rate of return
- calculate and use payback
- calculate and use net present value
- calculate and use of internal rate of return
- discuss the advantages and disadvantages of investment appraisal techniques
- use investment appraisal techniques to make supported investment decisions

KEY TERMS

Investment appraisal   Sunk costs   Accounting rate of return   Payback period   Net present value
Time value of money   Present value   Internal rate of return

Key skills exercises

Knowledge and understanding

To answer the questions in this chapter, you need to know and understand:

- investment appraisal is a process of assessing whether it is worthwhile to invest funds in a particular project
- investment appraisal techniques: accounting rate of return, payback period, net present value and internal rate of return
- the advantages and disadvantages of investment appraisal techniques.

You also need to be able to apply your knowledge and understanding of investment appraisal to calculate the accounting rate of return, payback period, net present value and internal rate of return.

Analysis

To answer the questions in this chapter, you need to be able to use investment appraisal techniques to make supported investment decisions.

Evaluation

To answer the questions in this chapter, you need to be able to evaluate non-financial factors in investment decision-making.

CAMBRIDGE INTERNATIONAL AS & A LEVEL ACCOUNTING: WORKBOOK

THE MAGICAL STUDIO

The Magical Studio was established in 1923 in California. From humble beginnings as a cartoon studio to its pre-eminent name in the entertainment industry today, Magical proudly continues its legacy of creating world-class stories and experiences for every member of the family.

What started as a cartoon studio has grown into a leading diversified international family entertainment and media enterprise. The Magical Company, together with its subsidiaries and affiliates, have the following business segments: Media Networks; Parks, Experiences and Products; Studio Entertainment; and Direct-to-Consumer and International.

Over the years, Magical has invested in many businesses and acquired many to get to the position they are in now to be known as one of the world's most valuable brands. Magical's success and growth have come from their time and money invested in new segments and their acquisition of existing companies.

There is always a risk involved when investing large amounts of money into new segments; however, companies such as The Magical Company will do an investment appraisal before making a final decision. Investment appraisal is a process of assessing whether it is worthwhile to invest funds in a project. These projects involve making choices, including whether or not to proceed with the project, which assets to buy, which new products to introduce and so on.

WORKED EXAMPLE 1

The Magical Company is considering investing in a new machine that will increase the profit of the merchandising segment. The machine will cost $190 000 and have a life of four years. After that time, it will be scrapped at no value.

The company policy is to depreciate the non-current assets by 25% using the straight-line method.

Expected cash flows from the new machine are:

Year	Cash inflow	Cash outflow
	$	$
1	96 000	42 000
2	84 000	38 000
3	92 000	40 000
4	100 000	45 000

REQUIRED

a Calculate the accounting rate of return for the new machine.

Additional information

The Magical Company is currently earning an ROCE of 12% and requires any new investments to earn at least the same percentage.

b State, with reasons, whether the business should buy the new machine.

CONTINUED

Answer

a **Step 1**: The cash flows and expected profit as a direct result of buying the machine are as follows.

Year	Cash inflow	Cash outflow	Net cash flow(W1)	Annual depreciation(W2)	Expected annual profit(W3)
	$	$	$	$	$
1	96 000	42 000	54 000	47 500	6 500
2	84 000	38 000	46 000	47 500	(1 500)
3	92 000	40 000	52 000	47 500	4 500
4	100 000	45 000	55 000	47 500	7 500
	Expected total profit over the life of investment				17 000

Workings

W1: Net cash flow = cash in − cash out

W2: Annual depreciation is $47 500 $\left(\dfrac{\$190\,000}{4}\right)$

W3: Annual profit = net cash flow − depreciation

Step 2: The average profit of the investment of calculating accounting rate of return is: $17 000 ÷ 4 (life of the project) = $4 250

Step 3: The average investment is: $\dfrac{\$190\,000}{2}$ = $95 000

Step 4: The accounting rate of return = $\dfrac{\$4\,250}{\$95\,000} \times 100 = 4.47\%$

b The Magical Company should not buy the new machine because the accounting rate of return of the new machine is below the company's minimum requirements of 12%. As the accounting rate of return is below the current ROCE, the machine will not improve the company's overall profitability.

Knowledge and understanding

1 Colby Ltd is proposing to introduce a new product that is expected to produce the following incremental profits over a period of four years:

	$
Year 1	56 000
Year 2	62 000
Year 3	66 000
Year 4	75 000

The project will require the use of a machine that was purchased some years ago at a cost of $120 000, and the use of a second machine that will have to be bought for $230 000. It is estimated that inventory held will increase by $40 000, and trade receivables will increase by $15 000.

REQUIRED

Calculate the accounting rate of return that will be earned from the new product.

> **TIP**
>
> Accounting rate of return takes depreciation of the investment into account.

CAMBRIDGE INTERNATIONAL AS & A LEVEL ACCOUNTING: WORKBOOK

WORKED EXAMPLE 2

The Magical Company is considering a project with an initial cost of $220 000. The company accountant has estimated its net cash receipts from the project for the next five years to be as follows.

Year 1	$35 000
Year 2	$44 000
Year 3	$45 000
Year 4	$56 000
Year 5	$63 000

The cost of capital is 10%. The discounting factors for the present value of 10% are:

Year	Discount factor at 10%
0	1.000
1	0.909
2	0.826
3	0.751
4	0.683
5	0.621

REQUIRED

Calculate the net present value for the project.

Answer

The calculation of the net present value of the project is:

Year	Net cash inflow/(outflow)	Discount factor	Discounted cash flow[1]
	$		$
0	(220 000)	1.000[2]	(220 000)
1	35 000	0.909	31 815
2	44 000	0.826	36 344
3	45 000	0.751	33 795
4	56 000	0.683	38 248
5	63 000	0.621	39 123
Net present value[3]			(40 675)

Notes

[1] The discounted cash flow is calculated by multiplying the net cash inflow for the year by the discount factor for the year. For year 1, the discounted cash flow is $35 000 × 0.909 = $31 815.

[2] The discount factor in year 0 is always 1.

[3] The net present value is the total of all the discounted cash flows for years 0 to 5.

The net present value is negative, showing that the project should not be undertaken.

Knowledge, understanding and analysis

2 Blake Limited is considering investing in one of two possible projects: project A or project B. Each project costs $190 000 and will have a four-year life with no residual value at the end of that time.

The net receipts for each project over the four-year period are as follows:

	Project A	Project B
	$	$
Year 1	72 000	55 500
Year 2	70 000	55 500
Year 3	46 000	55 500
Year 4	34 000	55 500

Blake Limited's cost of capital is 12%.

The discounting factors at 12% are:

Year	Discount factor at 12%
0	1.000
1	0.893
2	0.797
3	0.712
4	0.636

REQUIRED

a Calculate the net present value of each option.

b State which project Blake Limited should choose and why.

3 The main cutting machine of LH Limited needs to be replaced. A replacement machine will cost $260 000.

The current machine cuts 40 000 units a year. The number of units is expected to be reduced by 10% in year 1 due to the time taken to install the new machine. The number of units is expected to increase to 42 000 units a year for both year 2 and year 3.

The following information is available.

1 The cost of capital is 14%.

2 It is assumed that revenues are received and costs are paid at the end of the year.

3 Each unit of production costs $26 to manufacture. This will increase to $27.80 in year 2 and $28.50 in year 3.

4 Each unit is expected to sell for $30 in years 1 and 2, increasing by 5% in year 3.

5 It is assumed that all production is sold. The following is an extract from the present value table for $1.

	12%	14%	16%	18%	20%
Year 1	0.893	0.877	0.863	0.847	0.833
Year 2	0.797	0.769	0.743	0.718	0.694
Year 3	0.712	0.675	0.641	0.609	0.579

REQUIRED

a Distinguish between the net present value method of investment appraisal and the internal rate of return. [4]

b Calculate the expected net present value for the replacement machine. [9]

c Calculate the expected internal rate of return of the replacement machine. [7]

d Analyse the benefits to LH Limited of purchasing the replacement machine. [5]

Cambridge International AS&A Level Accounting (9706) Paper 32, Q6, March 2017

[Total: 25]

Knowledge, understanding, analysis and evaluation

4 Marie is considering a project to produce a new product. To make it she will need to buy a new machine at a cost of $250 000 with a useful life of 4 years.

The following information is available.

- Sales volume in units is expected to be:

Year	Units
1	20 000
2	22 000
3	23 000
4	18 000

- The selling price will be $30 per unit and will remain unchanged.
- The labour costs are $15 per unit. These are expected to increase by 2% in Year 3. There are no further expected changes in labour costs per unit in Year 4.
- The material needed for each unit is 3 kilos at $2.75 per kilo. Material cost per kilo will remain unchanged.
- The annual fixed costs are $107 500. This includes the depreciation charge for the new machine.
- The new machine will have no residual value.

REQUIRED

a Prepare a table to show the expected annual net cash flows arising from the project.

Additional information

Marie's cost of capital is 10%. Discount factors are as follows.

Year	Discount factor
0	1.000
1	0.909
2	0.826
3	0.751
4	0.683

b Calculate the net present value of the project.

c Calculate the accounting rate of return for the project.

Additional information

Marie expects an accounting rate of return of 20% on all projects.

d   Recommend whether or not Marie should proceed with the project. Justify your answer.
e   Calculate for Year 1 the sensitivity of the project profit:
    i   to the selling price
    ii to the material cost.
f   Explain the significance of the figures calculated in **e i** and **ii**.

5   Daniyar has run a successful manufacturing business for several years.

He currently has $140 000 in the business bank account.

Daniyar is considering replacing one of his current machines with either Machine A or Machine B.

The following information is available:

	Machine A	Machine B
Cost	$210 000	$161 500
Expected life	5 years	4 years
Annual net cash inflows	?	$51 000
Payback period	2 years and 11 months	?
Net present value	?	$7 412
Average rate of return	?	?

All revenue and expenditure is expected to accrue evenly throughout the life of each machine.

Annual net cash flows for each machine stay the same every year.

The cost of capital is 8%.

The discount factors are:

Year 1	0.926
Year 2	0.857
Year 3	0.794
Year 4	0.735
Year 5	0.681

The company policy is to depreciate all non-current assets over their expected life using the straight-line method. Neither machine will have any residual value.

REQUIRED

a   Explain the difference between the net present value and payback methods of investment appraisal. [4]

b   Calculate:
    i   the payback period for Machine B [2]
    ii the net present value for Machine A [8]
    iii the average rate of return for both machines. [6]

c   Advise Daniyar which machine he should purchase. Justify your decision. [5]

TIP

Always round up if the payback period is to the nearest month.

Cambridge International AS&A Level Accounting (9706) Paper 32, Q6, March 2018

[Total: 25]

6   N Limited is planning a new project, which has an initial cost of $225 000. If the project runs for four years the marginal revenues and costs will be as follows:

Year	Revenues $	Costs $
1	100 000	31 000
2	110 000	40 000
3	125 000	59 000
4	90 000	48 000

The directors have two options.

Option 1 To stop the project at the end of year 2 when the scrap value of the project's assets will amount to $175 000.

Option 2 To continue with the project until the end of year 4 when the scrap value of the assets will be $75 000.

The company's cost of capital is 10%. Discount factors for this cost of capital are as follows:

Year	Discount factor $
1	0.909
2	0.826
3	0.751
4	0.683

REQUIRED

a   Calculate the net present value (NPV) of **each** option. [10]

b   Advise the directors which option they should choose. Justify your answer. [2]

Additional information

Before the directors make a decision, the finance director wishes to have further data on the project.

REQUIRED

c   Calculate, to **two** decimal places, the sensitivity of the option selected in your answer to (b) to changes in the initial cost of the project. [3]

d   Calculate, to **two** decimal places, the accounting rate of return (ARR) of the option selected in your answer to **(b)**. (Add scrap value to cost when calculating average investment.) [6]

e   Explain to the directors which is the more valid method of investment appraisal. Give reasons. [4]

Cambridge International AS&A Level Accounting (9706) Paper 33, Q5, October 2016

[Total: 25]

39 Investment appraisal A Level

EXAM-STYLE STRUCTURED QUESTIONS

1 Jason is considering investing in building a property in order to receive rental income.

He could buy the land now (year 0) for $100 000. Construction costs of $180 000 would be paid in year 1.

The building would have 10 flats and each would have an annual rental of $5 000. Jason thinks that he could rent out flats as follows:

Year	Number of flats rented out
1	Nil
2	7
3	8
4	10

Total annual maintenance and management charges for the flats would cost $12 000 plus 10% of the rent received. At the end of year 4 he would sell the building. Jason has consulted two different property dealers, Alan and Bob. Alan estimates the building could be sold for $290 000. Bob estimates it could be sold for $315 000. Jason's cost of capital is 10%. The discount factors to be used to account for this are as follows.

Year 1	0.909
Year 2	0.826
Year 3	0.751
Year 4	0.683

All cash flows are assumed to take place on the last day of the year.

REQUIRED

a **i** Calculate the net present value (NPV) of investing in the building, using Alan's estimation of the sale proceeds. [12]

ii Calculate the net present value (NPV) of investing in the building, using Bob's estimation of the sale proceeds. [3]

b Calculate the sales proceeds at the end of year 4 that would result in a net present value (NPV) of zero. [3]

c Advise Jason whether or not he should proceed with investing in the building. Justify your answer. [5]

d State two reasons why the calculation of the payback period is a less useful investment appraisal technique than the calculation of net present value (NPV). [2]

Cambridge International AS&A Level Accounting (9706) Paper 32, Q5, June 2018

[Total: 25]

2 The directors of P Limited plan to launch a new product that has an expected life of 4 years. A new machine is required for this and the directors are considering buying Machine X. Details of Machine X are as follows.

	Year 0	Year 1	Year 2	Year 3	Year 4
	$	$	$	$	$
Cost	400 000				
Annual receipts		390 000	420 000	460 000	370 000
Annual payments		280 000	280 000	270 000	250 000

The machine has a useful life of 4 years with no residual value. It will be depreciated using the straight-line method.

CONTINUED

REQUIRED

a Calculate the accounting rate of return (ARR) of Machine X. [5]

b State **two** advantages and **two** disadvantages of using ARR. [4]

Additional information

P Limited's cost of capital is 10%.

The following are the discount factors for 10%.

Year 1	0.909		Year 3	0.751
Year 2	0.826		Year 4	0.683

c Calculate the net present value (NPV) of Machine X. [5]

Additional information

P Limited requires an internal rate of return (IRR) of 13% on any capital investment. If a discount factor of 16% is used, Machine X will have a **negative** NPV of $13 130.

d Calculate the IRR of Machine X. [3]

Additional information

A similar machine, Machine Y, is available. It also has a useful life of 4 years. The following information for Machine Y is available.

Initial cost $480 000

Net present value $33 200

Accounting rate of return   25%

Internal rate of return   13.5%

e Advise the directors of P Limited which machine they should buy. Justify your answer. [5]

Additional information

The directors are also considering buying another machine, Machine Z, at a cost of $110 000. This will be used to produce another product that has an expected life of 3 years. The annual receipts from the sale of the product will be $100 000. Annual payments will be $45 000. This will remain constant for each of the 3 years. P Limited's cost of capital remains at 10%.

The directors are confident about the accuracy of their forecast for annual payments. They are **not** confident about their forecast for annual receipts.

f Calculate the annual receipts that give a zero NPV for Machine Z. [3]

Cambridge International AS&A Level Accounting (9706) Paper 31, Q5, October 2019

[Total: 25]

CONTINUED

Improve this answer

This is a sample answer to **Q1c**.

> The project pays back even at the lower sales amount. If Jason is a risk taker he should proceed with the investment.

Your challenge

See if you can improve this answer. The sample answer does offer a decision, but more justification is needed to explain this choice.

A better answer is available online – but write yours out first!